Volume 9
Minnesota Monographs in the Humanities
Gerhard Weiss, *founding editor*
Leonard Unger, *editor*

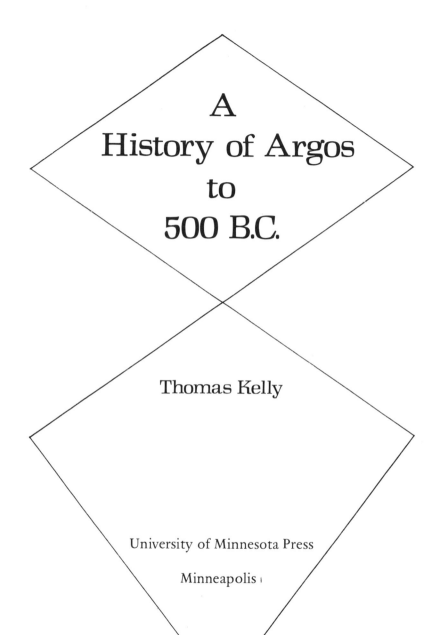

A
History of Argos
to
500 B.C.

Thomas Kelly

University of Minnesota Press

Minneapolis

Copyright © 1976 by
the University of Minnesota
All rights reserved.
Printed in the United States of America
at the University of Minnesota Printing Deparment, Minneapolis.
Published in Canada by Burns & MacEachern Limited,
Don Mills, Ontario

Library of Congress Catalog Card Number 76-11500

ISBN 0-8166-0790-7

/2-/8. 78

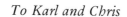

To Karl and Chris

Preface

For more than half a millennium after the collapse of Mycenaen civilization Argos was one of the most important states in ancient Greece.
Yet the history of Argos has been largely ignored by modern scholars.
Although this is unfortunate it is hardly surprising. There is no connected account of Argive history in the Greek historical literature that
has come down to us; only scattered literary references are to be found,
mostly in writers of later antiquity, and these are often hopelessly confused and contradictory. I have spent much time agonizing over these
references and have stated my views on a number of problems they
raise in various articles I have published over the past eight years. I have
drawn heavily upon these articles in the pages that follow. My work on
the literary sources led me to the conclusion that before early Argive
history could be understood a number of fundamental misconceptions,
myths really, that have been handed down since antiquity would have
to be discarded. The most important of these is the belief, held by
ancient and modern scholars alike, that the motivating force behind all
Argive history was the traditional enmity between Sparta and Argos.
This myth has dominated virtually every word that has been written
about Argive history since the fourth century B.C.

  If in the process of studying the literary evidence I have grown too
skeptical, especially of reports handed down by writers who lived after
Herodotus, I do not apologize. In fact, I have sought to trace the historical development of Argos by relying primarily upon archaeological

remains, and only after I had thoroughly familiarized myself with these did I turn to the literary evidence. Here we are fortunate, for Argos has been one of the most productive post-Mycenaen sites on the Greek mainland. Much of this material has not yet received final publication; yet it is well enough known from preliminary reports to be of inestimable value for the study of Argive history. Additionally, I have made use of any epigraphical evidence that was available.

Even with the combination of archaeological and epigraphical evidence and such literary reports as can be considered trustworthy, our knowledge of early Argive history is still meager. There is no possibility of treating it in any specific detail, and my aim has been to recover the broad outline and to isolate the main trends of development. Continuing archeaological excavation at Argos and final publication of previously uncovered material will surely add to our knowledge in the future and may necessitate revision or complete abandonment of many of my conclusions. This would be welcome, for too often a lack of information has led me to negative conclusions. For this I offer no apologies; with Beloch, I see nothing wrong with an honest profession of ignorance. I do, however, offer apologies for a certain amount of redundancy, but found it unavoidable. It has been necessary to cite some epigraphical evidence or literary report on more than one occasion where I felt it could be used for more than one purpose. I hope this will cause the reader less discomfort than it did the author.

Finally, for a work that has been too long in gestation any list of acknowledgments could grow to unmanageable proportions. Although it is impossible to thank individually everyone who has been connected with the work over the years, they have not been forgotten. Special thanks are due Professor Richard Nelson of Augsburg College for drawing the maps. My debt to Chester G. Starr, under whom this project was first undertaken as a Ph.D. dissertation, cannot go unnoticed. It was he who first suggested the topic to me, and although he has been far removed from it in the past decade, the work still bears the stamp of his influence as a teacher and scholar. Needless to say, he is in no way responsible for the finished product or for any of its blemishes; for these I take full responsibility.

Thomas Kelly

Minneapolis
May 30, 1976

Table of Contents

The Peloponnesus

10 0   20   40   60

10   0   20   40

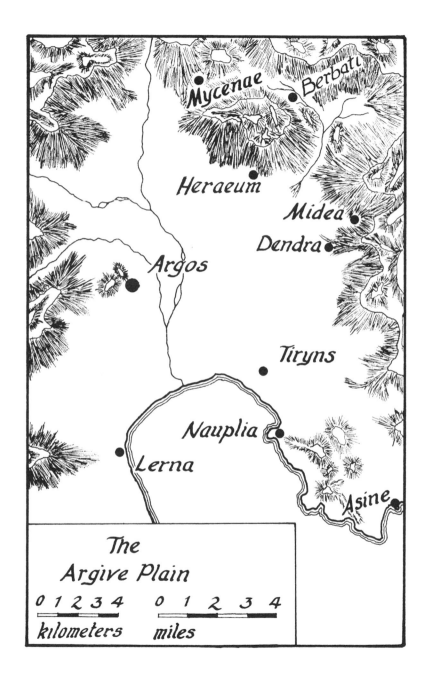

The
Argive Plain

0 1 2 3 4   0 1 2 3 4
kilometers   miles

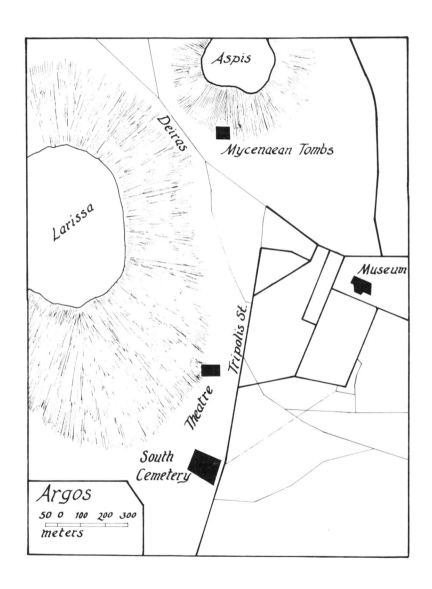

Aspis

Deiras

Mycenaean Tombs

Larissa

Museum

Tripolis St.

Theatre

South
Cemetery

Argos

50 0 100 200 300
meters

A History of Argos to 500 B.C.

Chapter I:

The Geography of
the Argive Plain and
the Early History of Argos

The area of Greece designated as the Argolid is located in the northeastern part of the Peloponnesus. Like most of Greece this area is made up largely of barren limestone hills and mountains. Only here and there does a small low-lying plain or an upland plateau break the monotony of the dull gray hillsides. One exception to this generalization is the Argive plain, a zone of subsidence in recent geological history,[1] but now a flat, triangular-shaped expanse of black alluvial soil which has been washed down from the surrounding mountains.[2] The Argive plain is not large; it covers about 200 square kilometers. It is smaller than the plain of Messenia and that of the Eurotas Valley. Nonetheless, this small area has had a remarkable and illustrious past. It has been inhabited continuously since the Neolithic period, and in the latter half of the second millennium before Christ, the civilization that flourished there was the most magnificent on the entire continent of Europe.

The Argive plain formed a separate geographical entity in antiquity. It is bounded by high mountains to the east and west, and is virtually cut off from the rest of the Peloponnesus.[3] Only to the north where the narrow Dervenaki pass affords comparatively easy access to Nemea, Cleonae, and Phlius, and to Sicyon and Corinth farther north, is communication with other areas of the Peloponnesus relatively easy. East of the plain, Mount Arachanion rises to nearly 4,000 feet and partially separates it from the eastern Argolid with its cities of Epidaurus,

Hermione, and Troezen. The separation is not complete, for south of Arachanion is a high plateau which permits some communication with the eastern coast of the Argolid. For the most part, however, one area is effectively separated and isolated from the other, and historically each area has formed a separate geographical and political unit. Similar conditions exist to the west of the plain where Mount Artemision rises to about 5,900 feet and blocks easy access to Arcadia. Although Mantinea to the north and Tegea to the south can be reached by passes through the mountains, the route is a difficult one. South of Artemision, Mount Parnon rises to nearly 6,500 feet and effectively separates the Argive plain from Laconia and its chief city Sparta, southwest of the Argive plain.[4] Contact with areas outside the plain proper can be more easily made by sea. On its southern extremity the plain borders on the Gulf of Argos, which opens out in a south by southeasterly direction. Crete lies south and a bit east of the plain, and the Cyclades are almost directly east.

The area of Greece in which the Argive plain is situated receives little rainfall—less than twenty inches annually and none at all during the summer months.[5] Generally speaking, therefore, the Argive plain is dry, and the rivers that course through it provide the best indication of this condition. There are three of consequence, the Inachus, the Charadrus, and the Erasinus. Of the three, however, only the Erasinus, a short river which arises at the springs of Kephalari on the western edge of the plain, carries water for most or all of the year. The others carry water only during the winter rainy season and until the winter snows have melted on the mountains west of the plain; then they cease to flow and become merely dry beds.[6] The general dryness of the area should not, however, be exaggerated. Although Homer refers to "thirsty Argos," even in antiquity we have reports to the contrary.[7] There are numerous springs in the area, and these provided an ample supply of fresh water for drinking purposes; in addition we know that until quite recently the coastal regions were marshy and swampy.[8] Although the surrounding mountains loom naked and treeless in the distance,[9] the plain itself with its thick layer of black alluvial soil is fertile and was always capable of supporting a relatively large population.[10] In fact, as early as the Neolithic period there is evidence of habitation of no fewer than eight settlements—Argos, Tiryns, Lerna, Prosymna, Nauplia, Mycenae, Berbati, and Kephalari[11]—in and on the fringes of the Argive plain.

In addition to fertile soil and an ample supply of fresh water, the Argive plain possessed one other feature that promoted settlement, at least in the second millennium B.C. In the plain itself and on its immediate fringes, a number of hills rise steeply enough to be easily fortified and defended but gentle enough to allow access to their peaks.[12] At least eight such sites dot the plain and the territory immediately adjacent to it. Seven of these are located on or near the eastern side of the plain; on the western side there is but one such location. It was here that the city of Argos was situated, virtually in the geographical as well as the natural center of the plain.[13] No point in the plain is more than ten miles distant from this location, and the entire area, as well as the Gulf of Argos, can be clearly surveyed from the summit of the Larissa, the 950-foot acropolis of the city. The advantages of such a location are manifest, and it is not surprising that Argos was settled at an early date.

There is, however, little that need or can be said about Argos before the beginning of the Middle Helladic period about 2000 B.C. Neolithic and Early Helladic remains have been found there, but in no great quantity. Only in 1967 was the first Neolithic material reported from the site. Remains of a Neolithic house have been found, as well as pottery dating from the Middle and Late Neolithic periods. This pottery is similar to that found at other sites in the Argive plain and at Corinth.[14] Habitation was not centered on the towering Larissa, but in the plain itself, as was characteristic of sites chosen for settlement at this time. Remains from the Early Helladic period are hardly more numerous. In fact, most of them date from late in the period, and although it is likely that the city was continuously inhabited from the Neolithic period onward, this cannot be proven. It is possible that some Early Helladic pottery has been found on the second acropolis of the city, the gently rising and much lower Aspis,[15] but most of the remains from this period have also been found in the plain. A single tomb was discovered below the Larissa, a few sherds have been found on the Deiras, the low ridge separating the Larissa from the Aspis, and an Early Helladic stratum is reported in one section of the modern city.[16] In addition, there is evidence of another settlement about three quarters of a mile west of the

Aspis and the modern city. There on a small rise called the Makrouvouni, at a site which had no prior or later occupation, Early Helladic pottery has also been uncovered.[17] The Early Helladic remains from Argos are not so impressive as those from Zygouries in the valley of Cleonae north of the Argive plain or from Tiryns and Lerna in the plain.[18] Moreover, it is not known whether Argos suffered a fate similar to Lerna, Tiryns, and Asine, where there is clear evidence of destruction by fire between the periods designated Early Helladic II and Early Helladic III, shortly before the end of the third millennium;[19] in all probability, this did happen. The city was certainly inhabited in the Early Helladic III period, however, for the tomb mentioned above dates from this time, as do the sherds from the Deiras, some of which are probably of eastern origin.

There is no clear break discernible between the Early Helladic period and the Middle Helladic period, which extends from the early years of the second millennium to about 1600 B.C.[20] Although nothing has yet been found that can compare with the earliest shaft graves at nearby Mycenae, the Middle Helladic period is well represented at Argos. Unfortunately, the remains have not yet been published in detail. The bulk of the pottery uncovered in the early excavations on the summit of the Aspis was of Middle Helladic date; both Minyan ware and Matt-painted ware were common, and a few imports from Crete were also reported.[21] These same excavations revealed house foundations which were labeled simply "pre-Mycenaean" by the excavator, but they undoubtedly date from the Middle Helladic period. More recent excavations on the Deiras and in the plain have yielded foundations that can be dated to this period with certainty, and house remains of crude brick also have been found.[22] It is possible that a fortification wall surrounded the summit of the Aspis, for traces of a wall enclosing an area approximately 720 feet in diameter have been uncovered there, and a Middle Helladic date has been suggested.[23] Early excavations also revealed Middle Helladic remains on the higher acropolis. Although no foundations preceding the Mycenaean era have been found on the Larissa, an ample amount of Middle Helladic pottery has turned up. It was found in such abundance that the excavator suggested that the higher acropolis had been inhabited for a longer time or at least had been more densely settled in this period than in the succeeding Mycenaean period, though recent soundings in the area may not support this conclusion.[24] In the plain itself at the foot of the Larissa three superimposed Middle Helladic strata have been found. Two of these were habitation layers, and the most recent represented a burial layer. In this latter stratum, as well as elsewhere in the city, numerous tombs, both cist and pithos, have been uncovered.[25]

Additional material from the Middle Helladic period uncovered during the course of the recent excavation of the Mycenaean burial ground on the Deiras ridge must also be taken into consideration. This material has been published by Jean Deshayes, who dates most of the pottery to the Middle Helladic I phase. He notes, in addition, that the period of the rich shaft-grave burials at Mycenae, that is, the latter years of the Middle Helladic period and the early years of the Late Helladic period, is completely unrepresented at Argos. He concludes that although Argos was the site of a substantial settlement in the early Middle Helladic period and for a time may even have been the leading settlement of the Argive plain, the city was abandoned well before the period came to an end, and it remained deserted for several centuries thereafter.[26] The evidence for the complete desertion of Argos seems less conclusive than Deshayes believes, however, and his conclusions would seem to require some modification. It is true that in one section of the city there is evidence of fire and a period of abandonment in Middle Helladic times, and in another section there is no record of occupation between a Middle Helladic level and a Geometric level.[27] In another area, however, Middle and Late Helladic potsherds are mixed together in the same stratum, and beneath this stratum is another that has yielded pottery assigned to the late phase of the Middle Helladic period.[28] Moreover, at the time Deshayes wrote, no remains from the Late Helladic I period had ever been found at Argos; but since then, a single tomb dating from the period has been excavated.[29] It is no longer absolutely clear, accordingly, that the site was deserted in the middle centuries of the second millennium as Deshayes believes. It is clear, however, that remains from these centuries are scarce, and the paucity of such remains stands in sharp and stark contrast to the abundance of remains from the early phases of the Middle Helladic period. Apparently Argos did suffer some serious reversal which decimated its population. Deshayes's suggestion that it may be more than coincidence that this occurred at approximately the same time that the inhabitants of Mycenae were beginning to reap the benefits of their newly established contact with Crete is tempting, but it must be noted that Middle Helladic remains are far more numerous than remains of Late Helladic I date at a number of sites both in the Argolid and throughout the Greek world generally.[30]

The Late Helladic or, as it is commonly called, the Mycenaean period of Greek history extending from about 1600 to 1100 B.C. was a time of unprecedented prosperity throughout the Greek world in general and within the Argive plain in particular. The most impressive settlement in the plain was of course Mycenae, immortalized by Homer and the excavations of Heinrich Schliemann. Located in the uppermost reaches of the plain and guarding entrance to it from the north, the site had important natural advantages, primarily from a defensive standpoint. Its palace, grave circles and rich shaft graves, tholos tombs, massive fortification walls, and Lion Gate are items too generally familiar to require further elaboration here. Suffice it to say that for half a millennium Mycenae was the most famous and most wealthy settlement in all Greece.[31]

Although the impressive remains of Mycenae are quite well known, the other settlements of the plain and its environs, with the possible exception of Tiryns, are less famous and deserve brief identification here. Three miles southeast of Mycenae lay Prosymna, a Mycenaean settlement of considerable importance, and later the site of the Argive Heraeum. Here a tholos tomb and more than fifty chamber tombs dating from the Late Helladic period have been excavated.[32] At an isolated site east of Prosymna, near but not precisely within the plain, the settlement of Berbati, where a tholos tomb has also been found, prospered for a relatively short period.[33] A bit to the south of Prosymna was the settlement of Midea with its walled acropolis. Nearby two of the richest tholos tombs yet excavated in Greece were discovered, as well as a number of chamber tombs. One recently excavated chamber tomb contained an almost complete set of bronze armor dating from the fifteenth century B.C.[34] Situated south of Midea, not far from the coast of the Gulf of Argos, was Tiryns with its palace and massive fortification walls;[35] and on the coast itself lay Nauplia, a settlement of some consequence in the Late Helladic period and later the port city of Argos.[36] Farther down the coast, but located just beyond the southern extremity of the plain, was the small settlement of Asine.[37] On the western side of the plain there were far fewer sites suitable for settlement in this age when high, easily defensible locations were preferred. Here, Lerna[38] was located near the coast and Argos in the interior. In addition, a number of smaller sites such as Priphtiani, Aria, and Skinchori deserve at least to be mentioned.[39] All of these settlements were located within the 200 square kilometers which make up the Argive plain, and all existed contemporaneously. Clearly, in the Late Helladic period the Argive plain was a densely populated area; the settlements located within its confines prospered. The rulers of these communities supported themselves resplendently in palaces behind massive fortification walls where their scribes kept elaborate records on clay tablets, and they were able to prepare imposing beehive tombs in preparation for their own burials. At Argos skeletal remains suggest that the inhabitants of the city enjoyed relatively good health, and even ordinary male citizens might expect to live from forty to forty-five years of age and could on occasion pass the age of sixty.[40]

The archaeological remains firmly fix the apogee of Mycenaean civilization to the two centuries between roughly 1425 and 1230 B.C., that is from the end of the Late Helladic II through the Late Helladic III B styles of pottery. At both Tiryns and Mycenae the fortification walls would seem to date from this period, as do the most impressive tholos tombs and the Lion Gate at Mycenae.[41] Smaller settlements such as Prosymna and Berbati seem to have been enjoying periods of unprecedented and unparalleled prosperity, and, as we shall see, so too was Argos. It was during this period that the peoples of the Mycenaean world began to carry on extensive overseas trade. In the east, Late Helladic II pottery has turned up in Syria and Egypt, and it is found in smaller quantity in Sicily and Italy in the west. This overseas trade reached its peak in the Late Helladic III A period,[42] when in addition to trade there might have been some colonizing activity as well, particularly in the east. Greek literary tradition points in this direction, and sometime it is confirmed by archaeological excavation.[43] It was, moreover, toward the end of this period that the Greeks supposedly rallied behind Agamemnon and launched a combined expedition against Troy, though, as has frequently been pointed out, such an expedition is difficult to reconcile with the archaeological evidence.[44]

The physical remains suggest that Argos was not as important as Mycenae or Tiryns in this period; but it was not an impoverished village, and its inhabitants undoubtedly shared in the general prosperity that prevailed throughout the area. Late Helladic strata have been encountered only sporadically in various sections of the modern city, and we have no precise information concerning the exact location or extent of the Mycenaean settlement. It seems, however, to have extended up the slopes of the Aspis and at least as far south as the site of the modern museum.[45] House foundations have been uncovered in the city,[46] but no Linear B tablets, no tholos tombs, and no traces of a royal palace have been found there. Yet, excavations conducted by Vollgraff on the Larissa a number of years ago suggest that there must have been a royal residence at Argos. In addition to a number of vase fragments, bits of amber, some gold leaf, and a cylinder seal of oriental origin, Vollgraff also uncovered remains of a wall constructed in typical Mycenaean fashion. He concluded that this acropolis was a fortified citadel with a Cyclopean wall about five feet thick surrounding its summit,[47] and presumably this wall enclosed a royal residence.

The excavations on the Larissa and in the modern city do not tell us much about Argos in the Mycenaean period, but fortunately there is other evidence to be considered. On the Deiras ridge is a burial ground that was apparently in continuous use for almost five hundred years, and most of our knowledge of Argive history in the Mycenaean period comes from nearly seventy tombs that have been excavated here.[48] These include both multiple-burial chamber tombs and single-burial pit tombs, and they are particularly important because they span virtually the entire Late Helladic period. Unfortunately, however, they do not tell us much about Argos before the latter part of the fifteenth century: only one tomb dates from the Late Helladic I period—its contents have not yet been published—and none of the tombs can be securely assigned to the early phases of the Late Helladic II period.[49] Most of them date from the period extending from the final stages of Late Helladic II right down to the very latest stage of the Late Helladic III C period. Although no detailed history of the city can be written on the basis of these tombs, they do permit some general observations about Mycenaean Argos. First of all, they firmly fix the apogee of the city to the period between the latest phase of the Late Helladic II and the Late Helladic III B styles of pottery, roughly between 1450 and 1230 B.C., precisely the period that was also the high point of other settlements in the Argive plain. Pottery and bronze utensils from this entire period are relatively abundant in tombs at Argos; jewelry in gold and other materials occasionally turns up, and ivory and other objects affirm Argive relations with the Levant. The skill of the Argive craftsman is amply illustrated by the fine quality of the exceptionally large dromos of Tomb X and by the elaborately painted doorway of another tomb.[50]

There is, in short, nothing in the physical remains to indicate that Argos differed materially from any of the other settlements in the plain, Mycenae included. This is not surprising, for it has long been recognized that Argos was culturally linked with Mycenae, a few easy miles away, and that the Argive plain formed a culturally unified area in the Late Helladic period. This is especially true in the Late Helladic III B period; it would appear that earlier, in the Late Helladic A period, Argos had closer contact with Crete than with Mycenae or any other community of the plain. The tombs at Argos closely resemble those found at Mallia, and Argive pottery of the period shows a certain similarity to that of Crete.[51]

Unfortunately, there is no evidence to help us determine whether or not Argos was an independent community in Late Helladic times. It has frequently been argued that the Greek world was politically as well as culturally unified in the Mycenaean period, but the evidence is at best equivocal. As Vermeule points out,[52] there is evidence suggesting that the Argive plain was politically unified at this time, but there is also evidence suggesting that each settlement in the area was a separate political entity. In favor of the latter suggestion are the numerous fortified sites which existed. Tiryns, Mycenae, Midea, Asine, and Argos all possessed thickly walled citadels, and if the rulers of Mycenae controlled the plain, they would hardly have permitted their subject cities to build such elaborate fortifications. Moreover, the tholos tombs at Midea, Prosymna, and Berbati, as well as at Mycenae, and the palace on the acropolis of

Tiryns and perhaps those at Midea and Argos as well suggest that each of these settlements was ruled by its own king, since only kings, presumably, could afford palaces or such elaborate places of burial. On the other hand, it must be remembered that the whole plain was served by a system of roads that radiated from Mycenae.[53] The presence of fortification walls at Argos may imply that the city was an independent kingdom, but at the same time it may not be irrelevant that Argos became a substantial settlement long after Mycenae had become a prosperous community. In the seventeenth and sixteenth centuries while the rulers of Mycenae were being buried in remarkably rich shaft graves, Argos was an insignificant village, impoverished by comparison and all but deserted. One might easily suppose that the growth of Argos in and after the fifteenth century occurred with the consent of the kings of Mycenae, and if this were true, it would imply a measure of subservience on the part of the rulers of Argos. In the final analysis, however, there is no definitive solution to the problem, and all that can be said with much assurance is that the plain was culturally unified at least until the end of the Late Helladic III B period in the latter half of the thirteenth century.

Before the Late Helladic III B period came to an end, unmistakable signs of trouble can be detected throughout the Argive plain. The remains from Argos do not show this, but those from Tiryns and Mycenae do. At both sites there were attempts to secure a supply of water within the fortification walls. At Tiryns the rulers twice found it necessary to extend their fortification walls, presumably to enable the inhabitants of the surrounding territory to find refuge behind them. Even before the end of the period, the houses outside the citadel walls at Mycenae were sacked and burned in a conflagration which represents the first of three distinct periods of destruction by fire at the site between the middle of the thirteenth and the latter half of the twelfth century. At the very end of the Late Helladic III B period the citadel itself was burned and presumably the palace destroyed; so too were the citadels at Tiryns and at Midea. The latter settlement was completely abandoned, as were Prosymna, Lerna, Berbati, and a host of smaller communities in the plain as well as Zygouries in the valley just north of Mycenae.[54] There were, in short, fewer occupied sites in the Argive plain after the wave of destruction, and those sites that continued to be inhabited were generally less impressive and presumably smaller than they had previously been. Within the plain only Mycenae, Tiryns, and Argos continued to be inhabited, and to this list Asine, on the southern fringe of the plain, might be added. It is quite clear that the population of the plain had declined considerably, and there is evidence that some of its inhabitants had emigrated to less troubled areas of the Aegean, such as Achaea and the mountains of Arcadia in the Peloponnesus, the island of Cephallenia in the west, Cyprus and the Asia Minor mainland in the east, and Perati on the east coast of Attica.[55] Overseas trade declined but did not cease, and the cultural unity of the Mycenaean world disintegrated rapidly following the devastation and was never regained. There is, in fact, no evidence to prove that the art of writing continued in Greece after the destruction. All Linear B tablets thus far discovered on the mainland have been found in a Late Helladic III B context, with the possible exception of Pylos where destruction took place perhaps at the very beginning of the Late Helladic III C period. Clay tablets can be preserved only under certain conditions, but it is worth noting that none of the inscribed pots and potsherds that we possess can be dated later than Late Helladic III B.[56] Although the settlements of the plain had obviously suffered severely, Mycenaean civilization was strong enough to recover from the setback it had received, but at best recovery was only partial. Culturally the Late Helladic III C period differed from the Late Helladic III B period only in degree not in kind. The same method of burial, primarily inhumation in chamber tombs, continued to be practiced, and the same burial grounds were used. Late Helladic III C pottery was an outgrowth and direct continuation of the pottery produced in the preceding period, though except for the so-called Close style, it was generally an inferior product.[57]

It is difficult to account for the widespread destruction that occurred throughout the Argive plain and indeed much of Greece at the end of the Late Helladic III B period. Various suggestions, including a sudden shift in the climate and internal strife within the Mycenaean world itself, have been offered.[58] But none of these suggestions is easily reconciled with the widespread destruction and devastation that took place, and an invasion by outsiders seems to be the only reasonable explanation. No section of Greece south of Thessaly was spared. From Phocis and

Boeotia in the north to Laconia and Messenia in the south, settlements were abandoned and presumably destroyed. This would seem to preclude any of these areas as the ultimate origin of the people who caused the destruction throughout the Argive plain. It is also clear that it could not have been caused by people indigenous to the plain and that it must have been caused by outsiders. The mighty fortresses of Mycenae and Tiryns had been penetrated and their palaces sacked and burned. If this had been the work of people residing in the immediate area, one would expect to find remains of a settlement exhibiting the necessary strength and resources to undertake a campaign against such heavily fortified citadels. So far, however, no such settlement has been found; on the contrary, all sites thus far excavated in the Argolid, with the possible exception of tiny Asine, show far less prosperity in the Late Helladic III C period than in Late Helladic III B times.[59] It seems reasonably clear that the destroyers, whoever they might have been, came from the north for a fortification wall was constructed across the Isthmus of Corinth in the Late Helladic III B period in an unsuccessful attempt to forestall an incursion from the north.[60] Otherwise, however, little can be said about them;[61] other than the destruction they wrought, they have left behind no tangible evidence of their presence, and it seems they did not settle in the Argive plain at this time.

Since the evidence comes primarily from tombs at Argos, there is no way to prove that the inhabitants of the city made any special preparations for their safety and defense as did the inhabitants of Mycenae and Tiryns. There is no indication in the physical remains that Argos suffered any devastation at all at the end of the Late Helladic III B period. There are traces of fire in a Mycenaean stratum in one area of the city. But it cannot be dated securely, and in any event it may well reflect a local rather than a general conflagration.[62] It has been suggested that Argos perhaps suffered less severely than any of the other settlements in the plain, but the picture might change appreciably if we had some evidence from the settlement or the walled acropolis. It seems highly unlikely that Argos escaped unscathed, and the possibility that some of the inhabitants of the city migrated into Achaea at the end of the Late Helladic III B period[63] suggests that the city suffered some devastation.

Far more impressive than the evidence for destruction, however, is the evidence for continuity at Argos. The burial ground on the Deiras ridge remained in use, and the same method of burial and the same types of tombs continued to be employed. In fact, at least two chamber tombs (Tombs XVI and XVII) were used without interruption, and several new chamber tombs were constructed in the Late Helladic III C period. There is direct continuity in figurines and in pottery styles, and many of the bronze objects of the period are based on earlier local models and also show continuity. The latter continue to turn up in quantity, and a few gold objects have also been found, which suggests that the inhabitants of the city were not completely impoverished. Nor did overseas trade cease. Ivory was found in one tomb, and foreign influence from diverse and widely scattered areas is evident in the bronze work. Some items show influence from central Europe, some pins are very similar to pins from the Orient, and a bronze votive wheel seems to have been imported from northern Italy. It seems clear, therefore, that although Argos may have suffered some devastation at the end of the Late Helladic III B period, the city was not totally depopulated or completely impoverished. There is, moreover, no evidence that an intrusive population element entered the city and took up residence. There are, however, indications that some changes did occur. Most important is the fact that the cultural unity that prevailed throughout the plain before the period of destruction broke down, and culturally Argos was less closely linked with Mycenae than it had been previously.[64] The Late Helladic III C pottery of the city is strikingly similar to the pottery manufactured in Achaea at that time, and no example of Close-style pottery, so prevalent at Mycenae and Tiryns, has ever been found at Argos. It has also been suggested that the mode of dress of the city's inhabitants underwent radical transformation at this time, but the evidence may not warrant such a sweeping conclusion.[65]

Of the final days of Mycenaean civiliation in the Argive plain and at Argos specifically, little can be said with assurance. After three generations of survival and partial recovery from the destruction that took place at the end of the Late Helladic III B period, the Granary at Mycenae was burned and the settlement reduced to ruins shortly before 1100 B.C. Although there is no positive evidence of any widespread destruction,[66] it is clear that from this time onward Mycenaean civilization ceased to exist, and the civilization that replaced it differed from it in many important respects. After 1100 there is habitation—and that in greatly reduced numbers—at but three sites, Mycenae, Tiryns, and Argos, within the plain, and at Asine a short distance beyond. According to Greek tradition it was the Dorians who were responsible for the destruction that occurred throughout Greece at this time,[67] and it is generally believed that they put an end to Mycenaean civilization and inaugurated the period of Greek history known as the Dark Age. There is little archaeological or anthropological confirmation for this tradition, and despite the fact that the Dorians have been a favorite topic of scholars, little can be said about them. In fact, even their homeland before their intrusion into the Peloponnesus is not known. It was most likely in the area north or northwest of Greece; Greek tradition places them in Epirus, and this has been widely accepted.[68] No material object can be distinctly singled out as having been brought into Greece by them,[69] and the recent suggestion of Desborough that they introduced the practice of single burial in cist tombs has been challenged on the basis of the tombs excavated at Argos and no longer appears tenable.[70]

Skeletal remains have frequently been cited as proof of an influx of northerners into Greece and the Argolid at the end of the Bronze Age. But these remains are not easy to classify and interpret, and one must wonder if this is even a sound approach to the problem. The Dorians, like the Mycenaeans, were Greeks, and to distinguish the skull of a Dorian Greek from a Mycenaean Greek can hardly be an easy task. The skeletal remains from the graves at Argos have been studied by Charles,[71] who seems to have difficulty deciding between Greek tradition and the physical remains. Although he states that there was an abrupt increase of northern-type skulls found in Argive tombs as a result of the Dorian invasion, the evidence, at least as he classifies it, suggests otherwise. He identifies only 1 of 13 skulls from the Protogeometric period following the invasion as northern, but he classifies 4 of 69 specimens from the late Bronze Age before the invasion as northern. Hence, the increase of northern-type skulls is from 5.9 percent in the Late Bronze Age to 7.7 percent in the early Iron Age; given the small size of the Protogeometric sample, this can hardly be regarded as very significant.[72] All anthropologists might not agree with Charles's classification of these skeletal remains, but it is clear that if his classification is accepted, there is no anthropological confirmation for the tradition that the city endured an influx of Dorians from the north toward the end of the Bronze Age. In fact, Charles himself seems to acknowledge this when he goes on to state that the population of the Argolid appears to have been only little affected by northern invaders.

In the final analysis we are left with Greek tradition as our chief source for the Dorian invasion. There is, however, the additional fact that the Dorians spoke their own particular dialect of the Greek language, and this dialect was spoken by the inhabitants of the Peloponnesus, Argos included, in historical times. The Late Bronze Age seems to be the most likely time for the introduction of this dialect into Greece and consequently for the Dorian invasion. About the invasion itself, however, little can be said. The course of the Dorian conquest of the Peloponnesus cannot be traced with any degree of accuracy, nor can the precise date of their settlement in the Argive plain be determined. They presumably moved south by land; but a combined land and sea movement cannot be ruled out[73] and may even be necessitated by the fact that the Dorians also settled in Crete, Rhodes, and other islands, and they could hardly have done this if they had not had some experience in seafaring. In the absence of precise dates for the fall of Troy, Thucydides's remark, even if accurate, that they took over the Peloponnesus eighty years after the fall of that city is of little help.[74] In any event, by the latter half of the twelfth century, they had apparently put an end to Mycenaean civilization throughout the Argive plain and taken up residence there. At this point a new era in the history of Argos begins.

By way of summary, Argos had been inhabited continuously for at least 1,000 years and perhaps more than 2,000 years before the arrival of the Dorians. For most of this period the city held a position of secondary importance within the Argive plain. In the Early Helladic period, Tiryns and Lerna seem to have surpassed it. For part of the Middle Helladic period, Argos may have been the chief settlement in the area; but it lost this distinction to Mycenae toward the end of the Middle Helladic period when it seems to have been all but deserted. For the next five centuries, Argos remained in the shadow of Mycenae, sharing generally in its culture but not without its own distinguishing characteristics. With the complete destruction of Mycenae shortly before 1100 B.C., however, Argos, though no longer so populous as it had previously been, was nonetheless the largest and leading settlement in the Argive plain. It retained this position throughout the subsequent history of Ancient Greece and in time was to become one of the most important states in the Peloponnesus.

Chapter II:

Dark Age Argos: The Archaeological Evidence

The Dorian invasion and the collapse of Mycenaean civilization inaugurate a new phase in the history of Greece, as well as in the history of Argos. The period extending from the late twelfth to the late eighth century is now commonly referred to as the Dark Age. This appellation derives from two considerations: it is a period about which we know very little, and it was a generally poor and backward age. As noted above, the art of writing disappeared completely from Greece perhaps as early as the end of the Late Helladic III B period, and it was not regained until the eighth century. There are, therefore, no contemporary written records or accounts to inform us about the day-to-day or even the century-to-century course of events across the Dark Age. When later Greek writers sought to fill this gap in their knowledge of their own past, they had no reliable information on which to base their views. Indeed, the only light cast on the history of Greece in this period is provided by archaeological excavation.[1] The collapse of Mycenae was, however, accompanied by a tremendous decline in all areas, and at a precipitous rate a number of fundamental changes occurred throughout the Greek mainland. The one that stands out most profoundly is the tremendous decline in population, a development that was to have serious economic consequences. For the first several centuries of the Dark Age we have very little evidence from settlements and none at all from places of worship. Gone from Greece are the impressive palaces and

19

tombs of the Mycenaean kings; the construction of monumental architecture had ceased entirely. The inhabitants of the mainland had neither the economic resources nor the ability to erect such imposing edifices. Gone too is the art with which the kings had once decorated their palaces, as well as the political system that had revolved about them. No longer were the potters so technically proficient as they had been in the Mycenaean period; overseas trade declined drastically, then ceased completely, and was not revived on any substantial scale for several centuries. In short, the archaeological remains from the Dark Age are neither plentiful nor elaborate, and they tell us much less about the period than we would like to know. In fact, we are forced to rely almost exclusively upon offerings, frequently scanty, of pottery and other objects that have been found in tombs.

Limited though the archaeological evidence may be, it provides the best evidence we possess for the history of Argos in the Dark Age, and a proper appreciation of Argive history in this period is essential if we are to understand the later historical development of the city. In this chapter the archaeological evidence for the period approximately 1125-750 B.C. will be considered, and an attempt will be made to extract some general conclusions about the course of Argive history in the Dark Age. But it must be made clear at the outset that all we can hope to accomplish is the reconstruction of Argive history in very broad outline.

For many years the Kerameikos cemetery in Athens was the only site in all of Greece that provided an unbroken archaeological record from the Dorian invasion throughout the entire Dark Age. In the past twenty years, however, excavations at Argos have shown that this site provides a similar record. These excavations are still in progress, and they continue to supply additional information, as do numerous accidental discoveries that are made in the city each year. Unfortunately, much of this material has not yet been fully published and is known only from sketchy preliminary reports. This is a serious handicap, but it is not an insurmountable one. More detailed information is available from other sites—Mycenae, Tiryns, and Asine—in the Argive plain and from the Greek mainland as a whole. From this material we now have a reasonably clear idea about the general historical development of Greece throughout the Dark Age, and the archaeological remains from Argos can be profitably viewed in this context.

Until recently it was common to refer to the first several generations following the Dorian invasion as the Submycenaean period of Greek history. This name is derived from the pottery then being produced, and it is a term denoting that this pottery, though closely related to that manufactured in Mycenaean times, was degenerate both in technical proficiency and aesthetic merit.[2] Within the past decade, however, Desborough has argued that Submycenaean pottery was not common to the whole of Greece but was rather a local style confined to western Attica and particularly to the cist-tomb cemeteries of Salamis and the Kerameikos. Elsewhere, he believed, Mycenaean pottery evolved directly into the Protogeometric style. This view would eliminate the Submycenaean period of Greek history, and it has won some acceptance.[3] Recently, however, even Desborough himself has retreated from it and acknowledged that "variations" of Submycenaean pottery were produced in other areas of the Greek mainland, among them Argos and the Argolid. Desborough has also retreated from his original position that Submycenaean pottery was associated only with cist-tomb burials, and he is now willing to follow Jean Deshayes in labeling some of the vases from the chamber tombs on the Deiras ridge at Argos as Submycenaean.[4] The same conclusion was reached by Carl Styrenius, who has studied the material of this period from all sites on the Greek mainland, and both he and Deshayes would go so far as to suggest that the Submycenaean style of pottery was initially developed at Argos and transported from there to Athens.[5]

Whether or not this was actually true rests on subjective considerations, and for the moment at least certainty is out of the question. For our purposes it is more important to recognize that Submycenaean pottery is not lacking in the Argive plain. It has been found at Mycenae, Tiryns, Asine, Nauplia, possibly Midea, and at Argos; but except at Argos only scant remains are extant. Styrenius lists a single vase from Nauplia; a single vase, possibly but not certainly Submycenaean, from Midea; three vases from Asine; five graves containing eight vases at Tiryns; and at Mycenae, two tombs with a total of nine vases, a few vases from isolated finds, and some fragmentary pottery. To these figures some recent discoveries must be added. A rich tomb containing seven vases, three fibulae, two pins, and a finger ring, all of bronze, has been found at Mycenae; it is dated to the very end of the period by Desborough. Four Submycenaean graves have been uncovered at Nauplia, but their contents await publication. So, too, do the contents of a cist tomb recently discovered at Tiryns, and four chamber tombs at that site are reported to contain pottery that is possibly but not certainly Submycenaean.[6]

Although the quantity of Submycenaean pottery found at Argos is not great in absolute terms, or even in comparison with the amount found at Athens or Salamis, it is considerable when contrasted with that found elsewhere in the Argive plain. Much of this material has been found in chamber tombs located in the old Mycenaean burial ground on the Deiras ridge. At least one tomb (Tomb XVIII) appears to have been constructed originally during the Submycenaean period; another (Tomb XVII) was in continuous use during the LH III C 1 and Submycenaean periods, and several others, constructed earlier in the LH III period, were reused in Submycenaean times. In all, some six chamber tombs containing twelve vases have been found; five of these tombs also contained bronze objects.[7] But not all Submycenaean material found at Argos comes from chamber tombs. Two amphorae, now identified as Submycenaean, were employed as burial containers. A simple earth-cut tomb with one vase was discovered in the area of the Geometric necropolis, and two others were discovered during the course of excavation for the new Argos museum. In addition, seven cist tombs have been found along Tripolis Street in the modern city; these tombs contained six vases which have not yet been fully published but which the excavator and Styrenius assign to the Submycenaean period.[8] Finally, fragmentary pottery has been found in several areas in the city.[9]

It is from these archaeological remains that our knowledge of Submycenaean Argos must be derived; any conclusions made on the basis of this limited evidence must obviously remain tentative. Both Deshayes and Styrenius would agree that the Submycenaean pottery from the chamber tombs spans the entire Submycenaean period and that it is approximately contemporary with the Submycenaean pottery found in the cist tombs at the Kerameikos cemetery in Athens. Unfortunately, the pottery from the cist and earth-cut tombs at Argos has been less fully described, but Styrenius believes that the vases from these tombs also span the entire Submycenaean period.[10] If this is in fact true, then it would appear that two different burial grounds and two distinct methods of burial were being employed simultaneously at Argos. It would be tempting to see this as proof that the city was inhabited by two different strains of people. One might easily believe that those who continued to inter their dead in chamber tombs in the Mycenaean burial ground were remnants of the earlier population of the city and those who opened up a new burial ground in the plain where they laid their dead to rest in earth-cut or cist tombs represent an intrusive element, the Dorian invaders. Such a belief might well be an over-simplification, however, for as mentioned above, Snodgrass has provided strong reasons for rejecting the notion that the Dorians introduced the practice of cist-tomb burial. Moreover, Deshayes believed he could detect Mycenaean pit tombs in the Deiras cemetery that had almost evolved into cist tombs.[11] It is possible, therefore, that the adoption of cist-tomb burials at this time was more the result of a slow evolutionary process than of a sudden influx of new settlers.

Yet there can hardly be any doubt that the population of Dark Age Argos was a mixture of Dorian and pre-Dorian elements. Not only was a new burial ground opened up, but a new area of settlement was also established in the Submycenaean period.[12] This would seem to rule out a perfectly smooth transition from Mycenaean to post-Mycenaean times. Some destruction undoubtedly occurred, and the population of the city obviously declined; but it is difficult to speak about either with any precision. For the subsequent history of Argos, it may be of greater consequence that the site was never completely abandoned. There is no discernible gap in time between the latest Mycenaean and the earliest post-Mycenaean remains, as the continued use of Tomb XVII and the new construction of Tomb XVIII in the Submycenaean period show. The archaeological evidence suggests that Mycenae, Tiryns, and possibly Nauplia and Asine were never completely abandoned either; but judging from the quantity of Submycenaean material found at Argos, it would appear that the transition was much less severe here than at other settlements in the Argive plain and elsewhere throughout Greece. It may not, however, be entirely accurate to say that Mycenaean civilization endured longer at Argos than at such places as Athens and Salamis,[13] where Submycenaean pottery has been found only in cist tombs. As we have seen, old and new methods of burial were being employed simultaneously at Argos, and even those inhabitants of the city who clung to older methods of burial in chamber tombs were now placing offerings in the tombs which are more representative of Dark Age Greece than of Mycenaean Greece. The pottery, although it had its roots in the past, was anticipating the Protogeometric style. The neck-handled amphora from Tomb XXIV, and a similar amphora from an earth-cut tomb in the plain, are good cases in point. They are almost Protogeometric in shape and not far removed from Protogeometric in decoration. Moreover, the metal objects, primarily pins, closely resemble those found in Athenian Submycenaean cist tombs.[14]

Not a great deal can be said about Argive history in the Submycenaean period. The archaeological evidence would seem to indicate that Argos was the most populous settlement within the Argive plain, but by Mycenaean standards it was a simple village without any great wealth or extensive power. On the basis of the stark simplicity of Submycenaean pottery it has been suggested that this was a simple as well as a poor and backward age.[15] This is undoubtedly true, but the simplicity of the age must not be exaggerated. There are indications that the inhabitants of Argos were something more than an assemblage of backward and primitive people struggling desperately to preserve their very existence. Again, the pottery of the period is a good indicator. Although Submycenaean pottery is generally lacking both in artistic merit and technical competence, not all of it reflects inferior craftsmanship. The potters of Argos were far from incompetent; some of their products were very well made, and although the vases of this period are generally small and unassuming, occasionally large and comparatively handsome works were produced. Vase shapes were not so highly refined as they had previously been, and although decorative motives were simple, by the end of the period these motives were being applied with care.[16] Argive metalsmiths continued to work at their trade, as bronze objects from both chamber and cist tombs testify. A variety of such objects have been found, including pins, fibulae, and rings.[17] Although some appear to have been imported, others were undoubtedly manufactured locally, for we know that metalworking remained on a high plane at Argos. One of the most striking archaeological discoveries made in the city was a furnace that was used for smelting ore at least as early as the very beginning of the Protogeometric period, if not slightly earlier. The smiths who toiled at this furnace extracted silver from lead ore by a process known as cupellation, a rather advanced and sophisticated technique that necessitates the use of a blast of air. This technique had been known and employed throughout Greece in the Mycenaean period, but before the discovery of this furnace at Argos, it had been assumed that knowledge of the process was lost with the coming of the Dorians.[18] We know now this was not true, and there is additional evidence from a tomb at Tiryns that indicates that the smiths of the period were considerably less backward than one might imagine. This tomb (Tomb XXVIII) contained parts of two iron daggers, a bronze spear tip and shield boss, and a fragmentary bronze helmet. This is an interesting discovery, for iron was rarely used in Submycenaean times, and military armor from the period is otherwise unknown. The fact, moreover, that these objects were buried with their owner is also significant, for it suggests that economic conditions were not entirely desperate.[19]

It is worth noting, too, that although overseas trade had declined drastically, it did not cease completely in the Submycenaean period. Foreign influence has been detected in the metalwork found in graves at Argos, and by the end of the period Argive potters were aware of developments taking place at Athens.[20] Yet the extent of overseas contacts in this period must not be overemphasized. This was primarily an age of self-sufficiency and localism; there is nothing to suggest that Argos enjoyed anything more than casual contact with areas beyond the Argive plain and that this contact may have involved a movement of ideas rather than a movement of goods. In this connection, it may be worth noting that there is clear evidence that some inhabitants of the plain, and undoubtedly from the city of Argos had fled the area before it was overrun by the Dorian invaders. These emigrants eventually settled in Asia Minor, Cyprus, possibly Attica, and elsewhere, but there is no evidence to prove and no reason to believe that they preserved any ties, commercial or otherwise, with their former homeland.[21]

Finally it remains to be noted that the Submycenaean period was not a lengthy one either at Argos or throughout Greece generally. It is difficult to arrive at precise dates because there are no securely fixed chronological points; but the period seems to have begun about the middle or latter half of the twelfth century and lasted until about the middle of the eleventh century, that is, from about 1150/1125 to about 1050 B.C. Though this was a short period, it was a crucial one in the history of the Greek mainland, especially if the transition from the production of Submycenaean to the production of Protogeometric pottery about 1050 has been correctly interpreted as implying a "veritable revolution," which carried within it the seeds of Classical Greek civilization.[22]

Protogeometric pottery, the dominant style throughout Greece from 1050 to 900 B.C., differs subtly but significantly from the preceding style. Although it was a direct outgrowth of the Submycenaean and even earlier Mycenaean styles, it displays a number of innovations and improvements, both technical and artistic. Thanks to the use of a faster wheel, Protogeometric vase shapes are much more refined and balanced than Submycenaean vases, and new and improved methods of firing were introduced. Equally subtle change is evident in the decoration applied to these vases and the manner in which it was applied. The hand-drawn circles of the previous period give way to compass-drawn circles painted with a multiple brush. Working with a very limited number of motives and shapes, the Protogeometric potter was able to produce a remarkably beautiful finished product, one which was a masterpiece of form and design.

The transition from the Submycenaean to the Protogeometric style can best be followed in the vases from the cist tombs in the Kerameikos cemetery in Athens. The material from Argos has not been published, and no stylistic division beyond early and late has yet been proposed. It can only be discussed in general terms, and largely in relation to the material from Athens. Yet Argive Protogeometric pottery is much better represented now than when Desborough wrote his excellent book *The Protogeometric Pottery*,[23] which must serve as the starting point for any discussion of the style. At that time not a single Protogeometric vase was known from Argos, and Desborough was forced to base his discussion of the Argive style on the few examples then known from Asine, Mycenae, and Tiryns. Since then, however, excavation has turned up a large quantity of material from approximately fifty tombs at Argos as well as lesser amounts at Mycenae and Tiryns, and fragmentary pieces at Asine, Lerna, and Nauplia.[24] Desborough believed that Protogeometric pottery originated at Attica and that it spread from there throughout the rest of the Greek world. Initially he was of the opinion that the spread was rather slow and that most areas lagged behind Athens by half a century or more. But he subsequently revised this opinion and advanced the notion that in certain areas of Greece, Argos and the Argolid among them, there was little if any time lag behind Athens. Various alternatives have been suggested, but in the main Desborough's views have been widely accepted.[25]

Yet the argument of Deshayes and Styrenius that Submycenaean pottery originated at Argos cannot be dismissed out of hand, and if it is valid it would have serious implications for the whole question of the origin of the Protogeometric style. Until the material from Argos has been fully published, it would be rash to suggest that Argos was the birthplace of Protogeometric pottery. The preliminary reports do indicate, however, that the Protogeometric period must have endured there for a considerable length of time, for in the south quarter of the city a Protogeometric burial ground was superimposed on an earlier Protogeometric level that apparently included a potter's establishment.[26] They also suggest that Argive potters were not so heavily dependent on Athenian potters for the decorative motives they employed and the vase shapes they manufactured as has on occasion been suggested.

As a general rule it is true that the decoration of Argive Protogeometric vases exhibits traits that are characteristic of pottery assigned to the Late Protogeometric phase at Athens. Light ground ware, for example, is almost entirely lacking at Argos; almost exclusively, Argive Protogeometric pottery is dark ground ware, and at Athens this was a later innovation. Likewise, though concentric circles and semicircles do turn up at Argos, they seem to occur less frequently than the cross-hatched triangle and the checkerboard pattern, both of which are hallmarks of the well-developed Athenian style. At the same time, however, there is evidence of experimentation before the fully developed Protogeometric style emerged at Argos. Initially Argive potters experimented with hand-drawn circles and semicircles before they advanced to those drawn with a compass. There was apparently some experimentation with different types of brush too; some vases were painted with a thick brush, and others were painted with a narrower brush which produced a more elegant finished product.[27] It would seem, therefore, that the Argive potter was learning by experience and not merely adopting techniques that had already been perfected at Athens. It is possible that we have further evidence of the Argive potter's ability to innovate in the appearance late in the Protogeometric period of a handmade, unpainted style of pottery which seems to have originated in the Argive plain.[28]

With respect to vase shapes it is true that certain Protogeometric shapes such as the high-handled pyxis, the lekythos, and the hydra turn up at Argos only during the later years of the Protogeometric period; they may well have been manufactured in imitation of Attic shapes.[29] Desborough himself, however, noted that other shapes, such as the trefoil-lipped oeonochoe and the high-footed skyphos had continuity from Mycenaean to Protogeometric times in the Argolid, and he even went so far as to acknowledge that Athenian potters may have drawn their inspiration for the latter from the potters of the Argolid.[30] Certain other shapes, such as the neck-handled and belly-handled amphorae, Desborough recognized as obviously derived from Mycenaean shapes,[31] but at the time he wrote, few examples were known from the Argolid. It now appears, however, that these shapes were being employed at Argos at least as early as the Submyceanean period,[32] and their use in the Protogeometric period might just as easily result from continuity of development from the Bronze Age as from any contact with Athens in the Protogeometric period.

In sum, although the evidence does not allow us to state unequivocally that Protogeometric pottery originated at Argos, it is sufficient to illustrate that Argive potters were capable of developing their own unique style. Aesthetically, this style does not command as much respect as the Athenian; but next to the Athenian, the Argive Protogeometric style was the most progressive and ambitious in all of Greece. It may be significant, too, that this generalization holds true for the pottery produced for nearly 200 years after the Protogeometric period came to an end about 900 B.C.

By this time the Protogeometric style had evolved into the Geometric, and this new style remained in production throughout the remainder of the Dark Age and beyond, until it gave way to various orientalizing styles toward the end of the eighth century. An enormous quantity of Geometric material has been excavated at Argos and at other sites in the Argive plain. The finds from burial grounds and isolated tombs from Mycenae, Tiryns, Asine, Lerna, Berbati, and Argos have been published in some detail, and Argive Geometric pottery has been exhaustively and definitively studied by Paul Courbin and independently by J. N. Coldstream.[33] Both Courbin and Coldstream have divided this pottery into three separate stages, Early, Middle, and Late. Although they do not always agree on specific details, each has further identified an early and late phase of each individual stage. Precise and absolute dates are not easily determined in this period, but Courbin has suggested the following divisions: Early Geometric 900-820; Middle Geometric 820-740; and Late Geometric 740-700 B.C. Argive Late Geometric pottery lies beyond the Dark Age proper and will be discussed in a later chapter. Here we shall consider only the Early and Middle Geometric stages, and since this material has been fully treated by both Courbin and Coldstream, no detailed discussion is necessary.

Argive pottery of the first phase of the Early Geometric period (EG 1) does not differ markedly from the latest Protogeometric pottery. There was a slow evolution in shape and decoration from the old style to the new. Many Protogeometric motives continued to be used, but new ones such as the meander and the zigzag began to turn up. The vase shapes produced were generally similar to Protogeometric shapes, but new varieties such as the vertical-handled amphora and several types of oeonochoe and pyxis began to appear. As in the late Protogeometric period, there is a striking similarity between Argive pottery and contemporary Athenian pottery; but at the same time there are significant differences as well. The late phase of this Early Geometric period (EG 2) is described by Courbin as a thoroughly conservative period during which the style continued to evolve, but at an excessively slow pace. The innovations of the previous period were consolidated; but few changes were introduced, and the similarity between the Argive and Athenian styles remains very close. Perhaps the outstanding development of the period was the final disappearance of all traces of the Protogeometric style.[34] The pace of change was hardly accelerated in the early phase of the Middle Geometric period (MG 1). Steady but slow development, especially in decoration, continued. New motives appeared, and painted decoration began to cover a greater portion of the vase and become generally more complex, so that more attention had to be paid to the overall composition of the decoration. By the late phase of this period (MG 2) we enter an era of rapid, even precipitous evolution. A variety of new shapes and motives began to appear, and before the period ended the first attempts at figured decoration had been made. Moreover, for the first time in several centuries Argive pottery began to diverge significantly from the Athenian.

The relationship between Argive and Athenian Geometric pottery in the period under consideration is worth a further word here. In general terms the Geometric style developed along similar lines throughout Greece as a whole, progressing from predominantly dark ground ware with little decoration restricted to the neck or shoulder of the vase to predominantly light ground ware with much of the vase covered with linear and figured decoration. Vase shapes, too, developed along a similar pattern, with a slow evolution toward more elegant, refined, and carefully balanced shapes. Although the Argive and Athenian styles were closely related, as they were in the Protogeometric period,[35] the relationship must not be overstated. It is misleading to regard the Argive Geometric style merely as an imitation of the Athenian, and it is equally misleading to suggest that it was the close relationship to the Attic style that accounts for the superiority of Argive Geometric over most other local styles.[36] Courbin has made a careful study of the relationship between the two styles, and his conclusions indicate that generalizations such as these go too far. He does acknowledge that there was a close stylistic resemblance, but at the same time he points out that exact and precise parallels are difficult to find. He acknowledges, too, that Argive potters did adopt some innovations of their Athenian counterparts, but he also notes that they rejected a great deal more than they borrowed.

Moreover, it is clear that Athenian potters adopted certain Argive innovations such as the hydra and the cup with vertical handles. In sum, Courbin concludes that although the two styles may have been related, the Argive style was something more than an imitation of the Attic; it possessed its own identity and individuality and had its own distinctive "personality."[37] These conclusions must be kept firmly in mind, for they emphasize that Dark Age Argos was not a carbon copy of Dark Age Athens; these were two different centers moving along similar but by no means identical paths. Perhaps the most obvious illustration of this is the mode of burial practiced at each site. Unlike the Athenians, who adopted cremation burial about the time that Submycenaean pottery was evolving into Protogeometric, the Argives continued to inhume their dead, in cist tombs in the Protogeometric period and either in cist tombs or pithoi in the Geometric period.[38]

Next to pottery, metal objects provide the largest body of material from Dark Age Argos. Metal objects from some sites in the plain, especially Mycenae and Tiryns, have been published in detail, as have those from the Geometric tombs at Argos. Unfortunately, the metal objects from the Protogeometric tombs have received only brief notice in the preliminary reports. All of this material, as well as metal objects found elsewhere in Greece, has recently been closely examined by Snodgrass, who observes that the number of iron objects increases both in relative and absolute terms in the more advanced sections of Greece, including Athens and Argos, in the Protogeometric period. He would date the true beginnings of the Greek Iron Age to this era,[39] but bronze continued to be employed in the manufacture of certain items. Throughout the Dark Age finger rings were numerous in the Argive plain and always of bronze; fibulae, though rare in this area, were also of bronze.[40] Before the Protogeometric period, pins were made only of bronze; in the Protogeometric period and early stages of the Geometric period they were made both of bronze and iron; in fact an Early Geometric tomb at Tiryns and several at Argos contained bronze and iron pins side by side.[41] In the manufacture of weapons, iron replaced bronze in the Protogeometric period, and from that time on they are almost all made of iron.[42] By the Early Geometric period gold reappeared in the Argolid for the first time since the Mycenaean Age. Three tombs at Argos contained gold jewels, and several at Tiryns contained more elaborate goldwork.[43] By this time, too, bowls of bronze were being manufactured, and certain tombs were remarkably rich in metal objects, as for example, Tomb XXIII at Tiryns which contained nine bronze rings, one iron and one bronze pin, three iron spear tips, and a fragmentary piece of another iron weapon, perhaps a dagger.[44]

In the production of metal objects, as in the production of pottery, there can be little doubt that Argos was one of the most progressive centers in Dark Age Greece. The discovery of a furnace used for extracting lead ore by cupellation and the implications of that discovery have already been mentioned. In addition, the products of Argive metalsmiths, particularly pins, are generally acknowledged to be more competently worked than those being manufactured elsewhere in Greece, Athens included. It has, in fact, been suggested that Argos was the leading and creative center of pin production in the Greek world.[45]

Exclusive of ceramic remains and metal objects there is not much evidence for Argive history in the Dark Age. Protogeometric and Geometric walls and house foundations are occasionally mentioned in the preliminary reports;[46] but these do not tell us much, and there are no other architectural remains for the period. Moreover, it is not possible to determine even approximately the extent of the city at any time during the Dark Age. We can, however, glean some information from the foreign objects that have been found in the Argive plain and from a consideration of the geographical distribution of Argive Protogeometric, and Early and Middle Geometric pottery.

Despite the fact that Argive pottery of the Dark Age is generally regarded as a fine product, second only to the pottery being manufactured at Athens, it was almost never exported. The Protogeometric pottery of the island of Cos shows some resemblance to the Argive style, and as we have seen, Athenian potters were influenced by developments at Argos both in the Protogeometric and Geometric periods. In addition, the Argive style may have had some limited influence at Corinth as well.[47] Yet for the entire century and a half of the Protogeometric period, the only Argive pottery found beyond the Argive plain is a single vase that has turned up at Aegina.[48] Nor does the picture change appreciably in the Early and Middle Geometric periods. This fact has not always been recognized, and as a result, the commercial contacts of Argos from the ninth century onward have usually been greatly exaggerated. The erroneous notion that Argos was deeply involved in trade and commerce has arisen largely from the excavations conducted at Perachora, where a temple of Hera was erected perhaps as early as 800 B.C. The excavator of the site, Humfry Payne, identified some of the pottery from the votive deposit of this temple as Argive, and he also believed that the locally manufactured pottery bore a close affinity to the Argive style. He noted, too, that many of the objects, such as small votive cups, terra-cotta votive cakes, and building or temple models, closely resemble similar objects found at the Argive Heraeum, and he concluded that the temple of Hera at Perachora was founded by Corinth with the collaboration of Argos.[49] Paul Courbin has reexamined the allegedly Argive material from the site, and his conclusions do not support the somewhat extravagant claims of Payne; in fact, Courbin is of the opinion that only a small quantity of the ceramic material can be identified positively as Argive, and none of this would seem to date much, if any, before 750 B.C.[50] It seems clear, therefore, that Argos had nothing whatever to do with the foundation of this temple. More important, however, is the fact that if the material at Perachora is dismissed as not Argive, there is virtually no evidence to prove that Argive Early and Middle Geometric pottery, despite its exceptional quality, was ever exported commercially. None has been found at Athens, and at Corinth there are only two Early Geometric vases.[51] Even at Cleonae, just beyond the Argive plain to the north, except for a single handmade, unpainted vase, possibly of Argive origin, the vases more closely resemble Corinthian than Argive workmanship.[52] Also, there is a single Middle Geometric sherd, perhaps of Argive origin from Corcyra, but that is all.[53] Although there was little export of pottery anywhere in the Greek world in these centuries, Athenian wares turn up on a limited scale, but over a rather wide area, and even Corinthian Geometric, though less pretentious than the Argive, has been found in quantity in the Megarid, at Delphi and Ithaca, and in lesser amounts at various other sites.[54]

A consideration of foreign objects that have turned up in the Argive plain reveals a similar pattern. For the Protogeometric period there is practically nothing. At Tiryns there are two obsidian arrowheads from a

Late Protogeometric tomb. An Athenian Protogeometric vase was reported from an Early Geometric tomb (Tomb 14)[55] at Argos, and a small marble statuette, strongly reminiscent of Early Cycladic plastic art, was also found. It is one of the earliest post-Mycenaean works of sculpture known from Greece, and although its place of origin is not known for certain, it is almost surely an import.[56] From the Early Geometric period there are a few Attic vases at Tiryns, a Corinthian vase from Tomb G 603 at Mycenae, and perhaps a few others from Asine, and there is a Cycladic vase from Tomb 4 Plessas at Argos.[57] Ivory was found in one of the earliest Geometric tombs (Tomb 2) at Tiryns, and this must have come from the eastern Mediterranean, as did the faience necklace from Tomb XXIII from the same site, and the faience beads from Tomb 32 at Argos.[58] For a three-hundred-year period this is not much,[59] and it suggests that although there may have been occasional and sporadic contact with other areas of the Mediterranean, there was no consistent or massive movement of goods into or out of the Argive plain at any time during the Dark Age. It seems necessary to conclude, therefore, that the Argive plain was a self-sufficient area throughout this period.

It is only in the wider context of our knowledge of the general historical development of Dark Age Greece that the physical remains from Argos acquire any meaningful significance. Admittedly, our knowledge of Greek history in the period between the twelfth and the middle of the eighth century is at best fragmentary and filled with lacunae; only the main outlines can be detected and often not even these can be securely isolated.[60] In general, however, it seems clear that aside from the drastic changes that accompanied the collapse of Mycenaean civilization, there were few revolutionary developments throughout the next three and one-half centuries. This is clearly illustrated in the ceramic material, where Submycenaean pottery gave way to the Protogeometric style, which in turn evolved into the Geometric. The transition from the production of Submyceanaean to Protogeometric pottery does mark a significant step forward; but once the innovations of a faster wheel and improved firing techniques were established, the dominant trend in ceramic production for the next three centuries was the slow but steady evolution of vase shapes and decorative techniques. In metal production the shift from bronze to iron early in the Dark Age was an important development, but iron did not supplant bronze immediately. The earliest iron products were crude and by no means superior to contemporary objects in bronze. But by the end of the Protogeometric period, their quality had greatly improved and their use became more widespread.

Apart from occasional innovations, however, the Dark Age appears to have been an essentially static period, and life remained uncomplicated. Writing was unknown and monumental architecture, except for a few unpretentious examples, did not exist. Trade ceased completely with the collapse of Mycenaean civilization. It was revived on an extremely limited scale before the end of the tenth century, and although it may have increased slightly in intensity for the next several centuries, it did not attain any appreciable proportions until the latter half of the eighth century. So far as we know, there was no highly organized governmental machinery, and although warfare was not unknown, this was not an age of grandiose schemes for ruling vast expanses of territory or carving out extensive spheres of influence. In short, during the Dark Age men lived simply, tilling their fields and ekeing out their livelihood from day to day.

The archaeological evidence surveyed in this chapter indicates that the history of Argos runs parallel to that of Greece as a whole throughout the Dark Age. With the Dorian invasion the city suffered some destruction, and the population declined drastically. It was not thoroughly depopulated, however, and there is no gap in time between the latest Mycenaean and the earliest post-Mycenaean remains found there. There are indications that the invaders settled down to live side by side with the remnants of the earlier population. Even as older methods of burial and the old Mycenaean burial ground continued to be employed, new burial grounds, including one that remained in continuous use until the Late Geometric period,[61] were being opened up, and the practice of single burial in cist tombs was being adopted. At the same time the Protogeometric style of pottery was evolving. There is no clear proof that Argos lagged much, if at all, behind Athens in the development and production of this new ceramic style, and it may even have been in the vanguard. In any event, throughout the remainder of the Dark Age, Argive potters consistently produced some of the best pottery then being manufactured in Greece. Only the workshops of Athens produced finer vases. The Argive metal industry was thriving, and Argive smiths were perhaps the most competent in the Greek world.

The similarity of pottery styles and metal objects found at Argos, Mycenae, Tiryns, and Asine, suggests that the Argive plain was a culturally unified area throughout the Dark Age. It would appear, however, that Argos was the largest and most important settlement in the plain and possibly in the entire Peloponnesus. Although neither the Aspis nor the Larissa was occupied, Protogeometric and Geometric potsherds and tombs have turned up in most parts of the city that were settled in later antiquity, and certain sections seem to have been inhabited only during this period.[62] Mycenae, Tiryns, Asine, and possibly Nauplia were, like Argos, continuously inhabited throughout the Dark Age. Tiryns has yielded substantial remains, though less than Argos, while Mycenae, Asine, and Nauplia were hardly more than settlements of a few families. Midea and Prosymna were entirely uninhabited, and only a few sherds and tombs, mostly from the Middle Geometric period, have been found at Lerna and Berbati.[63] Yet if Argos was by contrast a thriving and prosperous community, we must not be deceived into thinking that it was a bustling metropolis or that it exercised any control over the other settlements in the plain. Nothing could be further from the truth. Although the evidence indicates that the population grew steadily throughout the Dark Age, Argos was never more than a mere village in this period; its inhabitants were simple farmers, and there is nothing to suggest that they enjoyed any influence beyond the fields immediately surrounding their own settlement at the foot of the Larissa.[64] Indeed, there is no reason to believe that they desired anything more than that. The prime concern of most inhabitants of the city was earning their daily living, and there are indications that this was not always easy. Life expectancy was considerably shorter than in the late Bronze Age,[65] and natural disaster, disease, and accidents were not unknown. There is evidence of localized destruction by fire;[66] and though isolated, one of the most interesting finds from the city was a skeleton in an Early Geometric tomb. The skull bore clear evidence of infection, and beside the infected area was a carefully bored hole. The skull had been trepanned![67] Finally, there may have been some emigration from the plain—though not necessarily from the city of Argos—to the island of Cos in the Proto-geometric period.[68] Its causes cannot be determined. But it could not have been for commercial purposes, and no great numbers seem to have been involved.

Although the Dark Age was primarily a period of slow and gradual development, there are indications that substantial changes were begin-ning to occur by the late ninth or the early half of the eighth century. Sites such as Lerna and Berbati which had previously been uninhabited were once again settled. This may reflect a general increase in the popu-lation throughout the plain and some relocation of its inhabitants as a result. From this time, too, certain tombs with an extraordinary amount of grave offerings have been discovered,[69] and this may suggest that economic distinctions were becoming more pronounced. Undoubtedly, however, the most obvious and perhaps the most significant change is discernible in the pottery. After several centuries of slow evolution, the pace of stylistic development began to accelerate markedly. These changes signaled the inauguration of a new and important era in Argive history, and they can be more meaningfully considered when we deal with the archaeological evidence for the latter half of the eighth century.

With this discussion of the archaeological material behind us, we are now in a better position to assess the true place of Argos in Dark Age Greece. Although this material provides only limited information and leads to conclusions that are perhaps more negative than positive, it is, nonetheless, the best evidence we possess for the history of Argos in the Dark Age. The picture that emerges from this material differs consider-ably from the picture conveyed by the literary tradition and subscribed to by many modern scholars. The archaeological evidence suggests that Argos was a small, self-sufficient village in the Argive plain, not the capi-tal city of any wide ranging Dorian empire.

Chapter III:

The Role of Argos
in Dark Age Greece

Most modern attempts to reconstruct early Argive history have been based almost exclusively on ancient literary remains. As a result, they greatly misconstrue the role Argos played in Dark Age Greece. Indeed, the early history of Argos has been distorted since antiquity. From the literary evidence alone, one gets the impression that Argos was the center of an extensive empire during this period, that it was the mother city of numerous colonies founded throughout the Aegean, and that its traditional enmity with Sparta had already begun before the Dark Age came to an end. However, the literary evidence we have for the history of Argos across these centuries is fragmentary and limited; it dates from a period much later than the events it purports to describe; and it comes largely from writers who have no great claim to accuracy. To say that this evidence must be used with caution is an understatement; unfortunately, this has not always been done. Modern scholars have not only accepted the exaggerations and distortions inherent in the ancient literary tradition, but they have used these as a foundation upon which to construct an even more highly exaggerated and distorted picture of Dark Age Argos. Much of what passes as fact for this period of Argive history is not fact at all, and before proceeding, several erroneous notions must be briefly considered.

The most common misconception about early Argive history is that Argos ruled an extensive empire during the Dark Age. The earliest literary reference that might be interpreted as proof of such an empire is found in the Catalogue of Ships in the second book of Homer's *Iliad*.[1] Here we are told that Diomedes, king of Argos, controlled Tiryns, Asine, Troezen, Eionia, Epidaurus, Masses, and the island of Aegina. Most scholars now agree that the Catalogue of Ships is a genuine Mycenaean document and that it reflects, at least in a general sense, political conditions in Greece during the Mycenaean period.[2] The Catalogue may be a Mycenaean document, but the proposition that it reflects Mycenaean political conditions is not at all certain and would seem to have little to recommend it. It is difficult to believe that the rulers of the mighty fortress at Tiryns were subject to the control of the king of Argos, as the Catalogue indicates, and it is equally difficult to believe that the Argive plain was politically divided with part of it forming an Argive empire under Diomedes and another part forming a Mycenaean empire under Agamemnon. In an effort to escape this dilemma, it has been suggested[3] that the poet's reference to an Argive empire is a later addition to the Catalogue, an addition that reflects political conditions much closer to his own day, and the cities that acknowledge the suzerainty of Diomedes in the Catalogue must have acknowledged the supremacy of Argos about the time the poem was finally written down in the eighth century. This is a tempting solution to the problem, but unfortunately it rests on the assumption that an Argive empire existed during the Dark Age. Both the archaeological evidence from the Argive plain and our knowledge of Greece generally suggest that such an assumption is completely unwarranted. In the final analysis there is no greater likelihood that the empire attributed to Diomedes in the Catalogue of Ships can be assigned to the Dark Age any more easily than to the Mycenaean period, and it seems best to dismiss the passage entirely. Homer was, after all, a bard not a historian.

At the same time, however, it must be acknowledged that he had a tremendous influence on later Greek writers, and another passage of the *Iliad* seems to have contributed to the development of the ancient belief that Argos ruled an extensive empire in the Dark Age. At *Iliad* 2.108 we read that Agamemnon was "lord of many isles and of all Argos." A strictly literal interpretation of this passage would completely contradict the position assigned to Argos in the Catalogue of Ships. Here Argos is regarded not as an independent kingdom under its own king, but rather as a territorial possession of Agamemnon. The passage cannot be interpreted literally, however, for in it Homer is obviously using the term *Argos* to refer to a much larger geographical area than the settlement nestled at the foot of the Larissa. This has not always been understood, however, and Herodotus for one seems to have misinterpreted the passage. He reports that the Argives once controlled the entire western coastal area of the Gulf of Argos down to its southernmost tip at Cape Malea and the island of Cythera, as well as "the rest of the islands." This passage as well as other passages of Herodotus commonly cited as proof that Argos once controlled an empire will be discussed in greater detail below. Here it is necessary only to note that Beloch long ago recognized that Herodotus's inclusion of the offshore islands under Argive control was a reminiscence of Homer and specifically *Iliad* 2.108.[4] But Beloch did not go far enough, for if Herodotus believed that Argos once controlled the islands off the coast, he was all but compelled to believe that Argos also controlled the coastline opposite these islands. Accordingly, not just the latter portion of Herodotus's statement but the entire passage may well reflect nothing more than a Homeric reminiscence.

Yet it is not Homer and Herodotus that are usually cited to prove that an Argive empire existed in the Dark Age; in fact, most of the reports come from writers who lived in and after the fourth century B.C. It would be helpful to know where these men received their information about Dark Age Argos, but there is no definitive solution to this problem. It is surely suggestive, however, that a number of fifth-century writers chose Argive topics and settings for their works. Unfortunately most of these literary products have disappeared and survive only in fragments. Bronze Age Argos provided Aeschylus with the setting for his Danaid trilogy and several other plays. Acusilaus, an Argive native, wrote a work entitled *Genealogies*, in which he seems to have combined local legend and mythology with Greek legend and mythology generally. Hellanicus may have written a pseudohistorical work, the *Argolica*, as well as his *Priestesses of Hera*.[5] Two plays of Euripides, the *Temenus* and *Temenidae*, were actually set in Dark Age Argos, and a third, the *Archelaus*,[6] apparently dealt with the founding of the Macedonian monarchy by Archelaus, who was supposedly a son of Temenus. Temenus, in turn, was a direct descendant of Heracles who received Argos as his portion of the Peloponnesus after it had been conquered by the Dorians. It seems reasonable to suppose that the play named for him and his family dealt with this subject in a tragic setting. Tragedy is not, of course, history, and the likelihood that Euripides preserved any useful historical information is not great. Even Hellanicus, the most historically minded of these fifth-century writers, had little sound knowledge of events that occurred in the Dark Age. As I shall discuss at greater length in the next chapter, the Argive Heraeum was constructed only about the middle of the eighth century. But Hellanicus carried his list of priestesses of Hera well back into the Bronze Age, at least three generations before the Trojan War, and fully two of the three books he compiled on this subject[7] seem to have been concerned with the period before a temple of Hera was even constructed at the site. This should serve as fair warning that fifth-century writers had no reliable information on the Dark Age, and the fact that most of our specific references to an Argive empire come from still later works is hardly reassuring.

Appollodorus provides the most elaborate account of the establishment of the Dorians at Argos, but our chief sources for an Argive empire are the fourth-century historian Ephorus, who is quoted extensively by Strabo, and Pausanias. In both these works the empire that Argos supposedly controlled in the Dark Age is referred to as the Lot of Temenus.[8] The very mention of Temenus in this context suggests that Euripides was the ultimate source employed by these writers, but since the plays have been lost, this cannot be definitively proven.[9] What is clear, however, is that Ephorus's reference to this lot constitutes the earliest surviving mention of it in all extant Greek literature. Several versions of the story have come down to us, and although there is some variation in detail, the main outline seems fairly clear. The Dorians conquered the Peloponnesus under the sons of Aristomachus, a direct descendant of Heracles. These sons, Cresphontes, Aristodemus, and Temenus, divided up the Peloponnesus by lot after it had been conquered. Cresphontes secured Messenia; Aristodemus—or if he had already died as in one version of the story, his descendants—secured Laconia; and Temenus secured Argos. With the city of Argos as the seat of their power, Temenus and his descendants then supposedly went on to establish an empire, and it is this empire that is referred to as the Lot of Temenus. In accordance with the *Iliad*, this empire embraced the cities of Troezen and Epidaurus in the eastern Argolid, and, presumably, the island of Aegina since this island originally belonged to Epidaurus.[10] But it also encompassed much more. Phlius to the northwest of the Argive plain was also included, as was Sicyon[11] much farther to the north and only a short distance from the Gulf of Corinth. So, too, it almost goes without saying, were the various settlements within the Argive plain itself.

Most of our information on this Lot of Temenus comes to us from Pausanias, and there are several glaring inconsistencies in his account. First, he mentions in an often ignored phrase that Deiphontes, who supposedly led the force of Dorians against and captured Epidaurus, seceded from τῶν ἄλλων Ἀργείων upon the death of Temenus a short time later. Hence, even if Pausanias could be cited as proof of Argive control over this city in the eastern Argolid, his own words dictate that this control was at best ephemeral and lasted only for a brief moment. Moreover, he goes on to say that it was a group of Argives from Epidaurus who took control of the island of Aegina, and since these Argives had broken away from τῶν ἄλλων Ἀργείων, it follows that any control Argos might have exercised over Aegina must also have been ephemeral. Finally, his report concerning the capture of Sicyon and Phlius is equally disturbing. Supposedly, Sicyon was captured first, and only a generation later did Phlius succumb to a combined attack spearheaded from Sicyon and Argos. Phlius lies precisely on the most direct route between Argos and Sicyon. It is difficult, therefore, to imagine a force leaving Argos, bypassing Phlius, proceeding on to conquer Sicyon and annex it to Argive territory, while Phlius situated between them remained an independent settlement for yet another generation.

Such an incongruous account ought to be dismissed immediately.[12] Unfortunately, this has not always been done; ancient writers are not alone in creating empires where in fact none exist. Modern scholars have been equally adept. Those who accept the literary tradition at its face value are distressing enough, but still more disconcerting are modern attempts to enlarge upon the literary tradition by grasping at any bit of information that could be interpreted as lending support to it. A study of Greek mythology long ago led Gruppe to the conclusion that Argos must once have exercised control over a far-flung empire which included even the island of Rhodes.[13] Still more radical were the attempts of Vollgraff and Lenschau to concoct an Argive empire extending from Macedonia and Thrace in the north to Crete in the south and Asia Minor in the east.

The evidence on which these views are based is so shaky, however, that they need not be taken seriously. Vollgraff's evidence consisted of a third-century inscription that gave the names of the Argive phratries. Since he was able to trace many of these names to locations outside the Argolid and to heroes whom he considered to be non-Argive in origin, he concluded that the areas from which these names were derived must once have been subject to Argive control. Lenschau, having accepted the conclusions both of Vollgraff and Gruppe, went on to extend this empire even farther. He noted the presence of cults that he considered to be of Argive origin in widely dispersed areas of the Aegean and supposed that these cults were introduced into these areas when they were conquered by the Argives.[14] These are extreme views, however, and need be taken no more seriously than literary reports emanating from late antiquity. Yet even more cautious scholars are willing to credit Argos with controlling at least a good portion of the eastern Peloponnesus during the Dark Age,[15] and such views have little more to recommend them than do the more radical views of Vollgraff, Lenschau, and Gruppe.

Even if there were no other evidence to dispel the notion of a Dark Age Argive empire, the simplicity of life in Dark Age Greece would render it highly improbable. This was hardly an age in which political institutions had been perfected to a point where effective control could be exercised over a wide area; nor had political organization become sophisticated enough to allow any state to muster the strength and resources, nor to provide the continuity of policy, necessary for the creation and maintenance of any empire. This was, moreover, a period when trade was at a minimum and each geographical area was largely self-sufficient. In such circumstances Argos would have had little or nothing to gain from possession of the territory commonly assigned to her. The mountainous and generally unproductive eastern Argolid could have contributed little to the welfare of the inhabitants of the city of Argos, whose needs must have been all but completely supplied by the fertile Argive plain. Nor would possession of this area have contributed to the defense of Argos. Any attack originating overseas would have come via the Gulf of Argos rather than overland from the east coast of the Peloponnesus, and it is not likely that an invasion could have been launched upon the city of Argos from the eastern Argolid. Although only limited excavation has been undertaken in this area, there is as yet no trace of habitation either at Epidaurus or Troezen in the Dark Age. The same is true of Sicyon and Phlius, where no archaeological remains earlier than the eighth century have yet been found. Only at Aegina, where there is a complete sequence of vases from the tenth century onward, is the picture somewhat different. Although subsequent excavation might necessitate a substantial alteration or even complete abandonment of this view, in the light of our present knowledge, the greater portion of this supposed early Argive empire seems to have been uninhabited wasteland in the Dark Age.[16] Even if we acknowledge the possibility that Argos might have controlled the cities traditionally included within the Lot of Temenus, we would have to face the reality that such an empire would hardly have been profitable or practical.

Before leaving this subject there is some epigraphical evidence to be considered. Although this evidence dates only from the sixth and fifth centuries, it still has some bearing on earlier Argive history, for it was apparently during the latter half of the eighth century that the alphabet was diffused throughout the Greek mainland. For several centuries thereafter, local variations existed, and not until the alphabet became standardized in the fifth century were they finally eradicated. Thanks to Jeffery's excellent study of Greek scripts, we now know that a distinct Argive alphabet was employed only in a very limited geographical area and, most important, that this alphabet was not used in any of the cities traditionally included within the Lot of Temenus. The alphabet employed at Aegina closely resembles that employed in Attica; the alphabet used in the eastern Argolid was similar to and in all probability derived from the Spartan not the Argive alphabet. To the northwest of the Argive plain, at Sicyon, Phlius, and Cleonae, and even much closer to the plain at Nemea, the script employed closely resembled and was most likely derived from the Corinthian.[17] It would appear, therefore, that Argos had such limited contact with areas immediately adjacent to the Argive plain in the latter part of the eighth century that the inhabitants of this surrounding territory were more familiar with the alphabet in use at Corinth or Sparta than they were with the alphabet then in use at Argos. If the cities traditionally included within the Lot of Temenus were obviously not in very close contact with Argos toward the end of the Dark Age, we have no reason to assume that they could have had closer relations with Argos earlier in the Dark Age when conditions were still more primitive. Although there may be a germ of truth in legends that connect with Argos the establishment of Dorian kingdoms in such places as Corinth and Megara,[18] there is no reason to believe that Argos could ever have exercised hegemony over these regions or over a very substantial area during the Dark Age.

In the final analysis, the presumed existence of an Argive empire in this period rests on no solid foundations. Later literary references to such an empire cannot be accepted at face value, for the evidence offered is internally contradictory and not consistent with the simple conditions that prevailed throughout Greece in this period, and is not confirmed in contemporary archaeological remains or in the earliest epigraphical evidence we possess. In fact, the narrow and limited area in which a distinct Argive alphabet was employed in historical times is strikingly consistent with the narrow distribution of Argive Geometric pottery.[19] This evidence tends to support the conclusion deduced from the archaeological evidence discussed in the preceding chapter that throughout the Dark Age, Argos was a small, self-sufficient settlement with little power or even influence beyond its own village and the fields immediately surrounding it.

It was, in fact, suggested above that there is no reason to believe that Argos even controlled the Argive plain in the Dark Age, although such control is usually assumed along with the existence of an Argive empire, and select passages from Pausanias and Strabo are then cited as proof. Although Pausanias does tell us that Argos destroyed a number of settlements in the plain, he was certainly referring to events that occurred at a much later date. In all probability his information pertains to the destruction of Asine in the eighth century, Nauplia in the seventh century, and Mycenae and Tiryns in the first half of the fifth century.

Moreover, the passages of Strabo that are also cited apparently refer to these same events, for it has been pointed out that the information he supplied was pulled together from various periods with little regard for chronology.[20] Yet the Argive destruction of these various settlements in the plain, even though it occurred well after the Dark Age, cannot pass unnoticed here, for clearly at the moment of their destruction they could not have been firmly under Argive control. And if Asine, Nauplia, Mycenae, and Tiryns were so insecurely and tenuously controlled by Argos in the eighth, seventh, and fifth centuries that these mere villages could—even at their peril—disobey Argive wishes, then surely Argive control over them must have been even more insecure and tenuous during the Dark Age when political machinery was more primitive.

Together with the erroneous notion that Argos controlled an extensive empire in the Dark Age, we must consider the widely held belief that Argos served as the mother city of numerous colonies founded throughout the Mediterranean in this period. The two are surely linked, for any scholar, ancient or modern, who was convinced that Argos ruled an extensive empire could easily be led to believe that the city did indeed found a number of overseas colonies. There are numerous reports in ancient Greek literature of colonies supposedly founded by the Argives,[21] and although we cannot dismiss all of them out of hand, most would seem to have little to recommend them. It is highly unlikely that the conditions that gave rise to colonization in Greece—a surplus of population, a shortage of cultivable land, or some combination of both[22]—could have been operative at Argos during the Dark Age. The Argive plain was a fertile area; it supported a large population in Mycenaean times and in later Greek history as well. Surely it could support the greatly diminished population residing there in the Dark Age.

It is clear that some inhabitants of the Argive plain and perhaps even the city of Argos fled from this area in the movements of people that accompanied the waves of destruction that swept over the Greek mainland in the thirteenth and twelfth centuries. It is possible, but by no means provable, that later reports of Argive colonization on the island of Cyprus and along the southern coastal area of Asia Minor may derive from some vague recollection of these movements. We are told that the Argives founded colonies at Curium on Cyprus[23] and at several cities

(Tarsus, Soli, Aspendus, and Argeia) in Pamphylia and Cilicia on the Asia Minor mainland.[24] In each of these areas there is some evidence indicating an influx of newcomers late in the Bronze Age, but not at any other time before the Hellenistic period and especially not in the Dark Age.[25] Such movements of people cannot be regarded as deliberate colonization, however, and if Argives did settle in these areas late in the Bronze Age, the archaeological evidence and our knowledge of Greek history generally indicate that they had neither the need nor the ability to maintain contact with their former area of habitation. In this same connection, it is also possible that some Argives may have been involved in the Ionian migration and may eventually have settled in cities along the western coastal area of Asia Minor;[26] but again there is no evidence to suggest, and no reason to believe, that once they left the Argive plain they ever had any further contact with the people who continued to reside there during the Dark Age.

It is not my intention to review here all later literary reports of Argive colonization in this period. It could easily be shown that most of these reports find little support in the contemporary archaeological material. In this respect, reports of Argive colonization on the island of Crete provide a good case study. Supposedly, the Argives founded numerous colonies on the island.[27] As noted in the previous chapter, there appears to have been little if any contact between the Argive plain and Crete during the Dark Age. So far as I am aware no objects of Cretan origin have ever turned up at Argos and no Argive material has turned up on Crete. Nor is there any evidence that Argive potters were affected by Cretan works or that Cretan potters were affected by Argive works. There is important evidence from Cnossus where a complete record of Cretan ceramic development across nearly 500 years has been preserved, and the remains from this site can be considered representative for nearly the whole island in the Dark Age. The chief external influence on the local ceramic style, slight though it was, came from Attica, as did the bulk of the imported pottery. Moreover, the method of burial employed at Cnossus was almost universally cremation in contrast to the inhumation burial employed at Argos.[28] Cnossus is of especial importance, for it is one Cretan site that is widely acknowledged as an Argive colony.[29] The evidence on which this view is based, however, is less than compelling. It is derived largely from later literary tradition and a fifth-century inscription recording a treaty among Argos, Cnossus, and Tylissus. The inscription is badly mutilated and nowhere in the surviving portion is Cnossus specifically referred to as an Argive colony. It is only in a restoration of the missing portion of the text that we read that Cnossus and Tylissus were colonies of Argos.[30] In view of the archaeological evidence both from Crete and the Argive plain, and in view of our knowledge of the Dark Age generally, Argive colonization of Cnossus and Tylissus in the ninth century, as Vollgraff suggests, seems less than likely.

There is one area where Argive colonization has been reported that requires more careful consideration. It has already been mentioned that the Protogeometric pottery from the island of Cos is similar to the Protogeometric pottery from Argos, and it was acknowledged as possible that some inhabitants from the Argive plain, though not necessarily from the city of Argos, may have settled on the island in the Protogeometric period. There are also reports of Argive colonization on the nearby islands Cnidus and Rhodes and the Asia Minor coast opposite the island. It seems unlikely that Argives actually settled on the mainland in this period,[31] and the reports of colonization on Cnidus are hardly reliable.[32] For Rhodes, however, both Thucydides and Pindar[33] report that the island was colonized by the Argives. If such colonization actually took place, it must have occurred in the Dark Age. Rhodes seems not to have served as a refuge settlement in the Late Bronze Age. In fact, the island seems to have been abandoned completely sometime before the LH III C period came to an end. The earliest post-Mycenaean remains date from the Late Protogeometric period, and apparently new settlers moved into the area at this time. The archaeological evidence does not enlighten us about the origin of these settlers. The pottery they employed was similar to contemporary Attic pottery, but whereas the Athenians cremated their dead, these settlers on Rhodes apparently employed both cremation and inhumation burial until about the middle of the eighth century when cremation became almost universal.[34] Apart from the archaeological evidence, there is some evidence to suggest that these settlers might have come from the Argolid. The fact that the gods and goddesses worshipped at both locations were similar is of doubtful significance, but there are other indications. The Argive alphabet would seem to have been derived from this part of the world,[35] and at Lindus one phyle bore the name Argeia and one deme the name Argos. It seems probable that these names came into existence at a date much later than the Dark Age,[36] but it is not easy to explain why they were chosen if the inhabitants did not believe they had originally come from Argos. For what it is worth, there is epigraphical evidence from the third century B.C. in which a Rhodian clearly traces his origins back to Argos.[37] It must be admitted as possible that some settlers from Argos did arrive at Rhodes in the early part of the Dark Age, but beyond this we can say little.

In the final analysis, the literary evidence for Argive history in the Dark Age leads to conclusions that cannot be reconciled with those reached on the basis of the archaeological evidence. There would seem to be no reason to prefer later and often manifestly confused literary accounts to the contemporary physical remains. Yet the literary evidence has exercised a powerful influence on modern scholarship. It seems abundantly clear, however, that Argos was not the mother city of numerous colonies founded throughout the Mediterranean Sea and that it did not rule an extensive empire, or even a modest empire, in the Dark Age. In fact, Argos seems not to have been in complete control of the Argive plain.

If these conclusions are correct, there is one further notion about early Argive history that must be dispelled before we proceed. This is the view held by ancient and modern scholars alike that Argos and Sparta were bitter enemies in this period. The chief source for the notion that enmity existed between the two states in this early period is Pausanias, who tells us that Argos and Sparta fought over the territory of Cynouria even before the first Olympiad;[38] but there is no reason to take this report seriously. Thucydides[39] leaves no doubt that in the latter part of the fifth century at least the chief cause of conflict and hostility between the two states was this area of Cynouria, but it is important to understand why this was true. The area had no economic importance for either state: its agricultural land was limited; it possessed no known natural resources; and the coastline, with few good harbors, was inhospitable. It was, rather, the strategic location of Cynouria that was important to both states. Situated between the Argive plain and Laconia, it served to separate and divide Argos and Sparta. The Spartans had to have access to it before they could hope to invade the Argive plain successfully; conversely, the Argives had to control it if they were to prevent the Spartans from invading their territory.[40] Neither state could have been deeply concerned about Cynouria in the Dark Age, when Sparta had not yet fully acquired control over the Eurotas Valley and Argos had not yet gained complete control over the Argive plain. It was only after Sparta and Argos had advanced sufficiently to covet the holdings of the other that Cynouria became strategically important.

There is another report of warfare between Argos and Sparta just after 750 that might be mentioned here. According to Ephorus there was a war between the two states as a result of the usurpation of the Olympic games in 748 B.C. by the Argive tyrant Pheidon. The whole problem of establishing Pheidon's date will be considered at greater length in a later chapter, however, and it is only necessary to say here that he could not possibly have been ruling Argos in the middle of the eighth century.

Chapter IV:

The Consolidation of
the Argive Plain
in the Latter Half
of the Eighth Century

The latter half of the eighth century was in many respects one of the most amazing periods in all Greek history. During this short space of time the Greek world changed dramatically. After several hundred years of steady but slow progress, Greece began to break forth from the Dark Age, and from 750 onward rapid strides were made in all fields of human endeavor. Within the last half of the eighth century contact with the Orient was renewed on a large scale; the alphabet, which had only recently been taken over from the Phoenicians, was diffused throughout all of Greece; and the oldest literary products of the western world, beginning with the *Iliad* of Homer, were committed to writing. For the first time since the days of Mycenae there was monumental architectural construction. The population was increasing and doing so at such a rate that it became necessary to send out colonies from the Greek mainland. By the end of the century a degree of ordered life was attained as the polis was emerging, but at the same time warfare increased as individual poleis initially sought to consolidate the territory surrounding their polis and subsequently to extend their territorial holdings at the expense of other poleis. In certain states, too, social unrest and class conflict followed closely on the emergence of the polis, and primitive kings were giving way to aristocratically dominated governments. In these respects and others of equal significance this was a half century of great achievement, advancement, and change. It stands in sharp contrast to the gradual development that characterized the preceding 400 years of Greek history.[1]

Throughout the Dark Age, as we have seen, the history of Argos differed little from that of the rest of Greece. It was a settlement of modest proportions located in the rich and fertile Argive plain. Owing to the favorable agricultural conditions of the area and to the prevailing conditions of the period, Argive relations with the rest of Greece and the rest of the Aegean were narrowly circumscribed. Nonetheless, Greek tradition was at least partially correct in assigning to Argos a prominent position in post-Mycenaean Greece. Though it ruled no vast empire, Argos from all appearances was the leading settlement in the Peloponnesus and one of the most advanced and progressive in all of Greece. This statement is equally valid whether applied to the very beginning of the Dark Age about 1100 B.C. or to the very end of this period about the middle of the eighth century. The latter half of the eighth century was a period of striking change at Argos, as it was throughout the Greek world generally, but it was also a period of divergent, almost contradictory development. Although the position of Argos within the Argive plain was enhanced, its importance within the Peloponnesus and within the Greek world as a whole seems to have been declining at least in a relative sense. Argos remained aloof from overseas trade, and by 700 B.C., artistically at least, Argos was rapidly declining to a position of secondary importance.

There is very little literary evidence for this period in Argive history, and what we do have was written only at a much later date and often tends to confuse rather than clarify the issues. There is an abundance of archaeological evidence, however, and this evidence must continue to serve as our most trustworthy guide to Argive history. In this chapter I shall discuss briefly this archaeological evidence and attempt to relate it to the literary evidence. Finally, I shall attempt to sketch, in general terms, a history of Argos in this extremely important half century.

One of the most obvious developments occurring throughout Greece in this period was a dramatic increase in population. The archaeological evidence indicates clearly that this was true not only at Argos but throughout the Argive plain generally. Late Geometric pottery has been found at a number of sites which have not produced any Early or Middle Geometric pottery, and presumably, therefore, sites such as Dendra, Amoriani, Monastiraki, and Kandia were now inhabited or, more properly, reinhabited for the first time in several centuries, though from the small quantities of Late Geometric pottery found there, it would appear that this did not happen on any extensive scale. At other settlements such as Tiryns, Mycenae, and perhaps Lerna and Asine, there is a greater quantity of pottery, and presumably there was a larger population than there had been for centuries. Yet none of these communities exhibits evidence of the sharp increase in population detectable at Argos. Late Geometric pottery has been found in almost every excavation that has been made in the modern city; cemeteries were used intensively in this period, and it was necessary to open up additional burial grounds as well.[2] Unfortunately, however, even with numerous remains it is not possible to trace the precise extent of the Late Geometric settlement at Argos. It would seem, however, that it did not reach so far to the south or west as it did at a later date; but it did occupy a considerable area in the plain and probably extended farther to the north and east than it did in the archaic period or even in classical times. It also spread up the slopes of the Aspis and extended over part of the old Mycenaean burial ground on the Deiras ridge. The impression one gets when examining the archaeological evidence from this period is that after a steady but slow growth over several centuries during the Dark Age, Argos grew considerably in the latter half of the eighth century, and what had previously been a small village was transformed into an extensive settlement.[3]

Not only was the city becoming more populous in this period, but there are clear indications that it was becoming more prosperous as well. Several temples were apparently built within the city proper. No remains of these early structures have ever been found, probably because they were made of mud brick and wood, and so all trace of them has long since been obliterated. But their existence can be reasonably inferred from other archaeological evidence. On the Aspis, Late Geometric sherds have been found beneath the foot of the terrace on which the temple of Apollo later stood, and this implies that some deity was probably being worshiped on the site during the Late Geometric period. On the summit of the Larissa, where two temples existed in Pausanias's day, there are foundation remains that cannot be dated; but an abundance of Late Geometric sherds and a discarded votive deposit containing objects from the end of the eighth century testify to the existence of some religious cult here too.[4]

There is much more solid evidence for the building that was undertaken at the Argive Heraeum in the latter half of the eighth century. The site chosen for the construction of this temple was extremely irregular, and before a temple could be erected, a massive retaining wall, the so-called Old Temple Terrace Wall, and a terrace had to be built. Both these structures stand there today, almost as majestically as on the day of their construction. The Old Temple Terrace Wall was by no means a simple structure; over fifty-five meters in length and varying in height between three and five meters, it was composed of large, unworked blocks of stone which were laid up without mortar. The size of some of the stones used in its construction cannot pass unnoticed; some were as large as five meters in length and two meters high. The wall is strongly reminiscent of the Cyclopean architectural style used during the Mycenaean period, which deceived the excavators of the site into believing that the wall was contemporaneous with the walls at Tiryns.[5] In fact, however, it dates much later. Although no temple remains found at the site can be dated before the first half of the seventh century, it is clear that construction must have been carried on in the latter half of the eighth century. The earliest ceramic remains found there date slightly before the middle of the eighth century, but this does not prove that the temple was erected at that time, as has been suggested. Only a few sherds can be dated this early, and in any event the actual construction of the retaining wall, the temple terrace, and the temple itself must have taken a considerable amount of time. Accordingly, although work on the project may well have begun slightly before 750, the great bulk of it must have been done in the third quarter of the eighth century; soundings beneath the retaining wall and the floor of the temple terrace, conducted by Blegen, support this date. He recovered some Geometric sherds, but he does not report finding any Protocorinthian pottery; presumably, at least this portion of the construction must have been completed before the appearance of the Protocorinthian style about 725 B.C.[6]

For its day the construction of this complex was a gigantic undertaking; not since the great days of Mycenae nearly 500 years earlier had construction on such an impressive scale been attempted. Moreover, since the site of this building complex was situated some five miles away from the city of Argos, a roadway must have traversed the distance between the city and the temple, and before this roadway could have been constructed, the Inachus River had to be bridged. The construction of this temple of Hera was, in short, a major undertaking, which in and of itself clearly demonstrates the economic prosperity of the city of Argos in the latter half of the eighth century.

Other archaeological evidence supports this conclusion, and by far the most important body of this evidence is the ceramic remains. The latter half of the eighth century marks, without a doubt, the apogee of Argive activity in the production of painted pottery. Neither before nor after this period did the potters of Argos produce finer vases nor were they ever manufactured in greater abundance. Some of the tombs dating from this period are remarkably rich in ceramic remains, and, as noted above, almost everywhere that excavation has been undertaken in the modern city, Late Geometric pottery has turned up.[7] No less striking than the vast quantity of this pottery at Argos is its generally excellent quality. Two distinct phases of Argive Late Geometric pottery can be recognized, with considerable differences between them. In the earliest of these phases, LG I, there is still some resemblance to the products of the Middle Geometric period; but there are also some significant new developments, such as the appearance of new shapes, slight variations in standard shapes, the progressive improvement in painting technique, and the emergence of new decorative motives and more complex figured representation. It is difficult to generalize about the LG II style, which covers approximately the last quarter of the eighth century. This period has been characterized as one of massive production and precipitous evolution. There is the additional factor that a number of individual painters and workshops can be identified, and their styles vary greatly. Generally speaking, however, the style is characterized by the continuation of the developments of the preceding period, and it was during this phase that Argive Geometric pottery reached its zenith and within a relatively short time began to decline.[8] By the end of the eighth century, give or take a few years, vase shapes began to deteriorate; decoration, particularly but not exclusively on smaller vases, tends occasionally to be sloppy; sometimes the clay was inadequately prepared, and on occasion the pots were insufficiently fired. Such characteristics would appear, however, to be more representative of individual workmen and workshops than of the entire ceramic industry at Argos.[9] Argive Late Geometric pottery is generally of excellent quality, superior products representing fine workmanship by skilled craftsmen. The style was respected enough to exercise a predominant influence on the local style of Arcadian Geometric and had considerable influence at Sparta and Corinth and limited influence even at Athens. At the same time, it was a unique style with only a minimum of external influence exerted upon it, this influence coming particularly from Corinth but less frequently from Attica.[10] In sum, only the workshops of Athens were producing finer vases in the Late Geometric period, and it is generally acknowledged that the Argive school of Late Geometric pottery was the only one that could rival the Attic. The versatility of the Argive potters, moreover, is demonstrated by their occasional production of terra-cotta figurines that were as fine as any known from the Greek world.[11]

No discussion of Argive Late Geometric pottery would be complete without noting that it does exhibit some seemingly contradictory tendencies. In fact, Courbin[12] detects two distinct Argive Geometric styles, one which he calls the baroque and another the classic. The baroque is a rapidly executed, cursive style in which bold and none too precise brush strokes were used. It is a style that exudes energy, vitality, and vigor. The classic style, on the other hand, retains these qualities, but at the same time the work is done with much more care and precision. Both are thoroughly representative of Argive Late Geometric pottery, however, and there can be no doubt that in general this is a bold and confident style. Argive potters covered every square inch of exceptionally large vases with step meanders, rosette patterns, and other standard geometric motives, and they portrayed complex scenes of figured decoration depicting horses and other animals as well as human beings in typical scenes from everyday life. Yet by the end of the century, if not before, vigor and vitality had given way to a rather narrow conservatism. Occasionally Argive potters produced poor imitations of Corinthian products[13] and adopted an isolated orientalizing motif, but for the most part they were not receptive to new ideas or artistic innovations. This conservatism continued and indeed increased in the early decades of the seventh century, a development that will be discussed in greater detail in the next chapter. For the moment, however, it bears noting that no orientalizing style of pottery, as such, ever developed at Argos. Instead, Argive Geometric pottery simply evolved into a Subgeometric style that was almost wholly derivative from earlier Geometric traditions and except for the use of a few motives was almost wholly unaffected by the new styles of pottery making their appearance and the artistic revolution taking place throughout the Greek world by the last quarter of the eighth century.[14]

Whether any sweeping historical conclusions can be drawn from the fact that Argive Geometric pottery displays seemingly contradictory tendencies of boldness and confidence on the one hand and restraint and conservatism on the other is surely questionable; yet these same tendencies can seemingly be detected in other phases of Argive activity in this period. Thus, for example, the construction of the Argive Heraeum, which I shall have occasion to elaborate on further below, was a bold and confident measure, and Argive conservatism and restraint are perhaps reflected in the narrow distribution of Argive Late Geometric pottery and the generally limited overseas contacts of Argos, at least in a relative sense, in this period.

Despite the fact that Argive Late Geometric pottery was an exceptionally fine fabric, it was not widely exported nor was it exported in quantity. It has been noted above that before the latter half of the eighth century, Argive pottery was hardly ever exported beyond the Argive plain. But during this period for the first time it does begin to turn up over a more extensive area, though it was not so widely exported as has sometimes been suggested. Courbin's discussion of the subject remains vital.[15] He lists Argive vases or vase fragments dating from this period at Tegea, Aegina, Corinth, Perachora, Delphi, Athens, Melos, Ithaca, Megara Hyblaea, and Troezen. At first glance this would seem to indicate a substantial exportation of Argive Geometric pottery, but a closer examination of the material shows that this was not so. The entire amount found at all sites mentioned above constitutes only a minute quantity, and no one site produced more than a handful of fragments. Thus, for example, at Tegea there is a small oeonochoe and fragments of three other vases; at Delphi and at Troezen there is a single vase fragment at each site; even at Perachora, where strong Argive connections have long been taken for granted, and where Courbin acknowledges that numerous pieces strongly resemble Argive work, there is only a single fragmentary crater that he considers unquestionably Argive.[16]

On the basis of this evidence it must be concluded that there was no substantial exportation of Argive pottery in this period; rather, exportation was extremely limited and Argive Late Geometric pottery was not nearly so widely distributed as Athenian Late Geometric pottery or even Corinthian Late Geometric, a much less pretentious fabric. Given the quality and the quantity of the pottery found at Argos, this is indeed surprising; it seems to indicate that even in this age when most Greek states were rapidly increasing the tempo of their overseas trade, Argos had but limited commercial contacts. This conclusion, moreover, would seem to be confirmed by the small amount of foreign pottery that Argos was importing at the time. Except for vases from Corinth there are hardly any from other areas of Greece. A single fragment of a Cycladic vase, a single Laconian fragment, a few fragments from Athens, and a few others of indeterminate origin are all that have been identified.[17]

On the basis of ceramic evidence alone one might easily conclude that Argos remained totally aloof from overseas trade in this period, but this is not borne out by other archaeological evidence that must be considered. The Argive metal industry was thriving in the latter half of the eighth century; in fact Argos may well have been the leading center in all of Greece for the production of metal objects. Ancient literary reports indicate that the city was famous in antiquity for the manufacture of bronze objects,[18] and the archaeological evidence lends support to this literary tradition. We have already seen that the Argives were smelting silver in the Submycenaean period, and the manufacture of iron, bronze, and possibly even gold products apparently continued throughout the Dark Age. By the end of the eighth century Argive metalsmiths were, like their counterpart potters, skilled and competent craftsmen. Argive pins of the period are far superior even to those of Attica,[19] and chance has preserved for us what must have been one of the finest pieces produced at Argos in the late eighth century, a full suit of bronze armor complete with crested helmet.[20] Equally indicative of the strength of the Argive bronze industry are the finds from the Argive Heraeum. Nearly 6,000 metal objects were catalogued from the original excavation at the site, and subsequent work there has added many more. Most of these date from later than the period under consideration and need no detailed treatment here.[21] To illustrate the importance of metal objects for determining Argive contacts with other areas of the world, it will be sufficient to return for a moment to the bronze armor previously mentioned and the other metal objects found with it. The bronze breastplate shows familiarity with the bronzework of northern Europe or northern Italy. The helmet has striking similarities to contemporary Assyrian pieces, and two iron "fire-dogs" find their closest parallel in contemporary Etruscan works. A double ax found in the tomb is strikingly similar to axes from Crete.[22] There is no reason to believe that Argos was in direct contact with such wide geographical areas as the metalwork from this tomb might suggest, but it is obvious that foreign influence was being felt in the city. There is further confirmation of such influence in seal stones, which began to turn up in quantity at the Argive Heraeum in this period. It has been suggested that these seals had a Cycladic inspiration, that they were initially manufactured in the islands and from there were imported and subsequently imitated at Argos.[23]

There is, therefore, considerable evidence of contact between Argos and other areas of the Greek and non-Greek world in the latter half of the eighth century, but this contact should not be exaggerated. Seal stones were the work of only a limited number of craftsmen,[24] and the same is true of bronze objects as well. In relative terms, Argive contacts were much more narrow than those of Athens and Corinth. In fact, there is nothing to suggest that Argos had more than limited contact with the rest of Greece and even with the rest of the Peloponnesus. In many respects the Argive world was the rather narrow area of the Argive plain and not much more. There are indications that significant developments were occurring there.

In the production of painted pottery there seems to have been a trend toward localism within the plain. Pottery from the Protogeometric period and the earlier phases of the Geometric period found at the various sites within the plain is relatively homogeneous. But in the Late Geometric period each separate locality in Greece began to produce a type of pottery distinctly different from that being produced elsewhere, and the various settlements of the Argive plain were no exception. Compared with the workshops of Argos, those of Tiryns, Asine, and perhaps Midea were producing only inferior and provincial products.[25] Despite local variations, however, the Argive plain remained, as it had been throughout the Dark Age, a culturally unified area with Argos its center.

There is some evidence to suggest that Argos was enhancing its political importance within the Argive plain during this very period. As was pointed out in the previous chapter, settlements such as Mycenae, Tiryns, and Nauplia could hardly have been subject to Argos during the Dark Age; but before the latter half of the eighth century had passed, it seems clear that Argos was, at least in a limited sense, master of the Argive plain. Only two specific events that occurred in this period of Argive history can be spoken about with much assurance: one was the erection of the Argive Heraeum in the third quarter of the century, and the other was the destruction of Asine in the last quarter of the century. Neither can be treated as an isolated phenomenon. Rather, they must be considered together, and they must also be considered in the wider context of developments that were taking place in the Greek world as a whole.

The erection of the Heraeum was an important event in Argive history. The inhabitants of the city did not just begin to worship Hera at this time; indeed, it is commonly believed that her cult spread abroad through Greece from the city of Argos.[26] The intimate connection between Hera and Argos in the *Iliad* is of special importance,[27] for this poem in all probability antedates, or is approximately contemporaneous with, the construction of the Heraeum. Before the erection of this temple, Hera apparently had a temple or a shrine in the city of Argos proper, and possibly it was situated on the Larissa, where in Pausanias's day a temple of Hera Akraia was located.[28] The essential point to be stressed here, however, is that the construction of the Argive Heraeum signified a shift of Hera's chief shrine from the city of Argos to a site located five miles away from the city. Moreover, as noted above, this was a remarkable building project; nothing comparable had been undertaken anywhere in Greece for nearly 500 years. Stone blocks more than five meters long and two meters high are not easily moved over a distance of several miles. Dozens perhaps hundreds of workmen must have been required, and these men were asked to perform their services five miles from their homes. Even the construction of a bridge over the Inachus River and a roadway from the city to the temple was an ambitious endeavor. The state that undertook this project must have been wealthy enough to bear the expense involved; but more than wealth, the construction of the Argive Heraeum required manpower, cooperation, and, above all, planning and direction. Surely the erection of this temple[29] was a deliberate act, and we would like to know more about the circumstances and considerations that led up to it. Specifically, we would like to know why a new temple of Hera was erected at this particular time. And we would like to know, too, why it was erected at this particular site.

Although it may not be possible to answer these questions definitively, further consideration of them may prove useful. It bears noting that the inhabitants of the Greek world generally were becoming increasingly concerned with religion in the latter half of the eighth century,[30] and the inhabitants of the Argive plain were no exception. Religious scenes occur with great frequency on Argive vases of the period, and experiments with cremation were being made at Argos, Nauplia, and Asine.[31] Graves of the dead were being worshiped at Mycenae, in the city of Argos proper, and especially at the site of the Argive Heraeum, where no fewer than fifteen of the fifty-two Mycenaean chamber tombs nearby were found to contain deposits dating from the Late Geometric period.[32] In addition, mention has already been made of the construction of several temples within the city of Argos, and it should be pointed out, too, that at Tiryns the earliest votives from the deposit of the temple of Hera date from about the middle of the eighth century.[33] Finally, at Mycenae a shrine was built and a hero cult of Agamemnon established toward the end of the century.[34] It can hardly be doubted that the construction of the Argive Heraeum was in one sense at least another manifestation of an increasing concern with religion. However, the Argives may have been motivated by other concerns as well.

Although the question of why the Argives chose this particular site some five miles from their city for the location of the new temple cannot be answered definitively, we might guess that religious considerations played a part in the selection. But there is nothing to suggest that the site itself had any particular sanctity or religious significance. In the Mycenaean period a burial ground was located in the immediate vicinity, though the accompanying settlement has never been found. No burials at the site are later than LH III B, and presumably the settlement was abandoned at that time. It was unoccupied and possibly not even visited again until about the middle of the eighth century[35] when, as noted above, work began on the Heraeum. It was only at this time that the site became an important religious center—a fact not known to Greeks of the Classical period and one that is not always taken into account by modern scholars.[36] It was during the course of construction, undoubtedly, that the earlier chamber tombs were discovered and votive deposits placed in them. But there is no evidence to prove that the Argives were aware of these tombs before they began constructing the Heraeum, and we cannot use the presence of Late Geometric deposits in these chamber tombs to prove that the site had any particular sanctity or holiness in and of itself. Moreover, we do not know why the Greeks suddenly began to consider certain locations sacred and began worshiping certain gods or goddesses at them. So respected an authority as Nilsson believes that chance was often the governing factor.[37]

It would be cynical to suggest that political considerations alone lay behind the selection of the site chosen for the erection of the Argive Heraeum; yet the location cannot have been without significance. Situated some five miles from Argos, three miles from Mycenae, and approximately six miles from Tiryns, it was centrally located within the Argive plain.[38] A temple erected there could easily serve the inhabitants of all three cities, as well as those of Nauplia, a mile or so beyond Tiryns, and even Asine. It is well known that Hera was worshiped throughout the Argolid and in the plain particularly. She had a sanctuary, if not a temple, at Mycenae; and about 750 B.C. the Tirynthians dedicated a temple in her honor on their acropolis.[39] Presumably, therefore, the inhabitants of these communities would not have had any religious objection to the erection of a temple in her honor at this site centrally located within the Argive plain, and it is difficult to believe that the obvious advantages of this central location could have escaped the notice of those responsible for the erection of the Argive Heraeum. The location suggests that it was conceived as a shrine which could serve as a focal point of reverence and a center of worship not only for the population of the city of Argos, but for the population of the entire plain.[40] It may, in fact, not be going too far to suggest that the erection of this temple was part and parcel of a deliberate policy aimed at transforming Hera from a peculiarly local deity, the patroness of the city of Argos, into a sort of pan-Argive deity, the patroness of the entire Argive plain. In short, although the temple had religious implications, it may well have had political implications as well, for as Ehrenberg has recently reminded us, "the establishment and adoption of cults was a necessary concomitant of the formation and extension of political units. . . . "[41]

It cannot, unfortunately, be demonstrated that the temple was designed to serve the people of Tiryns, but there is some evidence that it was intended to accomodate worshipers from Mycenae as well as from Argos. Just east of the Heraeum and between it and Mycenae lies a deep ravine. Remains of a bridge that once spanned this ravine can still be seen there. Blegen[42] conducted some exploratory excavations around the foundations of this bridge, and although the precise date of its construction could not be determined, the only datable objects found were from the seventh century. From their location, however, Blegen concluded that they must have been deposited where they were found after the bridge had been constructed. Moreover, the architectural style of the bridge was similar to the style displayed at the Heraeum, and Blegen concluded that the two structures must have been erected at roughly the same time. The route of the road that once crossed this bridge cannot now be traced, but it is certain that it ran in the general direction of Mycenae and could, therefore, have served only one function: to provide access to the temple for worshipers coming from the general direction of Mycenae. It seems, therefore, that the temple was designed to serve the inhabitants of Mycenae as well as those of Argos; it is highly probable that it also served the inhabitants of Tiryns, Nauplia, and perhaps other settlements of the plain as well.

Moreover, we can be reasonably certain that at the time the temple was constructed in the third quarter of the eighth century, the Argives were on reasonably friendly terms with these other settlements. The erection of a temple at a completely undefended site five miles from the city of Argos was a bold and confident move. Clearly, the Argives anticipated that defending the shrine would be no problem. They would hardly have gone to the trouble and expense of erecting it if they had been at all concerned about an invasion of their territory by some other Peloponnesian state such as Sparta or if they had faced any serious opposition from other settlements in the immediate vicinity within the plain. Moreover, there is evidence indicating that these friendly relations continued into the last quarter of the eighth century. But there is also evidence that at the same time Argos had begun to encounter some limited local opposition. Mention has already been made of the foundation of a hero cult of Agamemnon just outside the citadel walls at Mycenae toward the end of the eighth century. The establishment of a shrine to this legendary king of Mycenae can only be regarded as an expression of Mycenaean rather than Argive sentiments, and it may well signify that relations between the two states were not as cordial as they had been a few years earlier.

A more important consideration for our purposes, however, is the destruction of Asine. The evidence for this event is both literary and archaeological. Pausanias informs us that the Argives attacked and destroyed Asine in the closing decades of the eighth century. By itself this report could hardly be considered decisive, but the archaeological evidence confirms it. The excavations at Asine have shown that the site was abandoned, if not in fact destroyed, about the time Pausanias says it was.[43] We cannot, however, take seriously Pausanias's report that the Argives destroyed Asine because the inhabitants of this village had aided the Spartans in an invasion of the Argive plain. As I have argued elsewhere,[44] this explanation is an obvious oversimplification and must be dismissed as erroneous. Nor is it likely that the Argives were motivated by a desire for territorial acquisition, for they did not occupy the town despite its favorable location for overseas trade and commerce. Rather, Asine was destroyed and its population expelled, after which presumably the Argives withdrew. Obviously, therefore, territorial acquisition as such was not behind the Argive attack on Asine any more than a desire to punish the Asineans for aiding the Spartans.

Any attempt to determine what the Argive motives in destroying Asine might have been must necessarily take into account the fact that relations between the two cities seem never to have been particularly close. Throughout the Dark Age, and even as recently as the time of its destruction, Asine, if the ceramic remains found at the site are any indication, seems to have had fully as much contact with Athens as with nearby Argos. The Asineans did not have a Dorian heritage, but were Dryopes, and they were still exhibiting pride in their Dryopian background nearly 1,000 years after the Argives destroyed their city. Moreover, they considered Dryops, their eponymous ancestor, to be the son of Apollo, and Apollo was the chief divinity of the site. So far as we know, Hera was never worshiped there.[45] It is clear, therefore, that there were significant differences between Argos and Asine long before the closing decades of the eighth century, and we must, accordingly, wonder why the Argives felt compelled to attack and destroy Asine at this time.

To answer this question we must first recognize that the destruction of Asine must be considered not as an isolated incident but rather in the light of evidence that suggests that warfare was becoming an increasingly important concern at Argos, as it was throughout the rest of Greece in the latter half of the eighth century. This is surely suggested by the archaeological evidence and especially by the ceramic remains. Mention has already been made of the bronze armor found in a Late Geometric grave at Argos, but the figured scenes on vases of the period are also significant. A number of diverse forms of combat and military armor are depicted on these vases; thus, for example, male figures in Argive art of the period are characteristically nude, the only detectable attire being defensive armor in a wide variety of styles and types. The only objects ever held in the hands of these figures, apart from the reigns or bridle of the horse, are military arms.[46] Horses are sometimes held in reign by helmeted warriors, and clay figurines of mounted warriors have been found. This would clearly suggest that the horse was used for military purposes in this period.[47] Interesting, too, is a sherd from the Heraeum depicting archers in action.[48]

The increasing concern with martial activity evident at Argos was not unique in the Greek world in the latter half of the eighth century, for warfare was becoming an increasingly frequent phenomenon at that time. It was in this period that Sparta and Messenia first engaged in combat over the territory of Messenia. In this period, too, Eretria and Chalcis first vied for control of the Lelantine Plain situated between them, and it is likely that Corinth and Megara went to war over the southern Megarid.[49] The causes of each of these wars are not difficult to find. As Greece emerged from the Dark Age, certain states were attempting to consolidate the territory around their particular polis, to increase their territorial holdings, and to extend their sphere of influence generally. It was a natural tendency for other states to resist such encroachment, and warfare resulted. The Argive destruction of Asine would seem to fit logically into this pattern, and it seems likely that Asine was destroyed because its inhabitants opposed Argive aims in the plain. In this connection, the strained relations between Argos and Asine stood in sharp contrast to the friendly relations between Argos and Tiryns and Nauplia. Both these cities were situated between Argos and Asine, and so far as we know neither state was disturbed when Asine was destroyed. Apparently, therefore, the act had their tacit approval at least, and perhaps they even cooperated with the Argives in the venture. We have strong evidence of close relations between Argos and Nauplia. The fact that the Argives had no interest in the harbor facilities of Asine can only mean that they had ready access to the closer port facilities at Nauplia.

It seems clear therefore, that with the destruction of Asine and the expulsion of its inhabitants, Argos was unchallenged master of the Argive plain, but the military aspect of Argive policy in achieving this position must not be overemphasized. Although warfare was undoubtedly an ever-present threat, the carefully selected site for the erection of the Argive Heraeum sugggests that religion was also an important aspect of Argos's overall policy. By and large, the Argives seem to have preferred to woo the other states of the plain by peaceful means, and they seem not to have attempted to gain direct control over them. There is important evidence to be discussed in the next chapter suggesting that both Tiryns and Nauplia retained at least a measure of independence in the seventh century, and even the inhabitants of tiny Mycenae could express independent sentiments when they began worshiping Agamemnon toward the end of the eighth century. Therefore, the evidence seems to suggest that the influence Argos had in the plain was only indirect; it derived no doubt, at least in part, from the fact that Argos was the most wealthy and populous settlement in the area and also that it probably enjoyed numerical and military superiority over its neighbors. But one other possibility must be considered.

It has frequently been suggested that Argos was the head of a religious association of states, an amphictiony.[50] The existence of such a league in the latter half of the eighth century is impossible to prove, and the evidence for its existence at any time in Argive history is far from conclusive. There is no direct evidence for such a league, and it can only be inferred from scattered references in a number of writers. Most important of these is Herodotus, who reports that in the early years of the fifth century, after Argos had been reduced to a second-rate power by Sparta, the Argives were able to levy fines against both Sicyon and Aegina because they had provided ships for the Spartan king Cleomenes in his invasion of the Argive plain. Although the Aeginetans refused to acknowledge the legitimacy of the Argive claim, the people of Sicyon actually made partial payment. Nowhere does Herodotus tell us on what basis or by virtue of what authority Argos levied these fines. But since Argos was not militarily powerful at the time, and since both Sicyon and Aegina were probably members of the Peloponnesian League, it is frequently assumed that the Argive claim derived from some religious authority that Argos possessed, and it is on this basis that it is commonly thought that Argos was once the leading state in a religious league.[51]

This is not much information to go on, and the issue is further complicated by the fact that there has been no general agreement about which god or goddess was the patron divinity of this league.[52] If Hera was the chief divinity of the Argive plain, Apollo was only slightly less important, and the view most widely expressed by present-day scholars maintains that the amphictiony had as its holy shrine a temple of Apollo. The tenuous nature of the arguments supporting this view, however, is well illustrated by the general disagreement and confusion about where this temple was located. The temple of Apollo on the Aspis at Argos, the temple of Apollo left standing by the Argives at Asine, and a hypothetical temple of Apollo located between Nauplia and Epidaurus have all been suggested and argued for, but none convincingly.[53]

If such a league did in fact exist, it seems much more likely that its sacred center was a temple of Hera, and it has on occasion been suggested that the Argive Heraeum served this function.[54] Although this suggestion cannot be proven, it may have more to recommend it than has previously been recognized. It would seem to be more than coincidence that this temple was erected at a site five miles from the city of Argos and located so that it could serve the inhabitants of all the communities of the plain at approximately the same time that Argos was enjoying a dominant position within the area. It is possible that political motives were as much a consideration in the erection of this temple as religious motives, that the Argives were attempting to capitalize on the intense religious feelings of the inhabitants of the plain by promoting the worship of Hera not merely as patroness of the city of Argos but as patroness of all the communities of the plain and by promoting the Heraeum as a sort of pan-Argive center of worship for the whole plain. Although this must remain an unproven hypothesis, it would provide a convenient explanation of why the inhabitants of Asine, who were not Dorian and whose chief divinity was Apollo, were reluctant to acknowledge not only the political supremacy of Argos but also the religious supremacy of Hera. It would also explain how Argos was able to gain ascendancy over the other settlements in the plain while allowing them to remain essentially independent communities. Finally, it should be noted that such a program is remarkably consistent with and may well reflect the dual tendencies of boldness and conservatism apparent in Argive Late Geometric pottery. The construction of the Heraeum was a bold and confident measure; yet the fact that the Argives were content with a certain amount of religious prestige derived from their connections with Hera and the maintenance of her temple and did not attempt to rule the cities of the Argive plain directly may well reflect a certain element of restraint that can also be detected in the products of the Argive potter.

Although the suggestion that the construction of the Heraeum was motivated as much by political as by religious considerations might reasonably be questioned, it cannot be objected to on the grounds that such deliberate planning was beyond the ability of the government of Argos in the latter half of the eighth century. The very construction of the Heraeum suggests otherwise. As noted above, this was a complex building project; it required both planning and direction, and this must have been supplied by the government of the city.

It is not easy, however, to make precise statements about the form and organization of this government or about the societal framework upon which it rested. Throughout the Dark Age the social and governmental institutions of Argos could have differed little from those of other Greek states. From the time of the Dorian invasion the city was ruled by a king who was neither absolute in power nor wealthy in resources.[55] He stood not far above his subjects, who were grouped into tribes or phylae. At Argos, as was common in Dorian states, there were three phylae, Dymanes, Hylleis, and Pamphyloi. There was also a fourth phyle, the Hyrnathioi, but this seems to have been instituted long after the Dark Age had come to an end.[56] Within each phyle there were a number of smaller, more personal associations, the phratries. Although essentially military brotherhoods, they assumed some importance in the government of the early Greek states and may, in addition, have been the single most important social unit in the early Greek states. We know little about the Argive phratries in the latter half of the eighth century, since the only information we have concerning them comes from a much later period. All that can be said for certain is that they were generally named after heroes from Argive or Greek mythology. But there were exceptions to this rule; some are clearly named after geographical locations in or near the Argive plain, others are named after members of the family of Odysseus, and the origin of the names of a few cannot be surely identified.[57] It is doubtful that any sweeping conclusions can be derived from this information,[58] and although the precise role of the phratry in the government of the city is not known to us, it might be reasonable to assume that since military activity was increasing in this period, the phratry was gaining additional influence as a result of its military importance.[59] All that can be said with much assurance about the government of Argos in the latter half of the eighth century, however, is that it was still at least nominally under the leadership of a king.[60]

It is impossible to determine how powerful a figure the Argive king was in this period, for there are clear indications that a wealthy class, an aristocracy, had by this time come into existence. This is affirmed by the richness of grave offerings which were buried with their owners. Some of the tombs that have been excavated in the city could not have been those of ordinary citizens. Certain cist tombs exhibit very careful construction and are of exceptional size. The ceramic remains associated with other tombs are even more impressive. Tomb I contained eighteen vases, and preliminary reports indicate that another tomb contained thirty vases.[61] The most impressive tomb of all, however, was the one that contained the full suit of bronze armor mentioned above. With this armor were ten fine vases, three gold rings, some fragmentary gold leaf, two double axes, twelve iron obeloi, and other iron objects.[62] Individual vases are equally revealing. One of the finest examples of Late Geometric Argive pottery is a very beautiful crater, half a meter in diameter, which served as a coffin for an infant. This vase, an absolute masterpiece of design and technique, is very carefully painted throughout, including four separate panels in each of which a man can be seen leading a horse. Even more conspicuous than the crater is a pyxis which was used as a pithos. It stands more than a meter high, and every square inch is covered with very carefully executed figured and geometric decoration. In place of the usual lid, it has as a cover an equally fine crater.[63]

These are impressive grave offerings and far beyond the means of any ordinary citizen; the men who lay buried with them were clearly men of means, and they offer silent testimony to the fact that an aristocracy had indeed come into being, not only at Argos but also at Tiryns and Nauplia and perhaps elsewhere in the plain as well.[64] This is similar to developments in other parts of Greece, for as prosperity increased tremendously in the late eighth century, some men benefited from it far more than others. The wealth of Greek aristocrats was derived more often than not from the land they owned; this was more characteristic of Argos than of other Greek communities, for here trade and commerce were carried on to such a limited extent that only a very small portion of the population could have been connected with it in any way. The rich and fertile land of the Argive plain provided the inhabitants of the city their wealth and livelihood, and only a few smiths and potters could have earned their living otherwise.[65] Although we know nothing specific about landholding at Argos,[66] the aristocracy, it must be assumed, owned most of it, but had little need to work the land personally. If representations on vases are any indication, they spent their days delighting in activities traditionally associated with Greek aristocrats everywhere: boxing, wrestling, dancing, playing or listening to music,[67] handling or riding their horses, and last but not least military activity.[68]

The use of expensive defensive armor and the horse as an implement of war seems to suggest that warfare was not yet carried on by all male citizens of the community fighting in hoplite armor in a phalanx formation, but was still an aristocratic preserve.[69] That the bulk of the fighting was borne by the Argive aristocracy in an age when military activity was intensifying suggests that this aristocracy was able to advance its political position within the state, but there is no way to determine whether it had become powerful enough collectively to challenge the power of the Argive king. In any event, the erection of the Argive Heraeum may well reflect the enhanced position of the aristocracy within the state, for there can be no doubt that the priestesses who managed the temple were chosen from among the daughters of the great noble families of the city.

What is perhaps of greater importance, however, is the realization that whether the government of Argos was controlled by the king or the aristocrats, the city was provided with sure, steady leadership. This government was responsible for some breathtaking innovations, the most striking of which was the construction of the Argive Heraeum five miles from the city, possibly designed to serve as a religious center for the plain. Otherwise, however, the aims of this government were limited. It was interested in the Argive plain, that is, in the territory immediately surrounding the city of Argos; there is nothing to indicate that Argive influence extended farther afield and nothing to indicate that the

Argives were even remotely interested in any wider area. As we have seen, they made no attempt to capitalize on the favorable location of Asine, and their commercial contacts, even with other Peloponnesian cities, were exceedingly limited. By confining their attention to the plain, the Argives had a nicely compact area with which to deal; and the limited objectives they sought could be achieved with relative ease. They were able to consolidate their position within the Argive plain by the end of the eighth century, and this was, accordingly, an important period in the history of the city.[70]

Chapter V:

Argos in
the Seventh Century

The task of reconstructing Argive history in the seventh century is not an easy one, and before this can be accomplished it will be necessary to dispel several erroneous notions that have led to serious distortion of Argive history in this period. The literary evidence is still limited and derives from writers who lived long after the seventh century came to an end. These writers rarely mention Argos except in connection with Sparta. It was a common belief from the fourth century B.C. onward that early Peloponnesian history revolved around an unending struggle between these two states. But as I have argued elsewhere,[1] this belief is clearly erroneous. It conflicts with what Herodotus tells us about early Peloponnesian history, and it ignores the geographical realities of the area.

Crucial to a proper understanding of seventh-century Argive history is the realization that Argos and Sparta did not have a common border in this period. It was noted in Chapter III that Herodotus's report that Argos once controlled the western coastal area of the Gulf of Argos as far south as the headland at Cape Malea as well as Cythera and other islands off the coast could not be taken seriously. It appears to have been derived ultimately from *Iliad* 2.108. There is additional evidence to be considered here that indicates this area was not dominated by Argos in the seventh century. Argive control of the offshore islands and even the area of the mainland along the Gulf of Argos, where land travel was and still is difficult, presupposes the existence of an Argive navy. There is no evidence to prove and no reason to believe that the city possessed one at this time. It is suggestive that the ship was one of the least frequently employed motives by Argive artists in the Late Geometric period. As noted earlier, Argos remained aloof from the vastly accelerated trade and commerce of the Greek world in the latter half of the eighth century, and as I shall have occasion to discuss at greater length in this chapter, Argive commercial interests remained equally limited in the seventh century. Moreover, in this period of extensive colonization the Argives did not establish even a single colony of their own.[2] In short, nothing we know about Argos in the seventh century suggests that the city possessed naval forces, and without a navy control of the offshore islands and the coastal area of the Gulf of Argos would have been all but impossible. To be added to this is the meager information we have about Prasiae, a city located along the coast but situated far north of Cape Malea. If Strabo's report that this city was one of the original members of the Calaurian Amphictiony can be trusted, it must have been an independent community when this league of states came into existence about the middle of the seventh century.[3] Presumably it remained independent until it came under Spartan domination about a century later,[4] and if the Argives did not control Prasiae, they obviously could not have controlled the coastal area south of that city. An appreciation of this places the whole problem of seventh-century Argive-Spartan relations in its proper perspective. The two states did not share a common border, and although an occasional military campaign between them would not have been entirely impossible, it seems less than likely that they could have been the bitter enemies of long standing that we have been led to believe they were.

A consideration of the geographical features of this area of the Peloponnesus reinforces this conclusion. The range of mountains situated between Laconia and the Gulf of Argos effectively separated Sparta from the Argive plain. It was indeed possible to travel from Sparta to Argos or from Argos to Sparta directly over these mountains, but this was not an easy route. The most frequently used route between the two cities, though longer, was much easier to traverse. It led north from Sparta toward Tegea; not far from that city it joined another road that ran from Argos to Tegea. It was then an easy matter to proceed along this road through Cynouria into the Argive plain and on to the city of Argos.[5] Since this road ran through Tegean territory and dangerously close to the city of Tegea itself, the Spartans undoubtedly did not have access to it before their conquest of that city. Indeed, Herodotus[6] implies that Argos and Sparta went to war only after Sparta had defeated Tegea, and even though this implication has been completely ignored by modern scholars, it cannot be cavalierly dismissed.

Although the course of Spartan expansion in the Peloponnesus is not a subject we are at all well-informed about, if we divorce ourselves 'from the views expounded by writers of later antiquity and modern scholarship based upon them,[7] the main outline of the extension of Spartan influence seems reasonably clear. According to Herodotus it was a much longer and more drawn-out process than most modern scholars have been willing to admit. Sparta's advance to a position of preeminence in the Peloponnesus can only have begun after the synoikismos of the Eurotas valley and the amalgamation of the five small villages there into the Spartan polis, probably about the middle of the eighth century or a bit later. This was followed, still in the eighth century, by the initial conquest of Messenia, and it is by no means certain that the Spartans achieved the conquest of the whole of this territory in the First Messenian War.[8] Moreover, the war itself seems to have given rise to serious internal troubles which the Spartans attempted to alleviate by shipping the malcontents off to found the colony of Tarentum late in the century. Even this did not settle all of Sparta's internal problems, however, and the Messenians were far from totally subdued. Although we do not know a great deal about Spartan history in the early half of the seventh century, what little we do know suggests that this was a period of severe internal problems and domestic concerns that led ultimately to the promulgation of the Great Rhetra.[9] Reports of warfare between Sparta and Argos in this period that come to us only from the pages of Pausanias must be considered in the context of this domestic strife. He tells us that the Spartan king Theopompus made an incursion into Thyrea, and he also tells us that the Argives fought and defeated the Spartans at Hysiae in 669 B.C.[10] As shall be discussed further below, neither report can be accurate. This has not, however, stopped modern scholars from speculating on the consequences of the latter campaign particularly. It is commonly assumed that it was Sparta's defeat at Hysiae which prompted the Messenians to revolt and touch off the Second Messenian War.[11] If we must look for a stimulus for this revolt, however, we would be better advised to attempt to understand it in terms of Spartan-Messenian relations, not Spartan-Argive relations. Whatever the cause, the war was not an easy challenge for the Spartans, and for two decades in the middle or latter half of the century they were busy trying to reassert their control over Messenia. Ultimately they were successful and in the process perhaps conquered that portion of Messenia they had not taken during the First Messenian War.[12]

The course of Spartan expansion after the Second Messenian War is not known in great detail either, but again the main outline seems clear. It was only with the successful conclusion of this war that Sparta was in a position to direct her attention farther afield. We know from Herodotus that the first target was not Argos but Arcadia and that the Spartans were no more immediately successful there than they had been in Messenia. The struggle was a bitter one and it lasted for some time. It began in the latter part of the seventh century when the Spartans confidently attempted to conquer the whole of Arcadia. When it became apparent they were not capable of the task, they consulted the Oracle of Delphi and were advised to concentrate their efforts on one Arcadian city, Tegea. Even here, however, success came slowly, and for several decades the Spartan advance was thwarted. They suffered at least one humiliating defeat in the Battle of the Fetters, after which they were forced to work the soil of Tegea in the very fetters they had brought with them to enslave the Tegeans. It was not until shortly before the middle of the sixth century that the Spartans were able to subdue Tegea,[13] and at this time the two states concluded an alliance.[14] This Spartan victory profoundly altered the political geography of the eastern Peloponnesus; it gave them access to Cynouria and an easy route to the Argive plain. Only at this point in time did the possibility of a direct military confrontation between Argos and Sparta become a reality.

We must, consequently, dismiss the notion that seventh-century Peloponnesian history revolved around a constant and bitter struggle between these two states. This view, to repeat, is derived only from writers of later antiquity beginning with Ephorus. At the same time, however, we must assume that these later writers did not maliciously distort early Peloponnesian history and that their belief in the traditional hostility between Argos and Sparta was sincere. This being true, we must ask what led them to this erroneous belief in the first place. Although many factors contributed to its growth, there seems to be no doubt that two of the elements involved were the mistaken notions that the Argive tyrant Pheidon lived and ruled in the eighth century and that he deprived the Spartans of hegemony over the Peloponnesus, thereby setting the stage for bitter hostility between the two states.[15] The evidence for dating Pheidon will be discussed in the next chapter, but it is necessary to say here that he cannot have been ruling at Argos in the eighth century as writers of later antiquity believed. Of equal importance, moreover, he cannot have been ruling the city in the early decades of the seventh century as many modern scholars hold, and in all probability his reign ought to be dated to the very end of the seventh and early part of the sixth centuries.

In short, if we are to understand seventh-century Argive history, we must dismiss as erroneous the two notions that have served as the keystone around which virtually all ancient and modern accounts have been written. When we do this it becomes quickly apparent that much of what passes as historical fact about seventh-century Argos is not fact at all. In truth, there is not much that can be said about the city in this period; its history can be treated only in broad outline and then by relying primarily upon contemporary archaeological evidence. Unfortunately there are far fewer physical remains from this period than from the latter half of the eighth century, and they tell us very little about Argive history generally and virtually nothing about Argive political history.

The archaeological remains suggest that the early decades of the seventh century were not a revolutionary period in Argive history; the clearest indication of this is found in the ceramic remains. By the end of the eighth century the Geometric style had run its course in Greece, and artists were beginning to move away from the restraint and confinement of the style and to experiment with new modes of artistic expression. New styles with heavy oriental influence began to appear first at Corinth, then at Athens, and by the seventh century in other locations as well. The potters of Argos remained largely unaffected by this development, however, and Argive Late Geometric pottery was not followed by the emergence of any true orientalizing phase like the Protocorinthian at Corinth or the Protoattic at Athens. Instead, Argive Late Geometric pottery evolved into a Subgeometric phase that continued to be manufactured until well into the seventh century.[16] Although this Subgeometric pottery was by no means an inferior product, it was little influenced by the artistic revolution taking place in the major centers of Greece. An orientalizing influence is noticeable on some Argive vases from the early half of the seventh century, but the new techniques adopted were of minor significance and usually confined to motives. The major aspects, artistically speaking, of the transition from the Geometric to the orientalizing style did not affect Argive artists to any meaningful degree.[17]

Shortly before the middle of the seventh century, however, a brilliant new Protoargive style of pottery emerged for a brief period. Although minor aspects of this new style such as the motives are surely Argive, for the most part the Protoargive style was not really a natural, logical development out of Argive Subgeometric pottery. The details of the figured representation, for example, bear a strong resemblance to contemporary pieces from the islands and owe little to previous Argive artistic traditions. By 650 B.C. this Protoargive style had attained amazing heights, as is palpably demonstrated by the most celebrated example which has thus far been found, the crater fragment depicting the blinding of Polyphemus. The style was produced for only a decade or so after the middle of the century, however, and our knowledge of it is presently limited to hardly more than a dozen small fragments.[18] In fact, its production may well have been limited to a single craftsman or at most probably to a single workshop. It would, therefore, be risky to attempt to draw any far-reaching conclusions from the sudden emergence and equally sudden disappearance of this Protoargive style.

For the second half of the seventh century our knowledge of Argive ceramics is limited, since very few pieces have yet been found. It would seem, however, that the production of painted pottery declined drastically; only a small quantity was produced after the middle of the seventh century.[19] Although a handful of Argive Black Figure sherds have been found, for the most part, Argive pottery of the late seventh and sixth centuries is unpretentious work, limited in both quantity and quality. It consists primarily of undecorated black glaze ware, simple monochrome containers, and miniature vases which were frequently sloppily decorated.[20] There was some imitation and importation of Protocorinthian pottery in the early part of the century, but as the century progressed pottery of Corinthian manufacture began to turn up in ever increasing amounts. In fact, ceramic production seems to have fallen off so markedly at Argos that by the latter half of the seventh century not even miniature vases were being manufactured in sufficient quantity to supply the local demand, and it became necessary to import them from Corinth.[21]

The decline and virtual demise of the Argive ceramic industry across the years of the seventh century is easier to note than to explain. For several hundred years Argive potters had kept pace with their counterparts elsewhere in Greece. But for some reason they were unable or unwilling to adopt the new orientalizing styles and techniques that were sweeping over Greece in the seventh century.[22] Possibly this was a reflection and continuation of the conservative tendencies detected in Argive ceramic products of the late eighth century. Yet it is worth remembering that in this period many Greek states found it more convenient to import Corinthian pottery than to continue producing their own.

The end of the production of painted pottery at Argos is a serious loss, for it deprives us of one very important source of historical information. This loss, unfortunately, is not offset by the fact that nonceramic archaeological remains are more abundant than in previous centuries, for these remains are more difficult to identify and classify. They are less securely dated than the pottery, and the historical information they provide is limited. Argive terra-cotta figurines provide a good illustration of these generalizations. Although a number of terra-cottas excavated on the Larissa and in the city of Argos proper remain largely unpublished,[23] literally hundreds found at the Argive Heraeum, Tiryns, and elsewhere have been published in detail.[24] These have been studied on several occasions, most thoroughly by Jenkins and Kaulen; their con-

clusions differ radically. Jenkins believed that few Argive terra-cotta figurines could be dated earlier than 650 B.C. and that very few were exported before the second half of the sixth century. He acknowledged
some orientalizing influence on certain terra-cottas, but he noted that
not one of the many figurines excavated at the Argive Heraeum was
fashioned in the Dedalic style, the most progressive style of the seventh
century. For the most part, Jenkins considered the terra-cottas from
this period to be rather primitive, handmade pieces with no great artistic or aesthetic merit.[25] Kaulen has proposed a completely revised chronology for these terra-cotta figurines, and many of the individual pieces
that Jenkins dated to the sixth century, he would place in the seventh.
Moreover, he believes that many of them were fashioned in the Dedalic
style and that they were being exported, at least to Perachora, as early
as the middle of the seventh century. If Kaulen is correct, the Argive
terra-cotta industry was not so backward in the seventh century as Jenkins's conclusions implied;[26] but it is difficult to choose between equally subjective arguments. What does seem to be reasonably clear is that
there was a dual tradition in the manufacture of terra-cotta figurines at
Argos in the seventh century, as there was in the manufacture of pottery. Certain Argive workshops were producing fairly primitive terra-
cottas which show little or no influence of the new Dedalic style; other
workshops were more progressive and their products were as advanced
as any in the Greek world. It is interesting, too, that there were two
schools of craftsmen who worked on seals in this period. One group continued to work in stone and was little affected by new stylistic advances,
and the other group worked in ivory and was more heavily influenced
by new orientalizing styles.[27]

Objects in metal are generally as difficult to categorize and date as
are the terra-cottas. Mention has already been made of the numerous
bronze objects found at the Argive Heraeum, many of which clearly
date to the seventh century.[28] Pins and spits still predominate, but
there are a number of human and animal figurines, personal objects
such as fibulae, rings, bracelets, and mirrors, and there are even a number of bronze containers. Equally striking, perhaps, are objects which
do not turn up at all or are encountered only infrequently at the site.
Military equipment is not represented, and only one griffin protome has

been found.[29] Other than offering incontrovertible evidence of the strength of the Argive metal industry[30] in the seventh century, these finds seem to tell us little about Argive history.

The same is true of one final category of archaeological evidence, architectural remains. Such remains are not numerous. In the south quarter of the city, foundation walls dating from the early decades of the seventh century exhibit careful construction and a sizable structure, but their precise function is unknown. At the Argive Heraeum the Old Temple of Hera seems to date before the middle of the seventh century, but only three or four blocks of the stylobate remain. Although built primarily of mud brick and wood, this was a large building with stone columns. It is believed by some to be the oldest peripteral temple in the Peloponnesus, but this opinion as well as a seventh-century date for the temple have recently been questioned.[31] Shortly after the middle of the century an altar was dedicated to Athena at Mycenae; from this altar we have some fragments of the metope. Though most likely the work of Corinthian not Argive craftsmen, the reliefs are masterpieces of the orientalizing style. They are, moreover, the oldest architectural reliefs yet found in Greece, and the altar from which they came is apparently the earliest known Greek altar with triglyph and metope arrangement.[32] There is evidence of other construction, such as a temple of Enyalius at Mycenae and an altar of Aphrodite later replaced by a temple at Argos,[33] and these remains provide evidence of the increasing economic resources of the Argive state. They also suggest that tremendous advances were being made in this period. To grasp the magnitude of these advances one need only compare the innovative attitude of the men who constructed the peripteral Old Temple of Hera with the conservative and tradition-bound attitude of the men who had erected the Cyclopean-like Old Temple Terrace Wall a few generations earlier. The difference between the two reflects a sharp shift in intellectual attitudes,[34] but beyond that we can say little.

There is one other observation of some significance that can be made on the basis of the archaeological remains: Argos continued to display little interest in trade and commerce in this period. Although the city enjoyed wider commercial contacts than it did in the late eighth century, these contacts were still extremely limited when compared with foreign contacts of other Greek cities. So limited were they, in fact, that one gets the impression that Argos did not play even a minor role in Greek commerce. Again, the finds from the Heraeum are instructive; here objects of oriental origin are not numerous either in a relative or absolute sense. The paucity of objects in ivory is striking. Only eighty-nine pieces have been catalogued; later excavation has added a few more, and one or two pieces were found in the city itself. But the total number is unimpressive when compared with the more than 400 that have been catalogued from the temple of Hera Limenia at Perachora and the considerable number from Artemis Orthia at Sparta.[35] The objects themselves are equally unimpressive; no free-standing sculpture was found, and the great majority of ivory objects are simply small discs, probably used as votive offerings, with inscribed decoration on both sides. The decoration bears a strong oriental influence—the griffin and lion predominate, but other designs seem to represent Mycenaean survivals or indigenous creations.[36] No less striking is the relative scarcity of objects from Egypt at the Argive Heraeum. Only sixty-one pieces have been catalogued compared with more than 900 at Perachora.[37]

Aside from Egyptian and ivory objects, almost all of which would seem to date from the first half of the seventh century, only a few bronze objects can be classed as oriental imports; so far as I am aware, only one Argive object, a griffin protome from Samos, is known to have been found in the eastern Aegean.[38] Indeed, even contact with nearby Crete can only be demonstrated by a handful of objects that have turned up at the Argive Heraeum.[39]

The evidence suggests that Argive contacts with areas outside the Greek mainland were extremely narrow throughout the seventh century. Even on the Greek mainland, the only evidence for Argive contacts outside the Peloponnesus is with Athens and Aegina. Little Attic pottery has been found in the city of Argos proper, and at Tiryns none seems to have been imported before the end of the Black-Figure style. But a few sherds, mostly from the second quarter of the seventh century, have been discovered at the Argive Heraeum.[40] Conversely, a few Protoargive vase fragments have been found at Athens.[41] Although it is possible that the Argives traded in goods that have not survived—grain in exchange for raw ores, for example—Argive connections during the seventh century, as earlier would seem to be limited largely to the Peloponnesus, and even here there is no evidence of large-scale commercial contact, except perhaps with Corinth.

Although it is no longer as certain as was once thought that a "common feeling" must have existed between Corinth and Argos in this period,[42] it is clear that the two states had frequent and close contact. Corinthian goods moved into the Argolid in quantity, and Argive products turn up at Perachora, but on a more modest scale and in no great quantity. The bulk of the pottery found at the Argive Heraeum was of Corinthian manufacture; in fact, Protocorinthian pottery is found in greater abundance at the site than even domestic wares of Argive manufacture. Recent excavations have also shown that it was imported into the city of Argos in quantity, and it was also the chief imported pottery at Tiryns.[43] Argive terra-cottas, though frequently difficult to distinguish from those of Corinth, were not widely exported in the seventh century, but they do occasionally turn up at Perachora. In addition, a few pieces of pottery and perhaps some ivory worked at Argos have been discovered there, and many of the bronze objects closely resemble pieces from the Argive Heraeum, though they are likely of local manufacture. Though not numerically impressive, it may be significant that they comprise the bulk of the imported objects found at the site.[44]

Except with Corinth, however, Argos seems to have had only little and infrequent contact even with other areas of the Peloponnesus. There is an "apparently" Argive Subgeometric crater from Cythera. A lead brooch and a few fragments of pottery from Sparta have been found at the Heraeum. Argive pottery, mostly miniature vases, and a considerable number of terra-cottas have been found at Phlius on the fringes of the Argive plain. A single terra-cotta has been found at Aegina, and Argive figurines clearly exerted a marked influence on the pieces made locally at Tegea.[45] Argive bronze objects are more difficult to identify securely, but few have been found outside the Argive plain that date before the last quarter of the seventh century when shield bands begin to turn up with some regularity at Olympia.

The archaeological evidence conveys the impression that Argos remained largely aloof from the vastly increased trade and commerce of the Greek states in the seventh century. This impression receives further confirmation from the fact that in this period of extensive overseas colonization the Argives did not found even a single colony of their own. Undoubtedly, the Argive plain was a fertile area that could provide sufficient food for the greatly increased population, and its inhabitants were never forced to send out colonies or to pursue vigorously trade and commerce, which were never as important at Argos as they were in many other Greek states. In fact, the Argives seem to have had even fewer commercial interests than Sparta in this period. Argos, in short, remained a largely self-sufficient agricultural state whose inhabitants, except for a few potters and smiths, made their living by farming.

The picture derived from the archaeological evidence indicates that economically at least Argos was not an important state in seventh-century Greece. This view conflicts sharply with the commonly held belief that Argos was one of the most important states, both politically and economically, in this period. As briefly noted above, however, this notion rests on insecure foundations; it presupposes that Pheidon lived in this century, that he was the inventor of weights, measures, and coinage, and that he was a vigorous military conqueror. These matters will be discussed at greater length in the next chapter; here it is necessary to consider other evidence which would seem to indicate that in the seventh century Argos was no more important politically than it was economically.

In this connection it may be significant that Strabo includes Nauplia but not Argos among the states participating in the Calaurian Amphictiony from its inception about the middle of the century.[46] If this report could be trusted, we would have important evidence that Nauplia was not under the direct control of Argos at the time. There is perhaps better evidence regarding Tiryns. An inscription from the site, claimed to be the earliest inscription yet known from the Argolid and most likely dating from the very end of the seventh century, is reported to contain the words *demos* and *aliia*.[47] Apparently the Tirynthians possessed their own assembly at the time the inscription was set up and were not under the direct political control of Argos.

If this was true, it seems clear that many of our notions about the political importance of seventh-century Argos must be reexamined. Quite apart from the myth surrounding Pheidon, literary evidence has been used to credit the Argives with playing an important role in the development of hoplite armor in this century. In fact, modern scholars have frequently employed the terms hoplite shield and Argive shield synonymously, and it has even been suggested that it was the Argives, under Pheidon, who first employed the hoplite phalanx.[48] The evidence upon which these opinions are founded, however, is far from convincing. It is true that a fragment of Pindar indicates that in his time Argos was famous for arms (ὅπλα), and we know that there existed at Argos at least as early as the fifth century B.C. a religious celebration, the Heraea, one of the features of which was a race in full armor with the victor receiving a bronze shield as his prize. In later antiquity these shields were referred to as Argive shields, and the games themselves as ἐξ ῎Αργος ἀσπίς.[49] But the earliest literary evidence we have that credits the Argives with the invention of the shield dates only from the first and second centuries after Christ. The claim is made by Pliny, and by Apollodorus, who attributed the invention to Proteus and Acrisius, two legendary figures in Argive mythology.[50] Additionally, Pausanias tells us that shields were first used in the battle between Proteus and Acrisius, and, finally, a papyrus from Oxyrhynchus dating from the second century after Christ lists Danaus or Proteus and Acrisius as the inventors of the shield, and attributes the first use of the porpax shield either to the Carians or the Argives.[51] Surely evidence as late as this cannot be invoked to prove that Argos played an important role in the development of hoplite armor in the seventh century B.C. There was a built-in factor that may well have led later writers to the conclusion that the shield was originally invented at Argos, for the lower acropolis of the city bore the name Aspis, that is, shield. The hill was appropriately named; its round, conical shape is strikingly like a round, convex hoplite shield. It is hardly surprising, therefore, that later writers attribute its invention to Danaus or Proteus and Acrisius. There is some evidence, though not conclusive, which suggests that the connection of Proteus and Acrisius with the invention of the shield arose only after the fourth century B.C. Pausanias reports seeing a pyramid-shaped building on the road from Argos to Epidaurus which he says was decorated with sculptured decoration consisting of shields of Argive shape. He believed this building was actually a common tomb for the dead who had fallen in battle when Proteus and Acrisius had fought for control of the Argolid. However, archaeological excavation has shown that the building was no tomb at all but a guard station that was constructed only in the latter half of the fourth century B.C.[52] At that time, accordingly, the building could hardly have been associated with Proteus and Acrisius, as it apparently was in Pausanias's day 600 years later.

Apart from this late literary tradition there is no evidence to suggest that the Argives played an important role in the development of hoplite armor. In fact, our knowledge of Argive weapons and armor generally is virtually nonexistent for the period between the late eighth and the last quarter of the seventh century.[53] By that time, however, shield bands begin to turn up at Olympia, and there is a continuous series of these shield bands from the last quarter of the seventh century to the end of the sixth century.[54] An Argive origin for these bands seems beyond doubt, but it is odd, indeed, that none have ever been found anywhere in the Argive plain, not even at the Argive Heraeum. The fact that the Argives were manufacturing shield bands by the last quarter of the seventh century does not prove that they were militarily powerful in this period, and it certainly does not prove that they played an important part in the development of the hoplite shield or hoplite equipment generally. By this time hoplite armor was fully developed, and it changed little for the next several centuries. In short, the manufacture of shield bands reaffirms what we have already said: Argos was an important center in the manufacture of metal objects; but beyond that these shield bands tell us little, and there is no archaeological evidence to prove that Argos was an important military state in the seventh century.

If we omit for the moment ancient reports concerning the alleged military activity of Pheidon and omit also modern attempts to date him to the seventh century, it becomes apparent that the only evidence for Argive military activity in this period comes from later writers, especially Pausanias. I have considered the trustworthiness of Pausanias as a source for early Argive history in some detail elsewhere,[55] and it is only necessary to restate my conclusions briefly. He reports that the Spartan king Theopompus, who ruled early in the seventh century, made an incursion into Thyrea and fought the Argives there. He also tells us that the Argives fought and defeated the Spartans at Hysiae in 669 B.C.[56]

Finally, Pausanias is our chief source for reports of Argive participation on the side of the Messenians in the Second Messenian War.[57] These must be considered in light of the fact that Pausanias wholly accepted the belief current in later antiquity that Sparta and Argos had been mutually hostile toward one another throughout the course of Greek history.

There is no way to prove or disprove his report that Theopompus fought the Argives in Thyrea, but at the same time there is good reason to discount it. His source for this campaign seems clearly to have been late and synthesizing in nature, and, as discussed above, a military confrontation between Sparta and Argos in Thyrea before the Spartan conquest of Tegea is extremely unlikely. It would be especially unlikely in the early decades of the seventh century when it would seem that Sparta was beset with serious internal problems. There is greater reason to reject Pausanias's account of the Battle of Hysiae. Although this battle has captured the imagination of modern scholars, the fact that it is not mentioned in any other ancient Greek literature that has come down to us from antiquity—the battle did not even make the *Chronicle* of Eusebius—must invite skepticism.[58] A Spartan incursion into the territory of Hysiae at any time before the Spartan victory over Tegea in the middle of the sixth century is inherently improbable, for the most direct route from Sparta to Hysiae runs through Tegean territory. Moreover, a careful consideration of Pausanias's account of this battle suggests that he knew little about it; he apparently learned of it from the guides who accompanied him through this section of the Peloponnesus. These guides could have known little about a battle that supposedly occurred 800 years earlier, and they may well have had in mind the destruction of Hysiae by the Spartans in 417 B.C. Pausanias's own words imply that he got his date for the battle from a different source, presumably an Athenian source. In so doing, it is entirely possible that he confused a campaign between Athens and Boeotia over Boeotian Hysiae with an Argive-Spartan campaign supposedly fought at Peloponnesian Hysiae. In any event, there is no trustworthy evidence for a battle between Argos and Sparta at Hysiae in 669 B.C. or for that matter at any other time in the seventh century. Reports of Argive participation in the Second Messenian War are no more well founded;[59] in fact, Argive participation in this war seems to have been unknown to writers who lived in the fourth century B.C. Historians of this period regarded the Messenian War as a local altercation between Sparta and Messenia, with the Arcadians aiding the Messenians at least for part of the war. Writers of the third and second centuries, however, such as Myron of Priene, Rhianus of Bene, and Apollodorus, regarded the Messenian War as a pan-Peloponnesian conflict that involved most of the important states of the Peloponnesus and even a few beyond the peninsula. Pausanias accepted these views unhesitatingly, but that does not mean we should.

In short, reports of warfare between Argos and Sparta preserved in the pages of Pausanias would seem to have little to recommend them either collectively or individually, and it must be admitted that there is simply no trustworthy information available that might help us determine the role played by Argos in the seventh-century Peloponnesus. That a certain amount of warfare was undoubtedly waged in this period seems beyond question. But it was not with Sparta, as later writers believed.

There is only one other report of warfare involving the Argives in this period. We are told that they attacked and destroyed Nauplia. Although this event is alluded to by Theopompus, most of our information comes from Pausanias,[60] who reports that the city was destroyed and its inhabitants expelled in the reign of the Argive king Damocritidas. He further provides an approximate date for the event by saying that it occurred in the time of, or perhaps just after, the Second Messenian War. Pausanias's chronology leaves much to be desired, but it may be strengthened by the fact that Theopompus also implies that the event took place after the Spartan conquest of Messenia. From the surviving fragment of his work, however, there is no way of knowing how long after the war, and in any event the problem is further complicated by the fact that we have no precise dates for the Second Messenian War itself.[61]

It is difficult to know how seriously to take this report, but if the evidence from Strabo listing Nauplia as one of the orginal members of the Calaurian Amphictiony is accurate, and if the city was independent about 650 B.C., its destruction by Argos later in the century is entirely possible. The destruction of Nauplia was an important event in Argive history; unfortunately we do not know what the motives behind it might have been. The only ancient author to provide us with a reason for the incident is Pausanias, who alleges that the city was destroyed because of the pro-Spartan sympathies of its inhabitants. This explanation cannot, however, be taken seriously, for Pausanias was obsessed with the notion that Sparta and Argos were always at odds. Moreover, the fact that he gives almost identical reasons for the destruction of both Asine and Nauplia is inherently more than a little suspicious. It seems much more likely that the actual cause of the destruction of Nauplia was a conflict of interests with Argos, but the nature of this conflict must remain a mystery.

One further point is worth making here: the destruction of Nauplia was clearly a localized conflict and did not involve the other settlements in the plain. The Argives apparently made no attempt to subvert Tirynthian independence at the time. It would appear, therefore, that Argos had no aggressive designs even upon cities within the Argive plain in the seventh century. The reason for this seems obvious enough. This was a fertile area, still capable of producing sufficient food for the inhabitants. There was, in short, no need to covet the agricultural land of neighboring states. The Argive lack of interest in overseas colonization demonstrates this clearly enough, and the fact that Tiryns remained independent throughout the seventh century reinforces this conclusion. It is well to remember, too, that the Argive plain was a relatively isolated area. Virtually surrounded by mountains on three sides and facing the sea on the other, it was secluded and small. It was not easily accessible to invaders, and defending it should have presented no great problems. If these assumptions are correct, it would seem to follow that warfare was not an important element in seventh-century Argive history. If we insist on assuming that it was, we must at least recognize that this assumption is not supported by any reliable evidence apart from the probable destruction of Nauplia late in the century.

If warfare did not play a prominent part in seventh-century Argive history, the course of the internal development of the Argive state was undoubtedly influenced by this. Unfortunately, we do not have a great deal of information to enlighten us on this topic. Generally speaking, however, we know that throughout the Greek world in this period there was a growing separation between the aristocracy and peasantry. Although the two classes may have cooperated from time to time in an effort to better their lot jointly,[62] aristocratic cooperation with the peasants usually stopped far short of admitting them to full partnership in the social, economic, and political life of the polis. In fact, as the position of the aristocracy was enhanced, exploitation of the peasants, not cooperation with them, became the rule rather than the exception.[63] Although it is difficult to prove, there is no reason to believe that this development did not continue throughout the seventh century at Argos.

In the absence of evidence from tombs dating from this period it is difficult to demonstrate that the economic separation between rich and poor visible at Argos in the latter part of the eighth century continued to grow throughout the seventh century. Yet there is some archaeological evidence which may be pertinent. Again the finds from the Argive Heraeum are suggestive if not decisive. The bulk of the ivory objects and all of the Egyptian objects found at the site date from the first half of the seventh century. Such objects are so limited in number that they must have been deposited there by only a small segment of the population. Presumably, they were too expensive for most worshipers at the site, many of whom had to content themselves with offerings much less pretentious. The votive most frequently dedicated to the goddess came neither from Syria nor Egypt, nor even from the workshops of Argive metalsmiths. It was, rather, the inexpensive miniature vase, manufactured exclusively for dedication as a votive. Thousands of these miniature vases have been found at the Heraeum, as well as at other sanctuaries in the plain, where they were deposited by poorer segments of the population.[64]

Although there is no direct evidence that can be cited as proof, it would be reasonable to assume that political differences also existed between aristocracy and peasantry in seventh-century Argos. As we have seen, aristocratic power seems to have been on the rise before the eighth century came to an end, and there is no reason to believe that this development did not continue in the seventh century. Several factors suggest that this did occur. First, it may be significant that the kingship was not abolished at Argos as it was throughout much of the Greek world in this period. No doubt this was because the Argive aristocrats were more than capable of controlling any individual who occupied the office. Moreover, if this was a period of relative peace, as suggested above, such warfare as the Argives engaged in might have been accomplished without the total mobilization of the Argive peasantry. Fighting may well have remained an aristocratic preserve,[65] and if this was true, if the peasantry was not needed to man the ranks of the hoplite phalanx, the aristocracy might well have been able to ignore their wishes and desires. Finally, the fact that Argos did not participate in colonial foundations is also suggestive. The intiative in leading out colonial expeditions and pursuing commercial interests was everywhere undertaken by dissatisfied and disaffected aristocrats. Colonization, moreover, was one of the chief means by which internal strife was alleviated in Greek states in the seventh century. It provided an outlet for oppressed peasants who could seek their own land in the new colony, but, just as important, it provided an outlet for dissident aristocrats who could become leaders in the new colony.[66] The fact that the Argive aristocrats were not interested in pursuing colonial and commercial interests suggests they were largely content with the status quo, reasonably satisfied with their lot, and, we must assume, well-off socially, economically, and politically. Evidently they owned or controlled the vast bulk of the fertile agricultural land of the Argive plain, and they were content to sit back and reap the benefits from it.

There is some other evidence that may confirm this conclusion, although, again, it is not decisive. There are indications that there was some emigration from the Argive plain, particularly in the early half of the seventh century. Archaeological evidence suggests that some Argives were residing at Syracuse in this period. Although no ancient authority credits the Argives with the foundation of this colony, Hippys of Rhegion reports that a certain Argive named Pollis was once king of the city. No other significant details are given, and Pollis is otherwise unknown. It would be odd indeed if an Argive were allowed to acquire the kingship of this Corinthian colony, and most scholars rightly tend to doubt the report.[67] Nevertheless, certain craters excavated many years ago in the Fusco Necropolis at Syracuse must be taken into consideration. These craters were long thought to be imports from Argos, but it is now quite certain that they were of local manufacture. Their affinity to contemporary Argive ceramic products is, however, beyond all doubt, and it is highly likely that they were manufactured at Syracuse by Argive craftsmen.[68] Since only a few vases fall into this category, there is no need to postulate that vast hordes of Argives resided in the city. But the presence of at least a few seems certain.

There is also evidence suggesting that a few Argives might also have settled on the island of Calymna. Although there is no literary evidence to confirm this, two fragments of an early seventh-century "Rhodian Geometric" style vase which have been found on the island are of interest. These sherds contain lettering, and the craftsman responsible for this lettering employed an alphabet which "appears to be that of Argos." Two possible explanations for this phenomenon have been offered: either the Argive and Calymnian scripts were derived from a common source or Argive craftsmen were residing on the island and painted these letters.[69] There is one additional bit of evidence that tends to support the latter of these alternatives. Argos is a geographical place-name on the island,[70] and presumably, though not necessarily, it received this name from settlers who came from the city of Argos on the mainland.

Finally, a report of Hesychius of Miletus that a contingent of Argives joined the Megarian settlers who founded Byzantium must be mentioned. Most scholars tend to doubt the accuracy of this information,[71] but in later times the calendar used at Byzantium shows Argive influence,[72] and it is indeed possible that some Argives settled there. If this report is correct, we would have additional reason to believe that some Argives were in fact emigrating from the plain in the early half of the seventh century, for according to the traditional scheme of dating this colony was founded about 660 B.C.[73] In any event, the archaeological evidence alone would seem sufficient to demonstrate that certain Argives did leave their homeland in the early half of the seventh century. Although many things may have prompted them to leave Argos, it does not seem unreasonable to assume, in the light of our present knowledge of Greek colonization generally, that they emigrated at least in part because they were not particularly satisfied with conditions in the Argive plain. We do not know if any substantial numbers were involved, and although it must be acknowledged that a few aristocrats may have accompanied these settlers, for the most part they would appear to have been craftsmen and not, therefore, members of the aristocracy. If this interpretation is correct, we have additional evidence of a growing separation between rich and poor, aristocrat and peasant in seventh-century Argos, but we have no way of knowing in any absolute sense the condition of the Argive peasant in this period.

By way of summary, there is not a great deal that can be said about Argive history in the seventh century, and most of our conclusions must of necessity be negative. For one thing, it would seem that the commonly accepted notion that Argos was an important state in this period is clearly erroneous. So far as the evidence indicates, the Argives were little interested in trade and commerce and not at all interested in colonization. There is no evidence to prove that they were continually at war with Sparta or that they engaged in anything more than occasional warfare with their more immediate Peloponnesian neighbors. Above all there is nothing to suggest that Argos was an important military power in seventh-century Greece. In fact, it is not even certain that they had complete control over the other communities in the Argive plain. It is not possible to trace the course of internal developments within the city in any precise manner, but there is no compelling reason to believe that the Argive peasants were any worse off socially, economically, or politically than were peasants elsewhere in the Greek world in this period.

Such a skimpy and sketchy picture of Argos in the seventh century may be disappointing to some; but if we are to be faithful to the evidence, we must recognize that no greater precision is possible, and attempts to arrive at it must be avoided. Such attempts have in the past led to serious distortion not only of Argive history but of Peloponnesian history generally. Perhaps the most significant observation to emerge from this consideration of the evidence for seventh-century Argos is that nothing we have encountered compels us to date Pheidon to this period. This is perfectly consistent with the literary evidence for dating Pheidon and will be the subject of the next chapter.

Chapter VI:

Pheidon: The
Evidence for Dating

The problem of dating Pheidon is one of the great enigmas not only of Argive history but of all Greek history. It is not exclusively a modern problem. Ancient writers were equally uncertain about when he lived and ruled Argos. By the fourth century B.C. no fewer than three dates, spanning a 300-year period, were already current. The ancient evidence, in fact, is so confused and contradictory that modern scholars have been able to find justification for dating Pheidon to practically every decade between the middle of the eighth and the middle of the sixth century B.C.[1] Although modern attempts to harmonize the ancient evidence have taken many directions, generally speaking scholars have tended either to ignore or completely reject the information provided by Herodotus, the earliest ancient author to refer to Pheidon. A few scholars have preferred to date Pheidon on the basis of information supplied by later writers such as Ephorus and Pausanias. However, the most widely accepted date for Pheidon—the early half of the seventh century—rests on no ancient evidence at all, but rather on a nineteenth-century emendation of the text of Pausanias. The reports of later writers may not be worth a great deal, but Herodotus cannot be so easily and cavalierly dismissed. The information he supplies has usually been explained away by maintaining, on no particularly good evidence, that he must have confused the Argive Pheidon with some other Pheidon.[2]

Although the ancient evidence for dating Pheidon has been reviewed many times, it will be necessary to review it once again, for usually this evidence has been considered in a very narrow context. Pheidon has not often been viewed in the broader context of several hundred years of Argive history, and when he has been, it has been assumed that no matter when he may have lived, the hostile state of Argive relations with Sparta must have been the dominant force that guided and directed his foreign policy. As I have argued in the previous chapter, however, Argive-Spartan enmity in the seventh century is not an established historical fact but an unwarranted and erroneous assumption; the two states could hardly have been seriously at odds with one another much, if at all, before the Spartan conquest of Tegea shortly before the middle of the sixth century. Pheidon must, consequently, be viewed in a completely different context.

In attempting to determine when Pheidon lived and ruled Argos, there are several possible approaches. First, we know that he usurped the Olympic games; if the date of this event could be established, we would have a fixed point in his career. Second, we have reports that he minted the first Greek coins; if we could establish the validity of this information and the approximate date of the introduction of coinage into Greece, we would have at least an approximate date for his reign, Finally, there is some genealogical evidence both for the Argive kings and for Pheidon's place within that genealogy, and there is some information regarding Pheidon's son Lacedes, who is connected with an event that can be approximately but not precisely dated. Each of these possible approaches has its own peculiar set of accompanying problems, however, and it will be necessary to consider and evaluate the evidence for each in turn.

There is no reason to doubt the reports of both Herodotus and Ephorus[3] that Pheidon marched on Olympia and secured control of the games there. Unfortunately, however, neither historian dates the Olympiad at which this event occurred. In fact, the only ancient writer to date precisely Pheidon's usurpation of the Olympic games is Pausanias, who tells us it occurred in the eighth Olympiad, that is, 748 B.C.[4] Pausanias, it must be remembered, lived and wrote about a thousand years after this date, and he can hardly be considered an authority on early Greek history. Indeed what little we know of the historical development of Greece suggests that the traditional date for the foundation of the Olympic games, 776 B.C., is far too early. At that time Greek society had not yet progressed far enough politically, socially, or economically to provide a proper setting for such a pan-Hellenic festival,[5] and even if the games were being celebrated as early as 748, it is not likely that they were anything more than a local festival that was hardly worth usurping.[6] Moreover, and perhaps more important, even if games were being celebrated at Olympia in the middle of the eighth century, it is doubtful that an accurate record of events was kept. Later writers would, therefore, have had a difficult time determining what might have happened at any specific Olympiad. In this respect, we have reports by writers who lived long before Pausanias that no records were kept at Olympia before the twenty-eighth Olympiad in 668 B.C., and the dating of historical events according to Olympiads was a method that came into use only in and after the fourth century B.C.[7]

Pausanias's date for Pheidon's march on Olympia, it must be noted, agrees well enough with the dating implied by Aristotle, Plutarch, and a scholiast on Apollonius of Rhodes, and also with the genealogical date for Pheidon supplied by Ephorus. Aristotle grouped Pheidon in a class of tyrants who were initially kings but were able to change their kingship into a tyranny. He says specifically that this was the earliest class of tyrants and that they were earlier than the Cypselids of Corinth, who belonged to a class of tyrants who were initially demagogues.[8] Hence, for Aristotle, Pheidon antedated the Cypselids, but by how much we cannot say. Plutarch tells a romanticized story about Pheidon and a plan to gain control of Corinth; he dates the incident during the period of Bacchiad control there, in the second generation before the foundation of Syracuse, traditionally dated to 733 B.C. The scholiast on Apollonius relates much the same story but with a number of variations. He makes no mention of Syracuse; rather, he places the event in the second generation before the expulsion of the Bacchiads and the foundation of Corcyra.[9] This incident does not appear in the remaining fragments of Ephorus, but as shall be considered more fully below, he does provide an approximate date when he states that Pheidon was tenth in descent from Temenus. This would place his reign about the middle of the eighth century. The real significance of the general agreement among these writers has been universally overlooked. It cannot be invoked to prove that the date must be accurate; rather, it can only be regarded as evidence that the date is a late and patent contrivance. Apparently Ephorus did not know the specific Olympiad in which Pheidon took over the games—at least this information is not recorded in the fragment of his work that has come down to us. He could only date Pheidon genealogically, and it seems clear that genealogical reckoning was the only information later writers possessed when they sought to date to a specific Olympiad Pheidon's march on Olympia. It is not surprising, therefore, that Ephorus's genealogical date and Pausanias's Olympic date are in agreement, for the latter was undoubtedly derived from the former. Moreover, from the time of Ephorus onward it was commonly believed that Pheidon lived at an early date, and it would be unlikely indeed if this belief, no matter how erroneous, was not accepted by writers such as Aristotle and still later men such as the scholiast on Apollonius and Plutarch. It has long been recognized, however, that an eighth-century date for Pheidon has little to recommend it, and although Pausanias's dating of his usurpation of the Olympic games to 748 B.C. was widely accepted in the nineteenth century, it is no longer taken seriously by most scholars.[10]

If Pheidon did not usurp the games in the eighth Olympiad, as Pausanias specifically says he did, we must seek to find another Olympiad at which his march on Olympia might have taken place. The major problem encountered in this approach, however, is that there is no reliable evidence concerning which Olympiads were actually celebrated under Elean stewardship and which were not.[11] The only evidence we have is from late authors, none of whom are especially renowned for their historical perceptiveness or reliability. The earliest author to give us any information on the subject is Strabo who believed that the games were held by the Eleans for the first twenty-six Olympiads, that is from 776 to 676 B.C. In the twenty-seventh Olympiad the games were taken over by the Pisatans, and they continued to oversee the celebration for some time thereafter, until the Eleans regained control over it. Strabo gives no specific number of years when the games were under Pisatan control, but the important point to consider is that on Strabo's reckoning alone, Pheidon's usurpation of the games cannot be dated before 672 B.C., though it might have occurred well after that date. Eusebius supplies some information that agrees well enough with this conclusion but which does not agree completely with all of the information given by Strabo. Eusebius,[12] quoting Julius Africanus, knew of no trouble in the twenty-seventh Olympiad, but he does say that the Pisatans gained control of the games in the twenty-eighth Olympiad in 668. We are not told who controlled the games in the twenty-ninth Olympiad in 664, but Eusebius adds that the Pisatans controlled them continuously from the thirtieth through the fifty-second Olympiad, that is, from 660 to 572. To recapitulate briefly, the information supplied by Strabo and Eusebius is only partly consistent. They agree that the games were not usurped at any time in the eighth century. According to Strabo they were first usurped by the Pisatans in 672, but Eusebius says this did not occur until 668. Both agree that the twenty-eighth Olympiad in 668 was an Anolympiad, and both knew of a continuous period of Pisatan control of the games. Whereas Eusebius dates this period of Pisatan control from 660 to 572, Strabo tells us only that it began in 672 and continued for an unspecified period thereafter.

This evidence must now be considered in the light of information supplied by Pausanias, the only other ancient writer who tells us about Anolympiads.[13] Pausanias knew of no continuous period of Pisatan control of the games. He believed rather that there were four isolated Olympiads in which Elean control of the games was usurped by the Pisatans. One of these was the one hundred fourth Olympiad, which is too late for our purposes and can, therefore, be disregarded. For the earlier period, however, in addition to Pheidon's usurpation of the games in the eighth Olympiad, Pausanias informs us that in the thirty-fourth Olympiad in 644 Pantaleon, tyrant of Pisa, secured control of Olympia and the games. These are the only Anolympiads Pausanias knew about; he does say, however, that there was a war between Elis and Pisa at the time of the forty-eighth Olympiad in 588, but the Eleans apparently did not then relinquish control of the games.

There is no other evidence regarding Olympic celebrations that were not conducted by the Eleans. Yet modern scholars, even though confronted with such late, conflicting and contradictory evidence, have been able to convince themselves with remarkable ease that Pheidon's usurpation of the games must have occurred in the twenty-eighth Olympiad in 668 B.C. They find consolation in the reports of both Strabo and Africanus that this Olympiad was celebrated under the direction of the Pisatans, and this can be made to harmonize with Pausanias simply by emending his text to read twenty-eighth rather than eighth. To clinch the argument another passage of Pausanias is invoked. He tells us that in 669, the year before the twenty-eighth Olympiad, the Argives fought and defeated the Spartans at Hysiae. It is commonly assumed that it was this victory that allowed the Argives to march to Olympia and take control of the games there without encountering any serious opposition from the Spartans. This solution was first proposed by Thomas Falconer in his edition of Strabo in 1807, and it provides even today the most widely accepted date for Pheidon.[14] No one seems to be embarrassed by the fact that no ancient author mentions Pheidon in connection either with the Battle of Hysiae or with the usurpation of the games in the twenty-eighth Olympiad. To complicate the situation further, no ancient author even suggests that Pheidon might have lived in the early part of the seventh century. Moreover, as I have argued in the previous chapter, there is no reason to believe that the Argives defeated the Spartans at Hysiae in 669 or for that matter at any other time during the seventh century. In short, the only evidence to support the commonly held belief that Pheidon usurped the Olympic games in 668 B.C. is the fact that Strabo implies and Africanus states that this year was an Anolympiad. But Strabo knew of other years when the games were under Pisatan control, and Africanus specifically tells us that the Pisatans were in control of the games in every Olympiad between 660 and 572 B.C. For all we know, Pheidon might have been involved in the games at any time during this period.[15] In point of fact, our knowledge about the Olympic games generally and the Anolympiads specifically is simply too scanty and confused to allow us to date Pheidon by this means, and the common belief that he usurped the games in 668 and that he must, therefore, be dated to the early part of the seventh century is fiction not history. We shall perhaps be in a position to speculate about when Pheidon's usurpation of the Olympic games might have occurred only if we are able to date Pheidon by other means.

As noted above, we have reports that Pheidon introduced coinage into the Greek world, and if these reports are accurate, we would have important evidence for at least an approximate date for Pheidon. The matter is not clearcut, however, for the literary evidence may not be that trustworthy and the introduction of coinage into Greece is not an event that can be dated with precision. Estimates have fluctuated widely over the years. A half century ago it was thought that the first Greek coins were to be dated to the early part of the seventh century, a date which was conveniently consistent with the widely accepted dating of Pheidon to the twenty-eighth Olympiad.[16] In the 1950s the date of the first Greek coins was moved down to 600 B.C. plus or minus,[17] and this new dating placed scholars on the horns of a dilemma. Acceptance of this dating meant either they had to disassociate Pheidon from the Battle of Hysiae and the twenty-eighth Olympiad or they had to disregard the ancient reports that he was the inventor of Greek coins. The latter was most effectively questioned. Most scholars preferred to dissociate Pheidon from the earliest coinage, but some, by dating the coins on the plus side of 600 B.C. and assigning Pheidon an artificially lengthy reign, still found it possible to connect him with the Battle of Hysiae and the twenty-eighth Olympiad and the introduction of coinage.[18] It now appears, however, that coinage was not introduced into Greece until sometime in the first quarter of the sixth century.[19] Even if this date should be universally agreed upon, we still cannot use it to date Pheidon until we have considered the reliability of the ancient reports that he was the inventor of the first Greek coins.

The evidence has been reviewed many times,[20] and it will not be necessary to treat it in elaborate detail here. It is important to note at the outset, however, that Pheidon's alleged connection with coinage cannot be separated from other ancient reports that also credit him with the introduction of a system of weights and measures. The three are so closely related in the ancient literary tradition that they must be considered together. The relationship between coinage and a weight standard is both intimate and direct; in fact the two are inseparably connected, for it seems that in antiquity weights were originally employed for parceling out precious metals.[21] A weight standard was, therefore, absolutely essential before coinage could have been invented. The relationship between a standard of measure and a standard of weight was not, however, all that direct, for everyday commodities were commonly doled out by measures of capacity, that is, by measures whose quantity was determined not by weight but rather by the capacity or volume of the container being used as the standard.[22]

Our earliest information on this subject comes again from Herodotus, who says nothing about a Pheidonian system of weights nor does he say that Pheidon had anything to do with coinage. He tells us only that Pheidon introduced a system of measures (μέτρα) into the Peloponnesus.[23] There is a good deal of evidence to support Herodotus's statement; a number of other ancient authors[24] also refer to a Pheidonian measure. It was apparently used at Athens before the reforms of Solon, and there is epigraphical evidence to prove conclusively that it was still being used at Apollonia in the fourth century B.C.[25] From this latter source, moreover, we learn the relative size of the Pheidonian medimnos, 3,000 of which were equal to 1,875 Delphic medimnoi; we learn also that, in this instance at least, it was a measure of grain. Additionally, there is a report by Aristotle preserved by Pollux that mentions a container called a "Pheidon," used for measuring oil.[26] The evidence strongly suggests, therefore, that Pheidon introduced a standard for both liquid and dry measure, and although it is by no means certain that this measure was employed throughout the Peloponnesus as Herodotus implies, its use at Athens and Apollonia suggests that it was used in a fairly wide area. The important point to note here, however, is that grain and oil were commonly parceled out by measures of capacity rather than measures of weight. The fact that Pheidon introduced a measure of capacity does not prove that he introduced a standard of weight measure. Nor does it prove, as has often been assumed, that he introduced a standard of linear measure.[27] His measure of capacity obviously derived from some linear standard, but it need not have been a standard introduced by Pheidon himself. He may well have employed a standard already in use.[28]

Of all the literary figures who credit Pheidon with the introduction of a system of measures (μέτρα), Ephorus is the only one to connect him with a system of weights (σταθμός).[29] The choice before us is whether we ought to regard a brief notice in a fragment of Ephorus as more important and trustworthy than the silence of all other ancient writers and especially those who speak of Pheidonian measures but not of Pheidonian weights. The silence of Herodotus is especially disturbing, and it may also be significant that nowhere in the surviving works of Aristotle, who twice mentions Pheidonian measures, is there any hint that he knew of a Pheidonian weight standard. Moreover, before we can accept Ephorus's statement, we must take into account the whole problem of the introduction of coinage. As mentioned above, weights and coins were inseparably connected, and anyone who believed that Pheidon introduced coins into Greece was likely to believe that he also introduced a weight standard upon which to base the coins.

It may be more than coincidence, therefore, that Ephorus, the only ancient author to tell us that Pheidon had anything to do with a system of weights, is also the earliest ancient author to tell us that Pheidon minted the first Greek coins. One other fourth-century author, Heracleides of Pontus, shared this belief. The information was repeated by the author of the Marmor Parium in the third century B.C.; by Strabo, quoting Ephorus, in the first century; and by Pollux and Orion several centuries later.[30] All these writers agree, moreover, that Pheidon did not mint his coins at Argos, as we might reasonably expect, but rather on the island of Aegina.

Numismatists agree that the first coins were in fact minted there, but before we can accept the ancient reports that Pheidon was the inventor of coins, two questions must be answered: first, how was Pheidon able to mint coins on Aegina?; second, why did he want to mint them there? The explanation most frequently advanced to the first question is that Pheidon and Argos must have exercised some control over the island. Although this view has been widely accepted, there is no evidence to support it. No ancient author tells us directly that Pheidon controlled Aegina, and such control can only be inferred from reports that he minted his coins there, from a strained interpretation of a passage in Herodotus,[31] from a brief notice in Pausanias where we are told that Aegina was included within the Lot of Temenus, and from Ephorus's notice that Pheidon recovered this lot for Argos.[32] So long as the introduction of coinage was dated to the early part of the seventh century, it was possible to believe that Argos might have exercised direct control over Aegina; but if the introduction of coinage is to be dated after 600

B.C., we must deal with a completely different set of circumstances. By this time Aegina was a prosperous commercial state; it was, moreover, an island, and from the early part of the seventh century onward, the Aeginetans were well versed in seafaring, and they must have possessed a navy that was both sizable and experienced. The one necessary prerequisite, indeed the sine qua non for Pheidonian control over Aegina, is the presence of an Argive navy. In the previous chapter it was noted that there is no evidence to indicate that Argos was greatly interested in naval matters in the seventh century; in fact, there is no reliable evidence that the city possessed a navy at any time in its history.[33] It is, therefore, difficult to imagine how Pheidon might have gained control over Aegina.

It has on occasion been suggested that he need not have controlled the island directly in order to mint coins there and that he might have been able to do so if he had had some sort of alliance with Aegina.[34] This is a reasonable suggestion, but there is no evidence that any such alliance ever existed. It does seem clear that the two states were on good terms in the early decades of the sixth century. Both may have been members of the Calaurian Amphictiony,[35] and they apparently had already cooperated in a war against Athens.[36] However, the fact that friendly relations existed between the two states is not an adequate explanation of how Pheidon was able to establish a mint on the island.

Even if we were to acknowledge the possibility of a Pheidonian mint on the island of Aegina, however, we would still have to consider the question of why he would want to establish one there. Modern scholars have usually held that Aegina was a natural and logical place for Pheidon to mint his coins because Argos was relatively isolated from trade routes and not within the mainstream of Aegean commerce, but Aegina was the leading commercial state of the period.[37] This is surely true enough, but such an explanation creates more problems that it purports to solve. What, for example, did the ruler of a commercially isolated and predominantly agrarian state hope to accomplish by minting coins in the first place? Coinage might have been both useful and beneficial to Aegina and Aeginetan merchants, but what Argos and the Argives stood to gain by it is not at all apparent.

Attempts to link Pheidon with the earliest Greek coins have too often failed to take into account the available numismatic evidence, particularly from Argos. Even a cursory inspection of this evidence reveals some curious and interesting facts. It is striking that the Argives did not begin to mint coins in their own city until about 500 B.C. or perhaps even slightly later.[38] The most reasonable explanation for this is surely that the Argives had no great need for coins and consequently no desire to mint them until this time.[39] In short, we must face the fact that the earliest Aeginetan coins antedate the earliest Argive coins by three quarters of a century. We must also recognize that when the Argives finally did begin to mint their own coins, they based them on the same weight standard as that being used at Aegina. It is commonly assumed that this was the weight standard introduced by Pheidon.[40] This assumption provides a convenient explanation of how later authors might have been led to the conclusion that Pheidon minted the first Greek coins.[41] However, as we have seen above, the evidence for a Pheidonian weight standard is far from conclusive. Indeed, the fact that Aeginetan and Argive coins were based on the same weight standard and the additional fact that Aeginetan coins antedate Argive coins strongly suggest that when the Argives first began to mint their own coins they simply borrowed the Aeginetan weight standard.[42] In this connection it is also important to note that although Argos and Aegina employed the same weight standard for their coins, they did not employ the same standard of measure; more to the point, the Aeginetans did not employ the Pheidonian medimnos.[43]

To sum up, there is good evidence that Pheidon introduced a system of measures as Herodotus reports, and although this measure was used widely throughout the Greek world, it was not employed at Aegina, where Pheidon was alleged to have minted his coins. There is no reliable evidence to prove that Pheidon also introduced a system of weights or that he had anything to do with the invention of coinage.[44] Ephorus is the only ancient author to connect Pheidon with a system of weights, and any tie between Pheidon and coinage was apparently unknown to writers who lived before the fourth century and was not shared by all writers of that century. Argos was in no position to have controlled Aegina either directly or indirectly in the early sixth century when the first Greek coins were minted there. It seems clear, therefore, that Pheidon had nothing to do with the introduction of coinage into Greece; accordingly, he cannot be dated by this means. We must turn to the final evidence to be considered, the genealogical information provided by the ancient authors.

Unfortunately, we are not well informed about the geneaology of the kings of Argos. Several versions of an Argive king list have come down to us from antiquity, but they are always given in connection with Macedonian not Argive history. It was a commonly held belief as early as the fifth century B.C. that the Argead monarchy of Macedonia was founded by descendants of Temenus who came to Macedonia from Argos. Herodotus and Thucydides are the earliest writers to express this view, but neither historian was aware of any connection between Pheidon and the founders of the Macedonian monarchy. Thucydides does not name the first Macedonian king; Herodotus tells us that it was Perdiccas, whom he places seven generations before Alexander I.[45] Later writers give a completely different account, and by the fourth century the Argive Caranus, who supposedly lived several generations earlier than Perdiccas, was recognized as the founder of the Macedonian monarchy. It is through Caranus that we get some information concerning the genealogy of the early kings of Argos and the genealogy of Pheidon. Our chief source is the Byzantine chronographer Syncellus, who quotes two variant versions of Caranus's genealogy. In one version, which he tells us was accepted by most ancient writers and specifically by Theopompus and Diodorus, Caranus was regarded as the son of Pheidon and eleventh in descent from Heracles and seventh in descent from Temenus. The other version that Syncellus knew about gives a completely different list of Argive kings, regards Caranus as eighth in descent from Temenus, considers him the son of Paeas, and does not mention Pheidon.[46] There is, finally, a third genealogy of Caranus that is preserved by the Hellenistic chronographer Satyrus. Although Satyrus follows essentially the same genealogy as Theopompus, he fails to mention Pheidon and apparently regards Caranus as the son of Aristodemus.[47] It would be naïve to believe that this late tradition provides us with any reliable evidence for dating Pheidon. Not only are these reports internally inconsistent and contradictory, but they conflict sharply with the tradition known to writers who lived in the fifth century B.C. The ancient belief that the Argead kings of Macedonia came originally from Argos has been examined many times, and most scholars agree that the story is myth not history.[48] It would seem to be a patent invention deriving in part at least from the similarity of the names Argead and Argos and also from a conscious desire on the part of the Macedonian kings to prove that they were in fact Greeks not barbarians. The aim of this later tradition was quite clearly to reaffirm the connection between the Macedonian monarchy and Heracles, and at the same time to connect the Macedonian kings with the most illustrious Argive of them all, Pheidon. The weakness of this latter connection is underscored, however, by the fact that although Syncellus reports in one place that Pheidon was the father of Caranus, elsewhere he refers to Pheidon as the brother of Caranus.[49]

If the genealogy of Caranus is no help in dating Pheidon, it does provide us with an excellent illustration of the magnitude of that problem. The confusion of later writers concerning Pheidon's place in the genealogy of the Argive kings is manifest, but it is important to recognize that this confusion existed as early as the fourth century B.C. As we have seen, Theopompus believed that Pheidon lived in the sixth generation after Temenus.[50] This view was also held by Diodorus, but it is specifically contradicted by Ephorus,[51] who reports that Pheidon was tenth in descent from Temenus. On Theopompus's reckoning Pheidon would have to be dated in the ninth century B.C., but Ephorus has him living in the early or middle part of the eighth century. Modern scholars have been reluctant to draw the obvious conclusions from this conflicting tradition. If Ephorus could date Pheidon four generations later than his contemporary Theopompus dated him, it is clear that these fourth-century historians provide us with no reliable information about Pheidon's date. What they do provide is positive proof that as early as the fourth century B.C. Greek historians had no reliable evidence of Pheidon's place in the genealogy of the Argive kings and, consequently, no reliable evidence of when he actually lived and ruled Argos. We cannot, therefore, place any faith in Aristotle's statement that Pheidon was an earlier figure than the Cypselids at Corinth, and it can surely serve no useful purpose to attempt to resolve our problems by relying on writers such as Plutarch, Pausanias, and the scholiast on Apollonius of Rhodes, who lived long after the fourth century. A good case in point is the third-century Marmor Parium, whose author says specifically that Pheidon was seventh in descent from Temenus and that he lived in the early part of the ninth century, 631 years before the chronicler's base date of 264-263.[52]

One other approach that has been employed in an attempt to date Pheidon by genealogical reckoning must be briefly discussed here. It is commonly assumed that the Argive kingship came to an end in the second generation after Pheidon. If this view were correct and if the end of the kingship could be dated within reasonable limits, we would have an approximate date for Pheidon. Unfortunately, the notion that the Argive kingship ended in the second generation after Pheidon is based more on modern conjecture than on any substantial ancient evidence. It is derived from a combination of information provided by three ancient authors, Herodotus, Plutarch, and Pausanias.[53] The technique of combining isolated passages from three such widely spaced and diversely reliable authors hardly inspires confidence. Pausanias is the only author to tell us that the Argive kingship came to an end in the reign of Meltas, and he further identifies Meltas as the son of Lacedes. He does not state specifically that Lacedes was king of Argos; for this information we must turn to Plutarch, who is the only ancient author to state categorically that Lacedes was once king of the city. According to Herodotus, Lacedes was the son of Pheidon, and it would seem to follow, therefore, that Meltas was the grandson of Pheidon and that he lived and ruled Argos two generations after the tyrant. Yet this conclusion cannot be hastily accepted. Pausanias, for what it is worth, seems not to have shared this view,[54] and as I shall discuss at greater length later, there was such a great deal of confusion concerning the circumstances leading up to the end of the kingship at Argos that the event must have been only dimly remembered at best.

Yet even if we could accept the propositions that Meltas was the last king of Argos and that he was the grandson of Pheidon, it would not help us significantly in dating the tyrant, for Meltas is even a more mysterious figure than Pheidon and he cannot be independently dated. The only evidence that can be cited is a fragment of Diodorus in which we are told that the kingship at Argos lasted 549 years. Unfortunately,

Meltas is not mentioned in the fragment, and it is not entirely clear whether Diodorus was referrng to the Temenid line of kings at Argos or, as has been suggested, "to the mythical kingdom of Inachus, Lynceus etc."[55] If Diodorus did mean that the Temenid monarchy lasted 549 years, we might easily calculate an approximate date for Meltas, for Diodorus seems to have accepted Ephorus's date of 1069 for the return of the Heracleidae and hence the beginning of the Temenid monarchy.[56] If the kingship began in this year and ended 549 years later, it would have come to an end about 520 B.C. If Pheidon lived two generations before this, it would be necessary to date his reign to the early years of the sixth century. Such computations do not inspire much confidence, however, and there is more reliable evidence that must now be considered.

It has long been recognized that the information supplied by later writers is far from reliable. As noted above, since the early years of the nineteenth century, scholars have found reasons to reject both the ninth-century date of Theopompus and the Marmor Parium and the eighth-century date of Ephorus and Pausanias, and to date Pheidon to the early part of the seventh century by emending the text of Pausanias. Although this solution underscores the inadequacies of the later literary evidence, it can hardly be regarded as an acceptable solution to the problem. On the one hand it rests on no ancient evidence, and on the other it completely ignores the information provided by Herodotus. Herodotus is the earliest ancient author to mention Pheidon and the only author to do so who lived before the fourth century B.C. In view of the confusion among later writers, it is surprising that modern scholars have not paid more attention to the information that he gives us. It is true that there are many chronological problems in Herodotus's history, and he does not always supply us with the chronological precision we should like.[57] It may even be that his chronology is not accurate, but there are many reasons for believing that he remains our best guide to the chronology of events before the fifth century.[58]

Herodotus mentions Pheidon only briefly, almost parenthetically.[59] He tells us plainly that one of the suitors for the hand of Agariste, daughter of Cleisthenes, tyrant of Sicyon, was an Argive named Lacedes.

He further identifies Lacedes as the son of Pheidon, and he specifically identifies this Pheidon as the Pheidon who usurped the games at Olympia and introduced a system of measures into the Peloponnesus. There are many problems surrounding Herodotus's account of the wooing of Agariste; its highly romanticized nature has often been noted. There can, however, be no doubt that Agariste was a historical figure and that she did, as Herodotus reports, marry the Athenian Megacles, son of Alcmaeon. Many have expressed doubts that the wooing took place in the manner described by Herodotus, and many have doubted that Lacedes was one of the suitors for Agariste's hand. Cleisthenes is known to have pursued a vigorous anti-Argive policy, and, therefore, it would be surprising to find an Argive prince residing at his court for a year and attempting to win acceptance as his son-in-law.[60] Yet, the important consideration for our purposes is the fact that Herodotus clearly believed that Pheidon had a son of marriageable age when Cleisthenes was tyrant of Sicyon.

Such dating is generally considered impossible for a number of reasons. It cannot be reconciled with the preconceived notion that Pheidon usurped the Olympic games in the twenty-eighth Olympiad. Second, it is impossible to reconcile a Pheidon ruling contemporaneously with the Orthagorids at Sicyon and the Cypselids at Corinth with our preconceived notions that he was a great conqueror who recovered an extensive empire for Argos.[61] But these are not serious objections at all. As we have seen, there is no reliable evidence for dating Pheidon's usurpation of the Olympic games to the twenty-eighth Olympiad or for that matter to any other specific Olympiad. The only evidence for a Pheidonian empire comes from later writers, Ephorus and Pausanias primarily, both of whom seriously misinterpreted early Peloponnesian history as a result of dating Pheidon to the eighth century.[62] I see no logical reason to prefer a modern emendation of the text of Pausanias or reports of an extensive empire in works of dubious value over Herodotus. His dating of Pheidon may not be accurate, but surely we ought to have better reasons for rejecting it than have thus far been advanced. Rather than disregarding the information he provides, as virtually all modern scholars have chosen to do, we must regard it as the best, indeed, as the only reliable evidence we have for dating Pheidon. Either we accept the date Herodotus provides or we admit that the entire problem is insoluble.

At the same time, however, it must be recognized that the best we can hope to arrive at is an approximate date for Pheidon; in the present state of our knowledge it is not possible to provide absolute dates for his reign. The evidence for dating the Orthagorid tyrants at Sicyon is far from secure; it has been examined many times and there is no need to treat it in great detail here.[63] We are told by Aristotle that the tyranny lasted for 100 years. But it is difficult to know how accurate this figure may be, and it is not easy to determine when it may have begun or ended. Modern scholars have advanced both a high dating, ca. 670/665-570/565, and a low dating, ca. 615/610-515/510, and it is not easy to choose between them. The dates of the reign of Cleisthenes within the period of the Orthagorid dynasty are more firmly but by no means definitively set. Most would agree, however, that he must have been tyrant between ca. 600 and 565 B.C., but it has been suggested that his reign lasted until about the middle of the century.[64]

The evidence we have is not sufficient to allow us to construct a relative chronology of events within his reign; it is not possible, therefore, to date the marriage of Agariste precisely. Herodotus's report that Cleisthenes announced his scheme for the wooing of his daughter at the Olympic festival in which he was victor in the chariot race is really no help because we do not know at which Olympiad this might have occurred. However, it probably took place sometime between 580 and 568 B.C., but other dates are entirely possible.[65] Our knowledge of the progeny of Agariste does not help to narrow the date. We know that her marriage to Megacles produced two sons, Cleisthenes and Hippocrates. Hippocrates was the grandfather of Pericles, who was born about 495 B.C. Cleisthenes was archon eponymous at Athens in 525/4 and was active there as a political reformer in the closing decade of the sixth century.[66] He could hardly have been born after the 550s and probably not before the 580s, but it is not possible to determine a precise date.

The evidence Herodotus supplies indicates that Pheidon had a son of marriageable age sometime between the 580s and the 550s. We have no way of knowing how old Lacedes might have been at the time of the wooing; it is hardly likely that he was much more than fifty or much less than twenty, but this does not help us in attempting to date Pheidon more precisely. Perhaps the clearest chronological indication we have is Herodotus's statement that the suitors were to remain in Sicyon for a full year competing for the hand of Agariste. It is not likely that Lacedes was ruler of Argos at the time, for he could hardly have absented himself from the city for such a long time without incurring serious political opposition at home. It is entirely possible, therefore, that Pheidon was alive and well and ruling Argos at the time of the wooing of Agariste; but in any event, the best evidence we have indicates that his reign must be placed in the late seventh and/or early sixth century. In the next chapter I shall attempt to show that there is nothing incongruous about such a date.

Chapter VII:

Argos in
the Time of Pheidon

All of the literary evidence for dating Pheidon, as we have seen above, is late, fragmentary, confused, conflicting, and contradictory. In using this material to date Pheidon, scholars have selected information that supported the particular case they were attempting to construct and ignored or conveniently explained away information that interfered with their conclusions. The same danger exists and the same mistakes have been made with respect to other aspects of Pheidon's career. Indeed, we must recognize at the outset that the evidence we have cannot be used to reconstruct a day-by-day account of his reign anymore than it can be used to date precisely the period in which his reign might have occurred. Although confused and contradictory, the evidence for dating Pheidon is far better than any evidence we have for determining the nature of his domestic or foreign policy. Not even the main outlines of his program are clear, and modern scholars have compounded the confusion by attributing far more to the man than the evidence warrants. In addition to being credited with the invention of weights, measures, and coinage, and the creation of a wide-ranging Argive empire, Pheidon has from time to time been given credit for the creation of the Argive phratries, for instituting the office of demiourgos and being the first one to hold that office, for building the Argive Heraeum and a fountain house in the city of Argos, for introducing hoplite warfare into Greece, for being the guiding force behind the fine style of Argive Geometric pottery being produced shortly after 750 B.C., and indeed for much more.[1]

To dramatize the nature of the problems we face, it may be convenient to begin by pointing out that it is not even easy to determine what position Pheidon held at Argos, for there were conflicting traditions on this point as early as the fourth century B.C. Our earliest evidence is again Herodotus, who says that he was tyrant of the city. Ephorus, however, refers to Pheidon not as tyrant, but as basileus, and this view was apparently shared by Theopompus and a number of later writers who included Pheidon among the descendants of Temenus in their lists of Argive kings. Finally, there is Aristotle, who says that Pheidon began his career as king but later became tyrant.[2] Although one might easily wonder if Aristotle were not merely attempting to harmonize conflicting traditions about Pheidon, his report cannot be dismissed out of hand. There is no reason to doubt Herodotus's assertion that Pheidon was tyrant of Argos, but neither he nor any other ancient author tells us that Pheidon inherited his tyranny. Accordingly, it seems safe to assume that Pheidon was not always tyrant of Argos; rather, at one point in his career he managed to establish himself in that position. To accomplish this he must have usurped the power of the Argive aristocracy, and if he were king before he became tyrant, as Aristotle believed, he must have been king in name only, with his effective power severely limited by the power of the aristocratic elements in the city.

In establishing himself as tyrant of Argos, Pheidon must have acquired his power at the expense of the Argive aristocracy. Unfortunately, we have no indication of the source and nature of his support and no indication of how he might have established his tyranny. It is, of course, entirely possible that he had some backing among his fellow aristocrats, but the bulk of his support came, presumably, as support for tyrants came generally, from the peasantry.[3] In return for their support Pheidon must have offered them something, but the only reliable evidence we have for his domestic policy is Herodotus's statement that he introduced a system of measures into the Peloponnesus. This is surely not much to go on, but we cannot overlook the potential political importance and implications of this innovation. Later writers by combining this Pheidonian measure with his alleged introduction of weights and coinage have obscured its true significance. We must not see his establishment of a system of measures as a program designed to stimulate trade and commerce,[4] though this may well have been of secondary importance. His main aim would seem to have been to improve the economic conditions of the Argive peasantry, for the Pheidonian measure, as we have seen, was used to measure grain and oil, and these were important commodities necessary for the day-to-day existence of the Argive peasantry. It is obvious that by fixing measures for commodities such as these, Pheidon made it much more difficult for the Argive aristocracy to exploit the peasantry. Henceforth, a measure of wine or grain, or some such commodity, was of a fixed and predetermined quantity and not a quantity perhaps arbitrarily determined by some aristocratic landowner. Such a program hardly qualifies as revolutionary, and it surely cannot be regarded as decidedly antiaristocratic; but it would appear to be an attempt to secure economic justice for the Argive peasantry, and as such its motive must have been as much political as economic.

Other reforms of a similar nature and with similar aims were undoubtedly introduced, but we do not know what they might have been. It is possible that some sort of legal reform, a code of laws perhaps, was part of Pheidon's program, but on this the literary evidence is silent.[5] It may be worth noting that Aristotle mentions a Pheidon of Corinth, whom he identifies as "one of the most ancient legislators,"[6] and it is always possible that Aristotle really confused a Corinthian Pheidon with an Argive Pheidon. However, this cannot be proven. In any event, if the danger of attributing more to Pheidon than the evidence warrants is to be avoided, it must be concluded that his domestic policy remains a mystery. There is no literary evidence to help us measure his success or failure as a political or social reformer, and the archaeological evidence adds nothing to our knowledge. It is not likely, however, that his programs and policies differed significantly from those of tyrants elsewhere throughout the Greek world in the late seventh and early sixth centuries. In attempting to solve Argos's internal problems, his aim was not to transfer complete political authority from the Argive aristocracy to the peasantry or to destroy the aristocracy as a class. He surely must have taken steps to lessen the distinctions between them, but he was probably careful to do so in such a manner that he retained the good will of significant numbers of the aristocracy as well as the peasantry.

It was not as a political or social reformer that later ages remembered

Pheidon but as a military conqueror. Yet it is striking that in all ancient literature that has come down to us, nowhere is Pheidon associated with any specific battle. It is only from later writers, initially and especially Ephorus, that we learn of any far-ranging Pheidonian empire. Ephorus's views on the subject are preserved in two passages of Strabo. In one we are told that Pheidon minted his coins on the island of Aegina; the other passage is more important and deserves to be quoted in full here:[7]

Pheidon the Argive, who was the tenth in descent from Temenus and surpassed all men of his time in ability (whereby he not only recovered the whole inheritance, which had been broken up into several parts, but also invented the measures called Pheidonian, and weights, and coinage struck from silver and other metals)—Pheidon, I say, in addition to all this, also attacked the cities that had been captured previously by Heracles, and claimed for himself the right to celebrate all the games that Heracles had instituted. And he said that the Olympian games were among these; and so he forcibly invaded Eleia and celebrated the games himself, the Eleians, because of the peace, having no arms wherewith to resist him, and all the others being under his domination; however, the Eleians did not record this celebration in their public register, but because of his action they procured arms and began to defend themselves; and the Lacedaemonians cooperated with them, either because they envied them the prosperity which they had enjoyed on account of the peace, or because they thought that they would have them as allies in destroying the power of Pheidon, for he had deprived them of the hegemony over the Peloponnesus which they had formerly held; and the Eleians did help them to destroy the power of Pheidon, and the Lacedaemonians helped the Eleians to bring both Pisatis and Triphylia under their sway.

It is clear from this passage that Ephorus regarded Pheidon as an impressive military figure: he deprived the Spartans of hegemony over the Peloponnesus and he recovered the Lot of Temenus for Argos. These assertions cannot, however, be accepted at face value. The whole story of the Lot of Temenus has been examined above and found to be fiction not history, and although the report that Pheidon deprived the Spartans of hegemony over the Peloponnesus has been universally accepted by modern scholars, it is nonetheless demonstrably false.

The main outline of Spartan expansion has been briefly traced above[8] where it was noted that as late as the early decades of the sixth century the Spartans were having an inordinate amount of trouble defeating the Tegeans; in fact, they were humiliated in the Battle of the Fetters. Indeed, it was only with the victory over Tegea and the conclusion of an alliance between the two states shortly before the middle of the sixth century that Sparta became an important state in the Peloponnesus. Thereafter events moved swiftly, and when the Argives were defeated in the Battle of Champions in 546 B.C.,[9] Sparta's prominent if not dominant position within the Peloponnesus was assured. In the remaining decades of the sixth century a number of other states were overcome by the Spartans, and toward the end of the century these states were drawn together into the Peloponnesian League.[10]

What the evidence clearly indicates is that the Spartans did not acquire much influence in the Peloponnesus until the latter half of the sixth century, and at no time before this period can they be said to have exercised hegemony over the Peloponnesus. If, therefore, we are to accept Ephorus's assertion that Pheidon deprived the Spartans of such hegemony, we shall have to date Pheidon to the latter half of the sixth century at the very earliest; such a date is obviously out of the question. We must, accordingly, reject Ephorus's assertion that Pheidon deprived the Spartans of Peloponnesian hegemony, and with it we must also dismiss the universally accepted belief that the keystone around which Pheidonian foreign policy revolved was the traditional hostility between Sparta and Argos.[11] If Pheidon did in fact create an empire it must have been created at the expense of some other Peloponnesian state or states.

In this connection, however, it is important to remember that Herodotus does not specifically mention any far-reaching Pheidonian empire; he tells us only that Pheidon took control of the Olympic games. There are, nonetheless, a number of passages in Herodotus commonly cited by modern scholars to buttress their notion that Pheidon did indeed create an empire. The most straightforward passage in this respect is one that has been cited several times previously, in which the historian states that Argos once controlled the western coastal area of the Gulf of Argos and the offshore islands; additionally, he indicates that at one time Argos had some influence in Cynouria. Although these are the only areas where Herodotus definitely indicates Argos had some influence, there are several other passages of his work that are commonly interpreted as implying some Argive influence or control at Epidaurus, Aegina, and Sicyon.[12] Despite the fact that Herodotus is extremely vague on chronology in each of these passages, modern scholars have simply assumed that if Argos ever controlled these areas it must have done so in the days of Pheidon. But this assumption conflicts sharply with the simple fact that Herodotus nowhere suggests that Pheidon created an empire.

It also conflicts sharply with Herodotus's dating of Pheidon as a contemporary of the Orthagorid tyrants at Sicyon and the Cypselid tyrants at Corinth. If Pheidon ruled when Herodotus says he did, it is extremely unlikely that he was the great military conqueror that later writers and Ephorus particularly remembered him to be. As argued above, we might reasonably reject Herodotus's dating of Pheidon, but we cannot reasonably do so simply because it conflicts with the belief of these later writers that he created an extensive empire. I see no practical alternative to rejecting these later views in favor of Herodotus's dating. Indeed, if we are to understand Pheidon's role in Argive history, we must recognize that he did not deprive the Spartans of hegemony over the Peloponnesus; he did not bring under Argive control the cities that were traditionally included within the Lot of Temenus; and he did not create an extensive Argive empire. This does not mean that Pheidon was not militarily active in the Peloponnesus, but it does mean that his military activity was much more limited than Ephorus and other later writers, including most modern scholars, would have us believe.

The whole question of Pheidonian relations with Corinth provides a good case in point. Herodotus's dating of Pheidon as a contemporary of the Cypselid tyranny at Corinth, and in all probability as a contemporary of the most illustrious Cypselid of them all, the tyrant Periander, indicates that so far as Herodotus was concerned, Pheidon did not exercise any control over Corinth. Indeed, any Pheidonian interference in Corinthian affairs during the period of the Cypselids would be out of the question. None of the surviving fragments of Ephorus refer to Pheidonian relations with Corinth, but there are reports in writers who lived long after Ephorus. Although they differ in details, both Plutarch and a scholiast of Apollonius of Rhodes[13] report that Pheidon had plans to overwhelm Corinth during the period of the Bacchiad oligarchy there, but he was not successful. Plutarch implies that this was one of the first acts, if not the very first act, of Pheidon's career; the only other evidence we have for Pheidon's relations with Corinth comes from Nicolaus of Damascus, who reports that Pheidon "out of friendship, went to help the Corinthians in a civil war. An attack was made by his supporters and Pheidon was killed."[14] This would place Pheidon's interference at Corinth at the very end of his career. It is difficult to take these late reports very seriously; they are not in agreement with each other, and they are in sharp conflict with Herodotus and other evidence that also suggests that relations between Argos and Corinth were cordial enough in the period about 600 B.C. Periander followed a policy of peace generally, and except with Epidaurus[15] we hear of no hostility between Corinth and neighboring states during his reign. It is clear from the archaeological evidence that commercial relations between Argos and Corinth remained relatively strong in this period,[16] and we know that the Cypselid ruler of Ambracia married an Argive woman, Timonassa. It may also be significant that the Pheidonian medimnos was later in use at Apollonia,[17] a Cypselid colony probably founded by Periander himself about 600 B.C.; and for what it may be worth, there is a report of a scholiast on Pindar that Corinthian measures were first struck by Pheidon the Argive.[18] Such evidence may not prove conclusively that Pheidonian Argos and Cypselid Corinth enjoyed friendly relations, but this conclusion seems more likely than one derived from the confused accounts of later writers.

From Corinth we can proceed in a clockwise direction to a consideration of areas surrounding the Argive plain. At first glance the eastern Argolid might seem like a logical area for any Pheidonian expansion. There was no major state to block an Argive incursion into this section of the Peloponnesus, and two cities in the area, Troezen and Epidaurus, as well as the island of Aegina off the coast, were traditionally included within the Lot of Temenus. The evidence commonly cited as proof that Pheidon once exercised control over Aegina has been examined in the preceding chapter where it was concluded he had not. There is no need to repeat that argument here, but Pheidonian control over the eastern Argolid requires further discussion. We know virtually nothing about

Troezen in this period[19] and not a great deal more about Epidaurus. With respect to the latter, however, we know that it was ruled by its own tyrant, Procles, whose daughter Melissa married the Corinthian tyrant, Periander. The marriage was undoubtedly political, but eventually relations between Corinth and Epidaurus deteriorated. Periander had Melissa murdered and then waged war against his father-in-law, took him prisoner, and captured Epidaurus.[20] Before this occurred, however, Procles must have been tyrant of the city for at least eighteen years, and Pheidon could not have been in control of Epidaurus during this period. He might have exercised some influence there before or after Procles's tyranny, but unfortunately we cannot say when his reign began and when it ended.[21]

There is one additional story in Herodotus involving Epidaurus and Argos, as well as Aegina and Athens, that requires further discussion. According to Herodotus,[22] Aegina was once subject to Epidaurus, but after acquiring ships, it broke away and proclaimed its independence. At this time the Aeginetans removed from Epidaurus the olive-wood statues of Damia and Auxesia which had been set up earlier on advice from Delphi. The olive wood had been secured from Athens, and in return the Epidaurians agreed to pay a sacred dues annually to Athena and Erectheus. After the Aeginetans removed the statues, the Epidaurians refused to continue payment and referred the Athenians to the Aeginetans, who also refused to make payment. A war between Athens and Aegina resulted, and in this war the Argives aided the Aeginetans. Herodotus knew of two accounts of the war, an Athenian version and another of the Argives and Aeginetans. Although they differ in details, both versions agree that Argos and Aegina enjoyed some measure of success against the Athenians. Unfortunately, Herodotus does not date the war, and all attempts to do so on the basis of the information he supplies have not been successful. Most important for our purposes is his report that as a result of their victory the Argives and Aeginetans passed a law making their brooch pins half as long again as they had previously been and that a prohibition was placed against the bringing of Athenian pottery into a certain temple at either Argos or Aegina or perhaps at both. Although pins were dedicated at the Argive Heraeum in vast numbers, they do not appear to have been a standard size; therefore, it is impossible to determine when, if ever, they might have been made half again as long as previously.[23] Nor is it possible to determine when Athenian pottery might have been excluded from either Aegina or Argos. There are few Attic imports at the Argive Heraeum from any period, and at Aegina there is no visible break in Athenian imports.[24]

Herodotus supplies one additional bit of information that may be of some significance. He tells us that before they crossed over to Aegina, Argive troops assembled at Epidaurus. Since Epidaurus and Aegina were at odds at the time, it is obvious that the Epidaurians did not willingly allow their city to be used as a staging area for troops going to the aid of their opponents. This would suggest that Argos was militarily powerful enough to impose its will upon Epidaurus. This does not, of course, provide a date for the war, but the temptation to resort to the argument that it seems unlikely that Argos was capable of exerting control over Epidaurus at any time other than the period of Pheidon's tyranny[25] is strong. If this actually was true, we would have important information regarding his foreign policy. But it must be emphasized that we can only guess that the war might have occurred in this period.[26] It cannot be proven.

The region to the south and southwest of the Argive plain along the western coastal area of the Gulf of Argos was another section of the Peloponnesus favorable for Pheidonian expansion. Here, too, there was no state powerful enough to resist Argive encroachment. It has on occasion been suggested on the basis of Herodotus's assertion that Argos once controlled this territory that Pheidon must have extended Argive influence into this region.[27] But as I have argued above, Argive control of this area was not possible since they did not possess a navy and since Prasiae apparently remained an independent community as late as the middle of the sixth century. Accordingly, there is nothing to suggest that Pheidon was able to exercise hegemony over the territory.

To the north and west of Prasiae lay the territory of Cynouria and beyond Cynouria, Tegea, Arcadia, and ultimately Olympia. Everything we know about Cynouria, however, and that is not much, suggests that it was certainly within the Argive sphere of influence, if not under direct Argive control. Yet there is no reason to believe that this development took place only during the period of Pheidon's ascendancy at Argos.

Herodotus suggests that the Argives had some influence in the area over a long period of time, and the archaeological evidence would seem vaguely to support this suggestion. There was a steady, if none too voluminous, commercial contact between Argos and Tegea throughout the period from the late eighth until the first half of the sixth century at least, and this commerce could only have proceeded through Cynouria.[28] This does not, however, constitute evidence that Argos actually controlled Cynouria; but it does suggest that it had some influence in the area and that this influence extended much further back in time than the period of Pheidon.

It would, nonetheless, be easy to assume that Cynouria was becoming an area of increasing concern for Argos in the early decades of the sixth century, but there is no evidence that this was in fact true. At this very moment the Tegeans were engaged in a life-and-death struggle to maintain their independence from the Spartans, and it must have been apparent to the Argives that the fall of Tegea would advance Spartan influence to the very gates of Cynouria and that this area would then become the final stretch of territory between Sparta and the Argive plain and the city of Argos itself. There is nothing to suggest, much less prove, however, that the Argives were overly concerned about this development; they might easily have adopted the attitude that since the Spartans were having an inordinate amount of trouble conquering little Tegea, Argos, a more powerful city and located at a greater distance from Sparta than Tegea, had little cause for alarm. In any event, if the Argives attempted to aid the Tegeans in their struggle against Sparta, we do not hear of it, nor is there any evidence indicating that Pheidon had designs on Tegea or any other Arcadian city. Although the argument from silence can never be conclusive, when coupled with other evidence it is at least highly suggestive. It seems manifestly clear that Sparta was not Pheidon's chief opponent or even his chief concern in the Peloponnesus, and there is no evidence to prove that he was militarily active in the area south and west of the Argive plain.

To the west we know he was interested in Olympia, but of his actions in this direction we know little. We have no reports of his relations with any of the states located between the Argive plain and Olympia that might enlighten us about his policy with respect to the large mass of the

Peloponnesus. In fact, his march on Olympia might better be discussed in connection with his relations with states to the north and west of the Argive plain. Two cities here, Phlius and Sicyon, were traditionally included within the Lot of Temenus. About Phlius we know virtually nothing apart from the fact that the city was ruled by a tyrant named Leon, possibly but not necessarily sometime in the sixth century.[29] Concerning Sicyon, however, there is the report of Herodotus[30] that early in the fifth century the Argives levied a fine on the Sicyonians for allowing Cleomenes to use their ships for transporting Spartan troops to the Argive plain. Unlike the Aeginetans, the Sicyonians actually paid the fine and by so doing acknowledged the Argive right to levy it. It has often been assumed that this right derived from some control Argos once exercised over Sicyon and further assumed that any such control could only have been a reality in the days of Pheidon. Since Cleisthenes and Pheidon were contemporaries, Pheidonian control over Sicyon is manifestly impossible, and if we are honest with ourselves we shall have to admit that we do not know why the Sicyonians paid the fine or by what authority the Argives imposed it. If we knew more about the history of Argos and Sicyon in the period between the end of Cleisthenes's tyranny and Cleomenes's invasion of the Argive plain, we might be able to explain both actions, but we do not. In any event, there is no reason to believe that Argos could have exercised any direct control over Sicyon at any time before or during the period of Cleisthenes's tyranny or for that matter at any time in Greek history.

To understand properly Argive-Sicyonian relations in the time of Pheidon, it is necessary to recognize that Cleisthenes and Pheidon had much in common, though the similarities between the two rulers have usually been overlooked. Both men were political reformers of sorts; they were interested in athletic games and religious celebrations; and they were known and respected by later ages for their military ability.[31] In connection with the latter, there is evidence to prove that in the early decades of the sixth century both Argos and Sicyon were becoming interested in a much wider area of the Greek world than merely their respective cities. Pheidon's usurpation of the Olympic games is one manifestation of this wider interest[32] and so too is Cleisthenes's interest in religious games and festivals, and especially his concern over the Oracle of Delphi. Although most of our evidence for this aspect of Cleisthenes's career comes from later writers and many of the specific details are open to question, apparently he participated in the First Sacred War on behalf of the Oracle of Delphi, and as a result of this war Crissa was destroyed and the autonomy of Delphi assured.[33] In the years following the war, there are reports that Cleisthenes was instrumental in founding the Pythian games[34] and that he oversaw the erection of the Sicyonian treasury at Delphi.[35] Indeed, it may not be irrelevant that Pheidon took control of the Olympic games while Cleisthenes fought on the side of Delphi in the First Sacred War. If the ancient evidence is even generally reliable, Cleisthenes and Pheidon would seem to have been almost natural opponents, and disagreement between them should come as no surprise but is, rather, exactly what we might expect. Indeed about 600 B.C. Argos had greater need to be concerned about an able, aggressive tyrant at Sicyon than about a Spartan state being bested in its struggle against Tegea.

Herodotus, who is certainly our most trustworthy source of information, implies that this was precisely the situation. He informs us that Cleisthenes engaged in a vigorous anti-Argive domestic policy, which he carried to incredible lengths. He forbade minstrel contests at Sicyon because the Homeric poems praised Argos; he attempted to expel the cult of Adrastus from the city, because Adrastus was of Argive lineage, but he was dissuaded from this by the Oracle of Delphi. Instead, he imported the cult of Melanippus from Thebes and began to exalt this cult at the expense of the cult of Adrastus, transferring to Melanippus the sacrifices and festivals previously celebrated in honor of Adrastus. Perhaps his most vehement and in many ways most inexplicable act, however, was to change the names of the Sicyonian phylae so that they would not be the same as those at Argos. In the process he gave them names that were anything but flattering to the Sicyonians.[36] But Cleisthenes was not content with merely pursuing an anti-Argive course at home; Herodotus reports that he also waged war against Argos. Herodotus does not, admittedly, tell us that Pheidon participated in this war; but his silence on this point is surely outweighed by the fact that he clearly believed that Cleisthenes and Pheidon were contemporaries.

There are a great many things we do not learn about Argive-Sicyonian relations in this period from Herodotus or from any other ancient author. We know nothing about the reasons behind Cleisthenes's Argive war or his immutable hostility toward Argos. The usual explanation is that this hostility derived ultimately from some control Argos once exercised over Sicyon, as a result of which the Argives still possessed some vague religious authority. War between the two states, it is argued, came about when Cleisthenes attempted to remove all traces of Argive influence from his city.[37] As noted above, however, this assumption presupposes that Pheidon lived long before Cleisthenes was tyrant of Sicyon. On the face of it, it would seem much more reasonable to look for the origin of Argive-Sicyonian hostility not somewhere in the dim past of their respective histories or in some vaguely defined religious prestige which Argos supposedly possessed but rather in contemporary events and situations.

Argos and Sicyon did not have a contiguous border. Several minor states, Orneai, Phlius, Cleonae, and Nemea, were situated in the area between them. Since none of these states were very large or particularly powerful, this section of the Peloponnesus was an area of potential expansion for both Argos and Sicyon. Unfortunately, we have little information about these minor states in this period. Apart from some evidence concerning the foundation of the Nemean games and a report that Phlius was included within the Lot of Temenus, we have only an isolated passage or two in Plutarch and Pausanias.[38] This would hardly constitute reliable evidence for the course of events in the sixth century B.C. under any circumstances, and the whole matter is further complicated by the fact that, except for the information concerning the foundation of the Nemean games, none of these reports carry any chronological reference. They can, therefore, be interpreted at will,[39] but to assume that they enlighten us about the course of events in the early decades of the sixth century is surely self-deception. Nonetheless, even in the absence of reliable information we might reasonably assume that Argos and Sicyon became involved in a war over the territory situated between them; no other explanation for their hostility is readily apparent. It is not likely that their rivalry was commercial, for Argos appears to have been little interested in commerce. Moreover, since both Cleisthenes and Pheidon were vigorous military men, it is easy to understand how their interests might have clashed in this area. Any war between Argos and Sicyon would certainly have involved at least Nemea and Cleonae, since these states are situated on the direct route between Argos and Sicyon. But we can say little else about the causes of the war.

It cannot be determined whether Pheidon or Cleisthenes was the aggressor in this war, and no ancient author tells us whether Argos or Sicyon emerged victorious. In view of the fact that Argos exercised some influence over Sicyon as late as the decade of the 490s, and in view of Cleisthenes's bitterness toward Argos and his anti-Argive domestic policy, we might suppose that the Argives were the victors. This is an assertion that cannot be proven; nor is it possible to date the war with any precision. Herodotus's report that Delphi not only opposed Cleisthenes's attempt to expel the cult of Adrastus from Sicyon but went so far as to deliver an insulting oracle to the tyrant when asked for advice might suggest that it occurred before the First Sacred War, which is generally dated to the 590s.[40] But this too can only be a guess.

In any event, it remains to be noted that Pheidon's usurpation of the Olympic games fits better in this context and in this period than at any other time in early Greek history. This event must be considered in the broader context of the general interest in the organization of the various Greek games in the decades between the 580s and the 560s. In addition to the first celebration of the Nemean games, the Pythian and Isthmian games were founded probably sometime in the 580s; and according to tradition, which is generally supported by the archaeological evidence, the first Panathenaic festival was celebrated in 566 B.C.[41] We do not know a great deal about the motivation behind the inauguration of these games,[42] but most scholars would agree that it was, at least in part, political. Peisistratus's interest in the Panathenaic festival is assumed as a matter of course. With respect to Pythian and Isthmian games it has been argued, on the one hand, that they were instituted by the tyrants to enhance their own glory and the glory of their cities, or, on the other hand, that they were founded as an expression of opposition to the tyrants and to celebrate and commemorate their overthrow.[43] Unfortunately, the chronology of events in this period is so insecure that neither argument is very forceful. Of greater significance for our purposes, however, is the testimony of Herodotus, who informs us that manipulation of games and festivals was one element of Cleisthenes's anti-Argive domestic policy, and, therefore, politically inspired.[44]

This is important information, for if Cleisthenes could use religious games for his own political purposes, so too could Pheidon. It is in this context that we must consider Pheidon's usurpation of the Olympic games and perhaps also the foundation of the Nemean games. Although scholars have long addressed themselves to the problem of attempting to find out at which Olympiad Pheidon secured control of the games, and they have advanced some ingenious solutions to this problem, they have tended to ignore the equally important question of the reasons for his action. Even the ancients were not overly concerned about this; of all the ancient authors who tell us that Pheidon usurped the games, only Pausanias and Ephorus give us any indication of why he did so. According to Pausanias Pheidon was invited to Olympia by the Pisatans and together with them conducted the celebration.[45] Ephorus, however, says Pheidon claimed the right to celebrate not only the Olympic games but all games instituted by Heracles, and in line with this, he invaded Elis and forcibly made good his claim. Ephorus goes on to say that Pheidon's action prompted the Eleans and Spartans to enter a military alliance, and together the allies defeated the Argives and drove Pheidon from Olympia.[46] On the basis of this information modern scholars have simply assumed that Pheidon's usurpation of the games was a military act aimed at the Spartans and tied up with his policy of replacing them as hegemon of the Peloponnesus and with his alleged victory at Hysiae. But if Pheidon's march on Olympia occurred before the Spartan conquest of Tegea and acquisition of hegemony over the Peloponnesus, this cannot have been true.

In fact, there is no evidence to prove and none to suggest that Pheidon's usurpation of the Olympic games was conceived as a military measure at all. All ancient writers agree that he took control of the games for one celebration only, after which, presumably, he withdrew to Argos. This would surely imply that he had no long-range interests in the games or in this area of the western Peloponnesus. In short, it seems reasonable and necessary to conclude that Pheidon's usurpation of the games was not a military act aimed at Sparta and in all probability was not conceived as a military measure. Indeed, it is much more readily understandable if it is viewed as a political measure aimed at Cleisthenes and Sicyon—that is, as one element in the Argive-Sicyonian hostility that permeated Peloponnesian history in the early decades of the sixth century—and more particularly, if it is seen as an attempt to counter the growth of Sicyonian prestige at Delphi. It is entirely possible that Pheidon did think the western Peloponnesus was of some military consequence, as both Pausanias and Ephorus seem to imply; but an alliance between Pisa and Argos would have been useful against Sicyon and need not have been directed against Sparta. Moreover, it makes greater historical sense. At this time Sicyon was ruled by an aggressive, hostile tyrant, while Sparta was unable to defeat the Tegeans.

Perhaps the founding of the Nemean games, which must have occurred not long after Pheidon's usurpation of the Olympic games, ought to be viewed in the same light. Although we have little actual information about the founding of these games, and even the traditional date may not be precise, it seems clear enough that they were founded at Nemea by the men of Cleonae.[47] This is suggestive in more ways than one. The creation of the games was obviously a cooperative venture. Although there is no evidence to prove conclusively that Argos was party to this cooperative venture, it is highly probable that it was. Relations between Cleonae and Argos were certainly close in the early decades of the fifth century.[48] More telling, perhaps, is the likelihood that Adrastus enjoyed an exalted role in the games and was closely connected to Argos and in absolute disfavor at Sicyon.[49] His aggrandizement at Nemea can only be interpreted as an affront to Cleisthenes, and this strongly suggests that Argos was in some way involved in the founding of the games. It may be worth repeating that Pheidon did not gain any lasting control over the games at Olympia. Whether he withdrew voluntarily or was driven out cannot be determined on the basis of the existing evidence, but it is tempting to suggest that once he had retired from Olympia he cooperated with Nemea and Cleonae in laying the groundwork for the inauguration of new games at Nemea. In the absence of any ancient evidence, however, this must remain purely conjectural.

One other conjecture readily suggests itself. We know from Herodotus that games were being celebrated at the Argive Heraeum in the early decades of the sixth century, but they may well have been instituted at a much earlier date.[50] The fact that these games had a decidedly military flavor—they included a race in full armor, and a shield was awarded as a prize[51]—may suggest that they were instituted or perhaps reorganized in this, one of the most aggressive periods in Argive history. In this connection, moreover, it may be worth noting that there is evidence of substantial building activity at the Argive Heraeum in the late seventh and early sixth centuries.[52]

Throughout this chapter an attempt has been made to show that there is nothing incongruous about an early sixth-century Pheidon; such a date, in fact, does less disservice to the ancient evidence than any other that has been suggested either by ancient or modern writers, who, with the exception of Herodotus, have simply assumed that the traditional enmity between Sparta and Argos was the guiding principle behind Pheidonian foreign policy. Yet this notion must be dismissed as erroneous, for the ancient evidence clearly leads to the conclusion that Sicyon and Argos, not Sparta and Argos, were natural opponents in the early decades of the sixth century. At the time, Sparta was a militarily insignificant state struggling, not very successfully, against Tegea and perhaps other Arcadian cities. Sicyon, on the other hand, was ruled by a militarily active tyrant who was bitterly hostile toward Argos.

Within this background I have been primarily concerned with attempting to point out what Pheidon did not do. There is precious little evidence for what he did do, and for the most part, I have deliberately resisted the temptation to substitute my misconceptions for those of others. Given the nature of our evidence there is not much we can say about the man. That he instituted some economic reforms seems clear, and perhaps these were accompanied by certain political reforms as well. Otherwise, however, the nature of his domestic policy is not known to us. Nor can we do more than generalize about his foreign policy and his reputation as a military conqueror. It is evident that there was no Pheidonian empire on anything approaching the scale referred to by Ephorus and a host of modern scholars; in fact, there is no clear evidence that there was much Argive expansion at all under Pheidon. He may have acquired some influence in Cynouria, but there is no evidence to prove that he was even interested in the area south or west of Cynouria. Also, he may have had some influence at Nemea and Cleonae and perhaps even at Phlius, but he certainly had no control over Sicyon or Corinth. He apparently enjoyed friendly relations with Aegina, but otherwise his relations with the cities in the eastern Argolid remain a mystery. Finally, it should be noted that even in the days of Pheidon the Argives may not have exercised complete control over the communities within the Argive plain. The inscription from this period indicating that the Tirynthians had their own assembly has already been referred to, and in this connection there is the text of a Delphic oracle that also implies Tiryns was an independent community.[53] In short, we must conclude that Pheidon's later reputation as a military conqueror is grossly exaggerated.

At the same time, however, Pheidon did engage in military activity. He fought a war against Sicyon, and there is an oracle from Delphi, probably to be dated to this period, which acknowledges the Argives as the finest fighting men in all of Greece.[54] His military might was not, however, aimed at Sparta but at Sicyon. Finally, it is much easier to understand Pheidon's usurpation of the Olympic games if we view it in the context of his relations with Sicyon and date it to the early part of the sixth century,[55] that is, to precisely the period when other religious games were coming into existence. The Olympic games, being older, undoubtedly increased in importance and prestige; they might well have become a prize worthy of acquisition, though it is difficult to imagine them as such at any earlier period and certainly not as early as 748 or 668 B.C., the two most widely accepted dates for Pheidonian interference at Olympia.

Chapter VIII:

Sixth-Century Argos after Pheidon

Since we cannot determine the precise dates of Pheidon's rule and we cannot draw a coherent picture of his domestic or foreign policy, it is not possible to assess the impact of his reign on the history of Argos. We would be in a better position to do so if our knowledge of Argive history after Pheidon and for the sixth century generally was more secure, but unfortunately this is not true.

What transpired in the city immediately following his death is not known. It was briefly noted above that modern scholars have employed a combination of ancient evidence to arrive at the conclusion that the Argive kingship came to an end in the second generation after Pheidon. This presupposes that Pheidon was succeeded by his son Lacedes, who was in turn succeeded by his son Meltas, who was subsequently deposed as the last king of the city. Despite the shaky ground on which this reconstruction is built, it has not been challenged. Yet, there is important epigraphical evidence that renders it most unlikely or at the very least will force us to compress the reigns of both Lacedes and Meltas into a very short space of years probably within the latter part of the first and/or the early part of the second quarter of the sixth century. This same evidence, moreover, clearly indicates that the second quarter of the sixth century, that is, the years following shortly upon the death of Pheidon, was a period of important political change at Argos. This may well indicate that the tyrant's programs and policies antagonized important elements in the city and that his successors were incapable of placating the malcontents.

The evidence consists of three Argive inscriptions which, admittedly, cannot be dated precisely but which L. H. Jeffery has assigned to the period between ca. 575 and 550 B.C. Although this can serve as an approximate date, there is, as Jeffery herself acknowledges, some room for error, and a slightly earlier or more likely a slightly later date cannot be ruled out entirely.[1] The earliest of these inscriptions is probably not complete; what we have, apparently, is the end of what was once a considerably longer inscription. The portion that remains is nearly intact, however, except for a few letters which can easily and almost certainly be restored. It reads as follows: ἐνν[έϝα δ]αμιοργοὶ ἐϝ[αν]άσσαντο. This is followed by a list of names, three with patronymics and six without, presumably of the nine demiourgoi referred to in the text. If the verb ἐϝανάσσαντο were to be taken literally, it could only mean that nine demiourgoi were in a position of supreme authority in the city,[2] and we should have to conclude that the leading official at Argos when the inscription was set up was not the king but the demiourgos or, more specifically, the nine demiourgoi referred to in the text.

Although this translation of the verb ἐϝανάσσαντο may be open to some question, the other two inscriptions leave no doubt that the demiourgoi were indeed important Argive officials. A second inscription is only slightly later than the one just discussed, and Jeffery has suggested that it was probably cut by the same hand at a later stage of his development.[3] The text, which is practically complete, concerns certain works (τὰ ποιήματα) and treasures (τὰ χρήματα) that were dedicated to Athena Polias in her sanctuary on the Larissa, when six men, whose names are included, held the office of demiourgos. Among the treasures were certain sacred utensils whose use outside the temenus of the temple was restricted to public officials and expressly prohibited to any private citizen. Another provision of the text states that if anyone should damage the utensils he shall be required to make good the damage, with the amount to be determined by the demiourgoi. It is clear from the wording of the text that the demiourgoi were serving as eponymous officials, and it also seems likely that they were serving as a college.[4]

The third inscription is of approximately the same date as the second; it was set up at the Argive Heraeum, and though badly mutilated, seems to have contained, among other things, a list of crimes against the state that were punishable by curse, banishment from the city, or death. The word demiourgos is clearly readable in the text, but the connection between the demiourgos and the provisions of the law is not at all certain. It is possible, however, that he had some authority to see that the sentence was imposed and carried out. There is also a provision for the procedure to be followed "if no one be demiourgos," but unfortunately the text breaks off at that point. It is perhaps worth noting that no college of demiourgoi is referred to here but rather an individual demiourgos, whose name is not given, at least not in the part of the inscription that survives.[5]

Although these inscriptions may ultimately raise nearly as many problems as they solve, individually and collectively they provide us with important if somewhat ambiguous information about the political history of Argos in the second quarter of the sixth century. Admittedly, they do not tell us as much about the duties and functions of the demiourgoi as we might like to know, but we do learn that they were important officials in the Argive state. They obviously had some religious duties, and apparently some judicial responsibilities as well, and at one point they served as eponymous officials.[6] Moreover, although it is by no means certain, the possibility remains that the verb ἐϝανάσσαντο should be taken literally, in which case we should have to conclude that the demiourgoi possessed supreme authority.

It is indeed striking that nowhere in these inscriptions is there any mention of an Argive king, not even of the eponymous variety we know existed there about the middle of the fifth century. If these inscriptions are properly dated, we must conclude either that the Argive kingship had already come to an end by the second quarter of the sixth century or that if there was an Argive king in this period he was a weak and ineffectual figure.[7] Choosing between these possibilities is not easy, but there is some negative evidence that tends to support the former. The Battle of Champions which occurred shortly after 550, and which will be discussed more fully below, is frequently mentioned in ancient literature. It is referred to by Herodotus and a host of Greek writers who lived after him, and it is the subject of several passages in the *Palatine*

Anthology.[8] But nowhere in any of these references is an Argive king ever mentioned in connection with the battle.[9] The argument from silence cannot prove that there was no Argive king at the time, but when this silence is considered in conjunction with the epigraphical evidence discussed above, it is, to say the least, strongly suggestive.

To sum up, the best evidence we possess for Pheidon—Herodotus—makes him a contemporary of Cleisthenes of Sicyon in the early decades of the sixth century. Epigraphical evidence indicates either that the Argive kingship had come to an end or that the kings had lost effective power by the second quarter or certainly before the middle of the same century. It makes no sense to reject this evidence in favor of modern interpretations of scattered references in later writers. Although nagging doubts are likely to remain, it seems reasonable to conclude that for all practical purposes the Argive kingship had come to an end by the second quarter of the sixth century. It is perhaps possible that Pheidon was succeeded by Lacedes and that Lacedes was in turn succeeded by Meltas; but if this did happen, we shall have to conclude either that they were weak figureheads with little or no effective power or that if they ruled, neither had a very lengthy reign. In fact, we shall have to compress both reigns into not much more than a decade or so late in the first quarter and/or early in the second quarter of the sixth century.[10]

However, there is additional information to be gleaned from the epigraphical evidence discussed above. Collectively these three inscriptions leave no doubt that at precisely this period Argos was undergoing important political and governmental changes. It is not easy to determine why one of the inscriptions refers to nine demiourgoi and another set up just a few years later mentions only six. Nor is it easy to determine why the nine seem to have been serving as individuals but the six, to judge from the wording of the text, seem to have been serving as a college.[11] Moreover, another inscription seems to imply that at least one demiourgos had some authority to act independently of the college. Although these discrepancies cannot be explained, their very presence suggests that this was a period of precipitous political change, perhaps even experimentation, at Argos, during which the number as well as the duties and functions of the demiourgoi were changing frequently. This is precisely the sort of governmental instability one might expect to find after a new government had taken power but had not yet solidified its position. It is, in short, precisely the sort of situation that was likely to follow immediately the end of a period of tyranny or the end of the kingship.

There is no reason to believe that the government of Argos in the second quarter of the sixth entury was a democracy.[12] We do not know who was eligible to hold the office of demiourgos, how they were selected, by whom, nor for how long. It has been pointed out that the nine demiourgoi correspond closely to the nine archons at Athens,[13] but it does not follow that Argos was a democratic state. The Athenian archons were symbols of aristocratic, not democratic, control of the polis. Although the government of the demiourgoi was apparently not a government without some concern for the Argive peasantry, as the publication of laws on stone and their erection in the temenus of the temple of Athena would seem to indicate, in all probability the demiourgoi reflected the wishes of the Argive aristocracy or more probably some of the Argive aristocracy. In short, it seems safe to conclude that the Argive kings had lost effective power to an oligarchy. Since this occurred shortly after the reign of Pheidon, it might be reasonable to suggest that his programs and policies antagonized important aristocratic elements in the city, and his successors were unable to reconcile the dissidents to their rule. There is, to be sure, no direct evidence to support this contention, and it must, therefore, remain a tentative suggestion, no more.

Before leaving the subject of the end of the kingship at Argos there is some literary evidence which, even though it does not tell us a great deal, deserves to be mentioned here. Plato relates[14] that the tyrannical nature of the Argive kings once gave rise to trouble in the city. It would be tempting to conclude on the basis of this report that the tyrannical nature of Pheidon's rule contributed materially to the end of the Argive kingship, but this temptation must be resisted. A closer examination of Plato's remarks indicates that he believed the trouble occurred at Argos at the time of Lycurgus, and it is difficult to believe that the report has any historical value. Yet Plato was not the only ancient author to comment on the tyrannical nature of the Argive kings. Plutarch tells us in one place[15] that the tyrannical temper of the kings coupled with the ungovernableness of the people were jointly responsible for the "overthrow of all existing institutions" at Argos. This report is tempered by the fact that Plutarch apparently knew another version of the end of the Argive kingship. Elsewhere he tells us that the Heraclid line of kings "became extinct" and a new king was selected with the help and advice of the Delphic Oracle.[16] In the final analysis the information supplied by Plutarch looks no more reliable than that provided by Plato.

There was also current in antiquity another view of the end of the kingship at Argos that placed less emphasis on the tyrannical nature of the Argive kings. Pausanias tells us that Meltas, the son of Lacedes and last king of Argos, was "deposed by the people," but he gives us no specific reason for the deposition and is not, therefore, much help in the matter. It has been argued, however, that Pausanias derived his information from Ephorus[17] and that his report must be considered in conjunction with a fragment of Diodorus, which is also thought to have been taken from Ephorus. Although Diodorus does not mention Meltas, he does preserve the most extensive account of the end of the Argive kingship that has come down to us from antiquity. It deserves to be quoted in full here:[18]

The Argives, since they had suffered serious reverses in the war which they together with their king had undertaken against the Lacedaemonians, and had been forced to hand over their ancestral homes to the Arcadians, laid the blame for this upon their king, on the ground that he had given over their land to the exiles and had not divided it in lots among them. And the mass of citizens rose up against him and in their despair laid violent hands upon him, whereupon he fled to Tegea, where he spent his days in the enjoyment of honours at the hands of those who had received his favours.

This account raises a number of problems that are not easily resolved. It is not clear why the citizenry should blame the king not for reverses suffered in the war but for handing over their ancestral lands (τὰς πατρίδας) to certain exiles. Nor is it clear why these exiles had taken up residence in Tegea nor even why the land should have been turned over to them. The loss of land to the Arcadians rather than the Spartans is also interesting. This implies that Sparta and Arcadia were cooperating in the war[19] and that it must, therefore, have occurred after the Spartan conquest of Tegea, the first Arcadian city to succumb to Sparta. Finally, it is not easy to understand why the Argive king would have been welcomed at Tegea if he had just waged war against that city. In sum, Diodorus's report seems so inherently inconsistent and improbable that it would be risky to put too much faith in the specific details he provides.

Yet there may be an element of truth in his implication that developments at Argos were directly influenced by events that occurred outside the city, events over which the Argives themselves had little or no control. Although Diodorus is the only ancient author to tell us that a war between Sparta and Argos set the stage for the expulsion of the Argive king, this possibility must be acknowledged;[20] in any case, it would be naïve to believe that Argive internal politics can be separated from Argive foreign policy.

We must, accordingly, keep firmly in mind the struggles between Sparta and the Arcadians in the late seventh and early sixth centuries that was outlined above in Chapter V. The Spartans suffered a series of defeats, first at the hands of the Arcadians generally and then at the hands of the Tegeans. Shortly before the middle of the sixth century Tegea was finally subdued, and at that time the two states entered an alliance. As previously noted, this Spartan victory profoundly altered the political geography of the eastern Peloponnesus, for it gave the Spartans direct access to an easily traveled route to the Argive plain.

It is difficult to believe that the Argives lacked the farsightedness to understand that the capitulation of Tegea would give rise to a serious threat to their own security. It is equally difficult to believe they stood idly by watching Sparta move into such an advantageous position without taking any positive steps to contain the growing menace to the west. Yet in all ancient literature that has come down to us there is not a single indication that the Argives attempted to aid the Tegeans against the Spartans.[21] Again, the argument from silence may not be compelling, and the possibility that they did offer aid to Tegea must be acknowledged. Even if they did, however, it was obviously not in sufficient quantity to turn the tide of the struggle or to arrest the advance of Sparta in the Peloponnesus.

It must be remembered, moreover, that these events were occurring in precisely the same period that substantial political change was taking place in the government of Argos. The two developments are so consistent with one another that it is difficult not to conclude that they are inseparably connected. It may well be that the Argives were preoccupied with internal concerns in the period, and it is equally possible that this preoccupation prevented them from playing an effective role in the struggle between Sparta and Tegea. It does seem clear, in any event, that the oligarchical government that controlled Argos in the second quarter of the sixth century was ineffective in dealing with the new realities of Peloponnesian politics and this ineffectiveness may, in turn, have contributed to further governmental instability and change.

That Argos was ill prepared to face the future is evident from subsequent events. Within a few years after the Spartan conquest of Tegea, Argos found itself at war with Sparta. Things did not go well for the Argives. The war involved the Thyreatide plain, a small area situated in Cynouria that had been under Argive influence, if not direct Argive control for some time. What touched off the war is not known. But the Spartans were obviously the aggressor, for we are told that they occupied the area. When the Argives came out to meet them, as Herodotus relates, a conference between the parties resulted in the decision that 300 handpicked men from each side should fight it out. When this limited engagement—the so-called Battle of Champions—proved inconclusive, a pitched battle between Spartan and Argive forces ensued. After heavy losses on both sides the Spartans emerged victorious.[22] Their influence in Cynouria was assured, and it was presumably at this time that they marched east to the Gulf of Argos and, if Strabo can be trusted, gained control of Prasiae and assumed its place in the Calaurian Amphictiony.[23] The Battle of Champions in 546, in short, assured Sparta of a predominant position within the Peloponnesus and at the same time reduced Argos to a position of secondary importance. With Spartan influence permanently established in Cynouria and as far east as Prasiae, the Argive plain and the city of Argos itself lay vulnerable, easily open to invasion.

In less than two decades the position of Argos within the Peloponnesus had changed drastically. It would be unlikely if this did not have profound political repercussions. It is tempting to suggest that events of these two decades did not enhance the position of the oligarchical government that directed the affairs of the city and that the position of the demiourgoi was undermined. There is indeed some negative evidence to support this contention; it is striking and it may be significant that the office of demiourgos is unattested at Argos after the latest of the three inscriptions cited above,[24] that is, after ca. 550 B.C. The demiourgoi may well have lost their influence as a result, directly or indirectly, of Argos's military setbacks at the hands of Sparta. Unfortunately, however, we know nothing about governmental institutions that may have come into being in this period, though there are reports of tyrants other than Pheidon who ruled at Argos, and in the fifth century we know that the Argives once again had a king.[25]

In retrospect, the Battle of Champions was a major turning point in Argive history. We cannot determine why the Spartans did not conclude an alliance with Argos as they had previously done with the Tegeans, nor can we determine why they did not thoroughly subjugate the Argives as they had previously subjugated the Messenians. Perhaps their victory in the Battle of Champions was not decisive enough to permit either action. In the half century following the battle, the Spartans went on to create their Peloponnesian League and to assume a more important role in the affairs of the Greek world as a whole. Admittedly we have little evidence of Argive history in this period; not even the main outline of the city's internal development or foreign policy can be traced. Most of our information for Argive history in the latter half of the sixth century comes from Aristotle, and he obscures its significance by interpreting it in terms of the traditional and long-standing enmity that supposedly existed between Argos and Sparta. Herodotus does indeed imply that the Argives took the loss of Thyrea seriously. He reports that as a result of their defeat they shaved off their long hair and passed a law, with a curse appended, that no Argive man could wear his hair long and no Argive woman could wear gold until the area was recovered. In fact, however, there is no compelling reason to believe that the Battle of Champions marked the beginning of the traditional enmity between Argos and Sparta. It would be more than half a century before the two states would once again go to war, and it would be more than a century before the recovery of Cynouria became the motivating force behind Argive foreign policy.[26]

The information we have for Argive history immediately after the Battle of Champions is related to us more in the context of Athenian than of Argive history. We are told that early in his career the Athenian tyrant Peisistratus married an Argive woman, Timonassa, who had previously been married to Archimus, the Cypselid ruler of Ambracia. It does not seem likely that the tyrants of Athens and Ambracia would marry an ordinary woman, and both marriages may well have been contracted for political purposes. It is not known if Gorgillus, Timonassa's father, held any official position at Argos; but two prestigious marriages for his daughter suggest that the family was influential economically or politically or both. Aristotle states specifically that the marriage was designed to promote Peisistratus's friendship with Argos, and he adds that as a result of this friendship 1,000 Argive mercenaries fought with Peisistratus at Pallene when he finally gained control of Athens. Aristotle goes on to maintain that close ties between the two states continued down to the end of the tyranny at Athens and that these ties were one of the factors that prompted the Spartans to interfere in Athenian affairs when they marched their army into the city to overthrow the Peisistratid tyranny.[27]

Yet Aristotle is surely confused and surely guilty of reading fifth- and fourth-century interstate relations back into the sixth century when Athens and Argos seem to have had little in common. Although the two states may have been members of the Calaurian Amphictiony, the Argives aided the Aeginetans in a war against Athens probably sometime in the sixth century and again in the very early years of the fifth century.[28] What Aristotle fails to note is that Timonassa's marriage to Peisistratus was apparently dissolved shortly after the first exile,[29] that is, long before the Battle of Pallene. If the marriage had been contracted for the purpose of promoting friendly relations with Argos, one would expect the divorce to have had an adverse effect on those relations. Moreover, it is clear that the Argives who fought at Pallene were not citizen-soldiers fighting for the glory of their city but mercenaries fighting for a salary. Finally, it is worth noting that they were commanded by Hegesistratus, one of the sons of Peisistratus and Timonassa, who was later rewarded by his father with control of Sigeum.[30] The fact that Argive mercenaries fought with Peisistratus at Pallene may offer additional proof that the family of Gorgillus had some influence at Argos. But it hardly proves, as Aristotle maintains, that there were close ties between the Argive state and the Peisistratid tyrants. There is no proof and little reason to believe that the venture was supported by either the government or the citizenry of the city.[31]

Yet the presence of Argive mercenaries at Pallene is potentially important information for Argive history in this period, though the lack of a precise chronology renders it difficult to interpret. The exact date of the Battle of Pallene is disputed; but most scholars would date it to the decade of the 540s, within a short time of, and quite likely to within the same year as, the Battle of Champions. Whether it occurred before or after that battle is not so easily resolved.[32] It is difficult to understand how Argive mercenaries could have been available for service at Pallene if this campaign occurred shortly after the Battle of Champions, where the Argives supposedly suffered heavy losses.[33] If, however, Pallene occurred shortly before the Battle of Champions and Argive mercenaries fought there, this might well indicate that the Argives were not concentrating all their efforts against the Spartans and that they were slow to react to the increasing importance of Sparta within the Peloponnesus after the Spartan victory over Tegea. There are, indeed, some negative indications that point to a similar conclusion. So far as we know, the Argives made no attempt to strengthen the defensive fortifications of their city in this period,[34] and there is nothing to suggest that they sought to strengthen their relations with other states. Although we know that they fought a war against an unknown opponent sometime in the last quarter of the sixth century,[35] when trouble once again arose with Sparta the Argives were forced to fight alone. Even their former friends the Aeginetans supplied aid to Cleomenes of Sparta when he defeated the Argives at Sepeia in 494 B.C.[36]

The defeat of Argos at Sepeia is, in many respects, the logical culmination of events that began more than a half century earlier with the Spartan conquest of and alliance with Tegea and the subsequent victory over Argos in the Battle of Champions. These events established Spartan preeminence in the Peloponnesus; the formation of the Peloponnesian League and the crushing victory over Argos at Sepeia insured the continuation of this preeminence. Indeed, so complete was the Argive defeat at Sepeia that it apparently resulted in fundamental governmental change and a complete social revolution within the city,[37] and the Argives used this defeat as an excuse for remaining neutral in the Persian Wars that followed shortly thereafter.[38] But these events form another chapter in Argive history and lie beyond the scope of this work.

NOTES

Abbreviations to Notes

AA	*Archäologischer Anzieger.*
AAA	*Athens Annals of Archaeology.*
AC	*L'antiquité classique.*
AD	Ἀρχαιολογικὸν Δελτίον.
AEH	Fritz M. Heichelheim. *An Ancient Economic History* 1 (Leiden, 1958).
AH	Charles Waldstein. *The Argive Heraeum* 2 vols. (Boston and New York, 1902-1905).
AHR	*American Historical Review.*
AJA	*American Journal of Archaeology.*
AJP	*American Journal of Philology.*
AM	*Mitteilungen des deutschen archäologischen Instituts: Athenische Abteilung.*
AP	Markellos Th. Mitsos. Ἀργολικὴ Προσωπογραφία (Athens, 1952).
AR	*Archaeological Reports.*
Arch. Eph.	Ἀρχαιολογικὴ Ἐφημερίς.
Ath. Pol.	Aristotle. Ἀθηναίων Πολιτεία.
BCH	*Bulletin de correspondance hellénique.*
BSA	*Annual of the British School at Athens.*
CAH	*Cambridge Ancient History.*
CGA	Paul Courbin. *La céramique géométrique de l'Argolide* (Paris, 1966).
CJ	*Classical Journal.*
CP	*Classical Philology.*
CQ	*Classical Quarterly.*

CRAI	*Comptes rendus de l'Académie des Inscriptions et Belles-Lettres.*
DAG	A. M. Snodgrass. *The Dark Age of Greece* (Edinburgh, 1971).
EA	*Études Archéologiques.*
EGAW	A. M. Snodgrass. *Early Greek Armour and Weapons* (Edinburgh, 1964).
EP	*Études Péloponnésiennes.*
ES	George L. Huxley. *Early Sparta* (Cambridge, Mass., 1962).
FGrH	Felix Jacoby. *Die Fragmente der griechischen Historiker* (Berlin and Leiden, 1922-).
FHG	Carolus Müller. *Fragmenta Historicorum Graecorum* (Paris, 1841-70).
GA	Robin Hägg. *Die Gräber der Argolis in submykenischer, proto-geometrischer, und geometrischer Zeit* (Uppsala, 1974).
GBA	Emily T. Vermeule. *Greece in the Bronze Age* (Chicago, 1964).
GDA	V. R. d'A. Desborough. *The Greek Dark Ages* (New York, 1972).
GG	Karl Julius Beloch. *Griechische Geschichte* (Strassburg, 1912-27).
GGP	J. N. Coldstream. *Greek Geometric Pottery* (London, 1968).
GGR	Martin P. Nilsson. *Geschichte der griechischen Religion* (Munich, 1955).
Gött. Nachr.	*Nachrichten von der Gesellschaft der Wissenschaften zu Göttingen.*
GPP	Robert M. Cook. *Greek Painted Pottery* (Chicago, 1960).
GRBS	*Greek, Roman, and Byzantine Studies.*
IA	Ioannis K. Kophinotou, Ἱστορία τοῦ ᾽Άργους μετ᾽εἰκόνων ἀπὸ τῶν ἀρχαιοτάτων χρόνων μέχρις ἡμῶν (Athens, 1892).
IG	*Inscriptiones Graecae.*
JdAOI	*Jahreshefte des österreichischen archäologischen Institutes in Wien.*
JHS	*Journal of Hellenic Studies.*
LMS	V. R. d'A. Desborough. *The Last Mycenaeans and Their Successors* (Oxford, 1964).
LS	Willem den Boer. *Laconian Studies* (Amsterdam, 1954).
LSAG	Lilian H. Jeffery. *The Local Scripts of Archaic Greece* (Oxford, 1961).
MKAW	*Mededeelingen der Koninklijke Akademie van Wetenschappen.*
Mnem.	*Mnemosyne.*
NC	*Numismatic Chronicle.*
Nem.	Pindar. *Nemean Odes.*
OGC	Chester G. Starr. *The Origins of Greek Civilization 1100-650 B. C.* (New York, 1961).
Ol.	Pindar. *Olympian Odes.*

Opusc. Arch.	*Opuscula Archaeologica.*
Opusc. Ath.	*Opuscula Atheniensia.*
Ox. Papy.	*Oxyrhynchus Papyri* ed. B. P. Grenfell and A. S. Hunt (1898-).
PGP	V. R. d'A. Desborough. *Protogeometric Pottery* (Oxford, 1952).
PP	K. Syriopoulos. Ἡ Προ-ιστορία τῆς Πελοποννήσου (Athens, 1964).
Praktika	Πρακτιὰ τῆς ἐν Ἀθήναις Ἀρχαιολογικῆς Ἑταιρείας.
Pyth.	Pindar. *Pythian Odes.*
RA	*Revue archéologique.*
RE	*Paulys Real-Encyclopädie der klassischen Altertumswissenschaft.*
REG	*Revue des études grecques.*
RFC	*Rivista di filologia classica.*
RhM.	*Rheinisches Museum für Philologie.*
SEG	*Supplementum Epigraphicum Graecum.*
SMA	Per Ålin. *Das Ende der mykenischen Fundstätten auf dem griechischen Festland. Studies in Mediterranean Archaeology* 1 (Lund, 1962).
SS	Carl G. Styrenius. *Submycenaean Studies* (Lund, 1967).
TAPA	*Transactions and Proceedings of the American Philological Association.*
Tiryns	Walter Müller and Franz Oelmann. *Tiryns: Die Ergebnisse der Ausgrabungen des Instuts* 1 (Athens, 1912).
UVA	Michael Wörrle. *Untersuchungen zur Verfassungsgeschichte von Argos im 5. Jahrhundert vor Christus* (Munich, 1964).

Notes

Chapter I

1. Any study of the geography of the Argolid must begin with Herbert Lehmann's excellent book *Argolis: Landeskunde der Ebene von Argos und ihrer Randgebiete* (Athens, 1937), which deals with every geological and geographical aspect of the area, and contains excellent charts, photographs, diagrams, and a map. Alfred Philippson and Ernst Kirsten, *Die griechischen Landschaften* 3 (Frankfurt am Main, 1959). I, Sec. IV, 93-154, remains invaluable. Somewhat outdated now, but still worth reading, are Antoniou Meliaruke, Γεογρεφία Πολιτική νεὰ καὶ ἀρχάια τοῦ Νομοῦ Ἀργολίδος καὶ Κορινφίας (Athens, 1886). and I. Kophiniotou, Ἰστορία τοῦ Ἄργους (Athens, 1892) 35-95. Herbert Lehmann, "Argeia. Das Anlitz einer griechischen Landschaft," *Die Antike* 14 (1938) 143-158, discusses the area from a more visual than a scientific point of view, and the same author's "Zur Kulturgeographie der Ebene von Argos," *Zeitschrift der Gesellschaft für Erdkunde zu Berlin* (1931), considers the impact of geographical factors on the history of the area. A good capsule view of the area is given by Raymond Matton, *Mycènes et l'Argolid antique* (Paris, 1966) 9-14, and by R. A. Tomlinson, *Argos and the Argolid from the End of the Bronze Age to the Roman Occupation* (London, 1972) 7-14.

2. Much erosion has taken place since antiquity; the earliest remains at Tiryns lay some seven meters below the present surface of the plain. Lehmann, *Landeskunde*, 29-31, estimates that the landed area of the plain now extends about 350 meters further into the Gulf of Argos than it did in antiquity.

3. Lehmann, *Zeitschrift der Gesellschaft für Erdkunde zu Berlin* 38-39, and *Landeskunde*, 138-143. Philippson and Kirsten, *Die griechischen Landschaften* 3: Pt. 1, Sec. IV, 94-95.

4. I have somewhat oversimplified matters here; the borders of the Argolid were not so clearly defined as I have presented them. Ancient authors often did not discriminate among the terms Argos, Argeia, and Argolis. Homer's use of Ar-

gos to mean Greece, or at least the Peloponnesus, as well as the city of Argos is well known; see Thomas W. Allen "Argos in Homer," *CQ* 3 (1909) 81-98, and Emil Smith, "Argos hos Homer," *Symbolae Osloensis*, 1 (1923) 71-86. On the ancient confusion of the terms Argolis and Argeia, see Guilelmus Lilie, *Quae ratio intercessit inter singulas Argolidis civitates* (Breslau, 1862) 3-4, and Lehmann, *Landeskunde*, 5.

5. Lehmann, *Landeskunde*, 41-50.

6. On the rivers in the plain, see Kophiniotou, *IA*, 48-54, and Lehmann, *Landeskunde*, 50-55.

7. Homer, *Iliad* 4.171, Aristotle, *Meterologica* 1.14.10 (352a), and Strabo 8.6.8 (371) all suggest that the area was not dry; Hesiod, *The Catalogues of Women and the Eoiae*, 16, says that the area was initially dry but was "made well-watered" by Danaus. There may be some archaeological evidence to suggest that heavy rain was experienced at least at times in antiquity. The eighth-century temple models excavated many years ago at the Argive Heraeum show steeply sloped roofs, as A. R. Burn, *The Lyric Age of Greece* (London, 1960) 13, has cogently pointed out.

8. Springs: Lehmann, *Landeskunde*, 54-57; Kophiniotou, *IA*, 61-66. Early travelers in the area report swampy conditions along the coast; see, for example, William M. Leake, *Travels in the Morea* (London, 1830) 2:348, and William Gell, *The Itinerary of Greece* (London, 1810) 83-84. More recently the marshy and swampy areas have been drained.

9. Pausanias 2.24.5 mentions trees on Mount Lycone west of the city of Argos, but as Lehmann, *Landeskunde*, 65, points out, he implies that this was the exception rather than the rule.

10. Herbert Lehmann, *Über die potentielle Volkskapazität im Peloponnese* (Berlin, 1927), stresses the point that the western Peloponnese was capable of supporting a greater population than the eastern part, but he estimates that the Argive plain could support a population density of 585 inhabitants per square kilometer. By contrast, he estimates that the Argolid as a whole could support only twenty nine inhabitants per square kilometer. Nils-Gustaf Gejvall, *Lerna: A Preclassical Site in the Argolid* 1: *The Fauna* (Princeton, 1969) has examined the animal bones from Lerna; these provide some information on the diet of the inhabitants of the site.

11. A list of sites in the Argolid that have yielded Neolithic remains is given by Fritz Schachermeyr, "Prähistorische Kulturen Griechenlands," *RE* (Stuttgart, 1954) 1384-1385; John L. Caskey, "The Early Helladic Period in the Argolid," *Hesperia* 29 (1960) 286-287; K. Syriopoulos, Ἡ Προ-ϊστορία τῆς Πελοποννήσου (Athens, 1964) 25-31. A number of recent discoveries must be added to these lists. Argos: *BCH* 91 (1967) 818; Nauplia: *BCH* 95 (1971) 867, and E. Protonotariou-Deïlaki," Ἀνασκαφὴ Ναυπλίας," *AAA* 4 (1971) 1-2; Kephalari: R. C. S. Felsch, "Neolithische Keramik aus der Höhle von Kephalari," *AM* 86 (1971) 1-12, and "Die Höhle von Kephalari," *AAA* 6 (1973) 13-27. For a discussion of these and other sites in the vicinity see Tomlinson, *Argos*, 15-47.

12. On the importance of such locations in ancient Greece, see Ernst Kirsten, *Die griechische Polis als historisch-geographisches Problem des Mittelmeerraumes* (Bonn, 1956), 44-45; Roland Martin, *L'urbanisme dans la grèce antique* (Paris,

1956) 31-32; and Max Cary, *The Geographic Background of Greek and Roman History* (Oxford, 1949), 48-52.

13. This point is stressed by Lehmann, *Landeskunde*, 6; Philippson and Kirsten, *Die griechischen Landschaften*, 3:142; and Wilhelm Vollgraff, "Fouilles d' Argos: Les établissements préhistoriques de l'Aspis," *BCH* 31 (1907) 144.

14. *BCH* 91 (1967) 818; on this period generally see Saul Weinberg, *CAH*[3] 1: Pt. 1, 557-608, and on the Peloponnesus generally see Syriopoulos, *PP*, 127-188. For what it may be worth, Diodorus 1.28.2 refers to Argos as practically the oldest city in Greece.

15. Wilhelm Vollgraff, "Fouilles d'Argos: Les établissements préhistoriques de l'Aspis," *BCH* 30 (1906) 5-45, divided the pottery he uncovered into six classes. Although it is difficult to reclassify it at this time, it is clear that while most of the material he published was of Middle Helladic date, his Class I would appear to contain a mixture of Early and Middle Helladic material. His classes IV and V may also contain some Early Helladic material. On the use of the name Aspis in later antiquity, see F. Croissant, "Note de topographie argienne (à propos d'une inscription de l'Aphrodision)," *BCH* 96 (1972) 137-154.

16. An Early Helladic tomb is reported in *BCH* 78 (1954) 176. An Early Helladic stratum is reported in *BCH* 83 (1959) 758. On the finds from the Deiras see Jean Deshayes, *Études péloponnésiennes* 4: *Argos: Les fouilles de la Deiras* (Paris, 1966) 112-115.

17. The material from this site is reported by A. S. Arbanitopoulos, " Ἐρευναι ἐν Ἀργολίδι," *Praktika* (1916) 75-82, where the pottery is identified as Neolithic, but Carl W. Blegen, *Zygouries: A Prehistoric Settlement in the Valley of Cleonae* (Cambridge, Mass., 1928) 209-210, considers it Early Helladic rather than Neolithic. It is doubtful that this site is to be identified with the φορωνίκων ἄστυ mentioned by Pausanias 2.15.5 as suggested by A. S. Arbanitopoulos, " Ἀνασκαφαί καὶ ἔρευναι ἐν Ἀργολίδι καὶ Θεσσαλία," *Praktika* (1920) 17-18.

18. On other Early Helladic settlements in the plain see John L. Caskey, "Greece, Crete and the Aegean Islands in the Early Bronze Age," *CAH*[3] 1:Pt. 1, 771-807; Emily Vermeule, *Greece in the Bronze Age* (Chicago, 1964) 29-36, and Syriopoulos, *PP*, 189-296.

19. The evidence for destruction throughout the Argolid at this time is summarized by Caskey, *Hesperia* 29 (1960) 285-303, and also "Lerna in the Early Bronze Age," *AJA* 72 (1968) 313-316.

20. On the Middle Helladic period generally see John L. Caskey, "Greece and the Aegean Islands in the Middle Bronze Age," *CAH*[3] 2:Pt. 1, 117-140; Robert J. Buck, "The Middle Helladic Period," *Phoenix* 20 (1966) 193-209; and Vermeule, *GBA*, 66-86. On the Middle Helladic remains found in the Argive plain, see Syriopoulos, *PP*, 299-309, 332-339, 362-369, 391-394.

21. The material from the Aspis is reported by Vollgraff, *BCH* 30 (1906) 5-45. On the Cretan material found there, see Wilhelm Vollgraff, "Arx Argorum," *Mnem.* 56 (1928) 326-327, and also "Opgravingen te Argos," *MKAW* 66 (1928) 98, 102-103. Recent excavation in the south quarter of the city has uncovered a Middle Helladic layer with Minyan ware and matt-painted pottery mixed; see J. F. Bommelaer and Y. Grandjean, "Recherches dan le quartier sud d'Argos," *BCH* (1972) 157-161.

22. Premycenaean house foundations: Vollgraff, *Mnem.* 56 (1928) 326-327. The Middle Helladic remains from the Deiras excavations are discussed by Deshayes, *EP* 4:15-21. More recent discoveries are reported in *BCH* 78 (1954) 177; *BCH* 79 (1955) 312; *BCH* 83 (1959) 769-770; *BCH* 91 (1967) 808, 818. Though Middle Helladic house remains are fairly numerous at Argos, they do not furnish proof that the city was actually an urban establishment in this period as is suggested by Robert P. Charles, "Étude anthropologique des nécropoles d'Argos," *BCH* 82 (1958) 309-310, who based his conclusion on the fact that the skulls he studied showed a preponderance of wisdom teeth, a characteristic more common of populations living in an urban than a rural setting.

23. Vollgraff, *BCH* 30 (1906) 7 and *BCH* 31 (1907) 150-151, reports finding traces of a fortification wall which he dated to the Middle Helladic period, but Schachermeyr, "Prähistorische Kulturen Griechenlands," *RE*, 1456, is not convinced that it dates from this period. Walls of Middle Helladic date have, however, been found in the modern city; see *BCH* 91 (1967) 1036 and *BCH* 93 (1969) 1017-1018.

24. These remains are reported and the suggestion made by Vollgraff in *MKAW* 66 (1928) 87-107, especially 103-104, and *Mnem.* 56 (1928) 324-325; but only a few Middle Helladic sherds are reported from recent excavations on the Larissa; see *BCH* 90 (1966) 932.

25. Middle Helladic strata: Paul Courbin, "Une rue d'Argos," *BCH* 80 (1956) 183-213, especially 207-210; see also *BCH* 80 (1956) 370; *BCH* 94 (1970) 765; *BCH* 95 (1971) 736; and *AD* 21 (1966) 126. Middle Helladic tombs are reported in *BCH* 78 (1954) 176; *BCH* 80 (1956) 376; *BCH* 91 (1967) 820; *BCH* 92 (1968) 1036; *AD* 19 (1964) 122, 126; and generally see Paul Courbin, "Discoveries at Ancient Argos," *Archaeology* 9 (1956) 166-174, especially 167-168.

26. Deshayes, *EP:* 4:15-21, 115-137, 236-237, 250-251.

27. For fire and abandonment in the Middle Helladic period see *BCH* 93 (1969) 989-991; on the absence of any remains between the Middle Helladic and Geometric periods see *BCH* 91 (1967) 808 and *BCH* 95 (1971) 740.

28. On these strata see Courbin, *BCH* 80 (1956) 207-210, and *Archaeology* 9 (1956) 168. Robert J. Buck, "Middle Helladic Mattpainted Pottery," *Hesperia* 33 (1964) 278, 300, dates one fragment from these strata to the closing years of the Middle Helladic period and believes it shows Minoan influence.

29. See E. Protonotariou-Deïlaki, "Δύο μυκηναικοὶ τάφοι εἰς Λάρισσαν 'Άργους," *AAA* 3 (1970) 301-303, and *BCH* 95 (1971) 867.

30. This point is emphasized by Buck, *Hesperia* 33 (1964) 282-283.

31. Among the many useful publications on Mycenae, see Alan J. B. Wace, *Mycenae: An Archaeological History and Guide* (Princeton, 1949); George E. Mylonas, *Ancient Mycenae: The Capital City of Agamemnon* (Princeton, 1957), and *Mycenae and the Mycenaean Age* (Princeton, 1966).

32. The chamber tombs are reported by Carl W. Blegen, *Prosymna: The Helladic Settlement Preceding the Argive Heraeum*, 2 vols. (Cambridge, 1937); one additional tomb is reported by E. Protonotariou-Deïlaki, " 'Ανασκαφὴ λαξευτοῦ Μυκηναϊκοῦ τάφου ἐν 'Ηραίῳ ''Άργους," *Arch. Eph.* (1960) 123-135. On the tholos tomb, see P. Stamatakes, "Περὶ τοῦ παρὰ τὸ 'Ηραῖον καθαρισθέντος τάφου," *AM* 3 (1878) 271-286.

33. Gösta Säflund, *Excavations at Berbati, 1936-1937* (Stockholm, 1965); see also Åke Åkeström, "Das mykenische Töpferviertel in Berbati in der Argolis," *Bericht über den VI. internationalen Kongress für Archaologie* (Berlin, 1939) 296-298.

34. Axel Persson, *The Royal Tombs at Dendra near Midea* (Lund, 1931), and *New Tombs at Dendra* (Lund, 1942). On the chamber tomb containing the bronze armor see Nicholas M. Verdelis, "Neue Funde von Dendra," *AM* 82 (1967) 1-53, and Paul Åström, "Das Panzergrab von Dendra. Bauweise und Keramik, *AM* 82 (1967) 54-67. The material from the acropolis is reported by Gisela Walberg, "Finds from the Excavations in the Acropolis of Midea, 1939," *Opusc. Ath.* 7 (1967) 161-175.

35. The material from earlier excavations at Tiryns was published in four volumes between 1912 and 1938 under the title *Tiryns: Die Ergebnisse der Ausgrabungen des Instituts.* Three additional volumes have been published since 1972, but they have not been accessible to me. See also the useful discussion of Georg Karo, "Tiryns," *RE*, 1453-1467.

36. H. G. Lolling, "Ausgrabungen am Palamidi," *AM* 5 (1880) 143-163; Seraphim Charitonidis, " 'Ανασκαφαὶ ἐν Ναυπλία," *Praktika* (1953) 191-204.

37. Otto Frödin and Axel Persson, *Asine: Results of the Swedish Excavations, 1922-30* (Stockholm, 1938). See also Per Ålin, "Unpublished Mycenaean Sherds from Asine," *Opusc. Ath.* 8 (1968) 87-105, and Carl G. Styrenius and Alvar Vidén, "New Excavations at Asine," *AAA* 4 (1971) 147-148.

38. The material from Lerna is reported by John L. Caskey and others, *Hesperia* 23 (1954) through 29 (1960).

39. Additional bibliography and discussion of the material found at all sites, large and small, in the Argive plain, can be found in Per Ålin, *Das Ende der Mykenischen Fundstätten auf dem griechischen Festland. Studies in Mediterranean Archaeology* 1 (Lund, 1962) 10-54, and R. Hope Simpson, *A Gazetteer of Mycenaean Sites* (London, 1965) 13-36.

40. These skeletal remains have been examined by Robert P. Charles, *Études anthropologique des nécropoles d'Argos. Contribution à l'étude des populations de la grèce antique. Études Péloponnésiennes* 3 (Paris, 1963) 65-76, where he notes among other things that life expectancy was lower for women than for men.

41. On this period generally see Vermeule, *GBA*, 156-231. For the sake of convenience I accept here the dates of Arne Furumark, *Chronology of Mycenaean Pottery* (Stockholm, 1941) 110-115; but his dates for the latter part of the Mycenaean period have been somewhat revised by V. R. d'A Desborough, *The Last Mycenaeans and Their Successors* (Oxford, 1964) 237-241, and others.

42. East: Frank H. Stubbings, *Mycenaean Pottery from the Levant* (Cambridge, 1951) 53-58; Helene J. Kantor, *The Aegean and the Orient in the Second Millennium B.C.* (Bloomington, 1947) 37-38. West: Lord William Taylour, *Mycenaean Pottery in Italy and Adjacent Areas* (Cambridge, 1958) 182-184.

43. Alan J. B. Wace and Carl W. Blegen, "Pottery as Evidence for Trade and Colonization in the Aegean Bronze Age," *Klio* 32 (1939) 131-147; Sara A. Immerwahr, "Mycenaean Trade and Colonization," *Archaeology* 13 (1960) 4-13. The literary and archaeological evidence has been fully discussed by Filipo Cas-

sola, *La Ionia nel mondo miceneo* (Naples, 1957); see also Michel B. Sakellariou, *La migration grecque en Ionie* (Athens, 1958).

44. Carl W. Blegen, *Troy* 4 (Princeton, 1958) 12, dates the destruction of Troy to the end of the LH III B period, but some sherds have recently been assigned to the LH III C period by Carl Nylander, "The Fall of Troy," *Antiquity* 37 (1963) 6-12. Nylander also points out that it is difficult to believe that the impoverished settlement known as Troy VIIA could have been important enough to provoke a Greek attack against it and suggests that Troy VI may have been the settlement attacked by the Greeks, even though we are assured by Blegen, *Troy* 3 (Princeton, 1953) 331-332, that Troy VI was destroyed by an earthquake. On the pros and cons of the historicity of the Trojan War, see Moses I. Finley, John L. Caskey, G. S. Kirk, and D. L. Page, "The Trojan War," *JHS* 84 (1964) 1-20.

45. On the extent of the Mycenaean settlement see Vollgraff, *BCH* 30 (1906) 7, and Courbin, *Archaeology* 9 (1956) 169. Late Helladic Strata: Courbin, *BCH* 80 (1956) 207, 210, and cf. 380; see also *BCH* 92 (1968) 1036 and *BCH* 93 (1969) 1017-1018. Tomlinson, *Argos*, 23, believes, however, that the settlement was within the fortification walls surrounding the summit of the Aspis.

46. *BCH* 93 (1969) 992.

47. Vollgraff's excavations on the Larissa are reported in *MKAW* 66 (1928) 87-104); *Mnem.* 56 (1928) 320-325; and "Nieuwe Opgravingen te Argos," *MKAW* 72 (1932) 71-120, especially 71-76; see also Anne Roes, "Une pierre gravée Syro-Hittite trouvée à Argos," *BCH* 61 (1937) 1-4. Mycenaean sherds from the Larissa are reported in *BCH* 90 (1966) 932.

48. Nine Mycenaean tombs were discovered early in this century and reported by Wilhelm Vollgraff, "Fouilles d'Argos," *BCH* 27 (1904) 364-399. He later excavated a tenth tomb which is reported in *MKAW* 72 (1932) 76-77. The pottery from these tombs has been twice reexamined by Jean Deshayes, "Les vases mycéniens de la Deiras (Argos)," *BCH* 77 (1953) 58-89, and "Les vases Vollgraff de la Deiras," *BCH* 93 (1969) 574-616. The tombs discovered since the resumption of excavation at Argos in the 1950s have been published by Deshayes, *EP* 4. Two tombs discovered since the publication of that work are reported in *BCH* 95 (1971) 867, and another is reported by E. Protonotariou-Deïlaki, "Μυκηναϊκὸς τάφος ἐξ ᾿Αργους," *Charisterion eis Anastasion K. Orlandon* 2 (Athens, 1966) 239-247. See also the useful discussion of Ålin, *SMA* 1:42-44.

49. LH I tomb: *BCH* 95 (1971) 867, and *AAA* 3 (1970) 301-303. Deshayes, *BCH* 77 (1953) 79-83, originally dated Tomb VIII to LH II A, but he has now assigned it to LH III; see *BCH* 93 (1969) 602-608.

50. The details contained in this paragraph are derived from Deshayes, *EP* 4, especially 23-28 and 201-213, and Vollgraff, *BCH* 27 (1904) 364-369 and 382-386. On a black hematite cylinder seal of oriental origin found on the Larissa, see *BCH* 61 (1937) 1-4.

51. These are the conclusions of Deshayes, *EP* 4:247-248. Arne Furumark, *The Mycenaean Pottery. Analysis and Classification* (Stockholm, 1941) 250-251, considers several vases from Tomb VI as Cretan; but Deshayes, *BCH* 77 (1953) 74-75, argues that they were manufactured at Argos but strongly influenced by Cretan work.

52. The most forceful statement of a unified Mycenaean empire is probably Desborough's, *LMS*, 218-220. The ambiguity of the evidence is noted and discussed by Vermeule, *GBA*, 232-237, and also by C. G. Thomas, "A Mycenaean Hegemony? A Reconsideration," *JHS* 90 (1970) 184-192.

53. On these roads see H. Steffen, *Karten von Mykenai* (Berlin, 1884) 8-12, and W. A. McDonald, "Overland Communications in Greece during LH III, with Special Reference to Southwest Peloponnese," *Mycenaean Studies: Proceedings of the Third International Colloquium for Mycenaean Studies* (Madison, 1964) 217-240; see also, J. M. Balcer, "The Mycenaean Dam at Tiryns," *AJA* 78 (1974) 141-149.

54. The evidence for the events discussed in this paragraph has been considered many times, but see especially Desborough, *LMS*, 73-84 and 217-241, and Ålin, *SMA* 1:10-54, with full reference to the archaeological material. Additional material from the Late Helladic III C period has come to light at both Tiryns and Asine since these works were published, however; see the works cited above in nn. 35 and 37.

55. On migration at the end of the Late Helladic III B period, see Desborough, *LMS*, 1-28, where full bibliographical references to the archaeological evidence are given. Desborough's belief that there was some immigration into Cyprus at this time has been confirmed by Hector W. Catling, *Cypriot Bronzework in the Mycenaean World* (Oxford, 1964) 50-52; Emily J. Vermeule, "The Mycenaeans in Achaia," *AJA* 64 (1960) 1-21, has shown that there was some migration from the Argive plain into Achaea at this time; and Deshayes *EP* 4:248 suggests that there may have been some migration to this area from the city of Argos.

56. Inscribed Mycenaean vases have been exhaustively studied by J. Raison, *Les vases à inscriptions peintes de l'âge mycénien et leur contexte archéologique* (Rome, 1968), who dates none of them later than Late Helladic III B.

57. On the continuity of culture between LH III B and LH III C see Desborough, *LMS*, 225-230, and Antony M. Snodgrass, *The Dark Age of Greece. An Archaeological Survey of the Eleventh to the Eighth Centuries B.C.* (Edinburgh, 1971) 28-31, 304-311, 360-365.

58. Rhys Carpenter, *Discontinuity in Greek Civilization* (Cambridge, 1966), argues that a climatic change was responsible for the collapse of Mycenaean civilization. The various suggestions that have been offered are summarized by Snodgrass, *DAG*, 304-313; see also Vermeule, *GBA*, 269-271.

59. For the events discussed here see Desborough, *LMS*, 220-230; Robert J. Buck, "The Mycenaean Time of Troubles," *Historia* 18 (1969) 276-298, especially 276-279; Mylonas, *Mycenae and the Mycenaean Age*, 224-229.

60. On this wall see Oscar Broneer, "The Cyclopean Wall on the Isthmus of Corinth and Its Bearing on Late Bronze Age Chronology," *Hesperia*, 35 (1966), 346-362, and "The Cyclopean Wall on the Isthmus of Corinth, Addendum," *Hesperia* 37 (1968) 25-35. It should, however, be noted that some scholars have questioned whether the wall was in fact a fortification; see, for example, Chrysoula P. Kardara, "The Isthmian Wall," *AAA* 4 (1971) 85-89, who suggests that it may have been a retaining wall for a road.

61. It has, however, frequently been suggested that the Dorians were respon-

sible for the devastation that took place at this time; see the list compiled by Buck, *Historia* 18 (1969) 280 n. 31.

62. See *BCH* 93 (1969) 992, where the possibility that the fire occurred in the LH III C period is suggested but with the admonition that additional work is needed before a definitive decision can be reached.

63. Lack of evidence for destruction at Argos is commented on by Deshayes, *EP* 4:248-249, where he also suggests the possibility of migration into Achaea.

64. On the breakdown of the cultural unity in the Late Helladic III C period, see Desborough, *LMS*, 225-230; Mylonas, *Mycenae and the Mycenaean Age*, 229-233.

65. The material discussed in this paragraph is derived from Deshayes, *EP* 4 *passim*; but see especially his conclusions on pp. 236-252; on the absence of any Close-style pottery at Argos and the resemblance to the pottery of Achaea see 195-196, 248.

66. On the destruction throughout Greece at this time see Desborough, *LMS*, 230-237, and also Ålin, *SMA* 1:148-150, where it is noted that the destruction of the Granary at Mycenae is an isolated event.

67. The literary evidence has been examined by Buck, *Historia* 18 (1969) 276-298; by N. G. L. Hammond, "The End of Mycenaean Civilization and the Dark Age," *CAH*[3] 2:Pt. 2 (Cambridge, 1975) 678-712; and by Franz Kiechle, "Die Ausprägung der Sage von der Rückkehr der Herakliden," *Helikon* 6 (1966) 493-517.

68. See, for example, N. G. L. Hammond, "Epirus and the Dorian Invasion," *BSA* 32 (1931-32) 131-179, and also his *Epirus: The Geography, the Ancient Remains, the History and the Topography of Epirus and Adjacent Areas* (Oxford, 1967) 365-395. For a different interpretation of the archaeological evidence, however, see Snodgrass, *DAG*, 257-261.

69. This is the forcibly argued conclusion of Snodgrass, *DAG*, 368-373, 394-401.

70. Desborough, *LMS*, 37-40, 259-260. Although the tombs from the Deiras are pit tombs rather than true cists, they are nonetheless single burial tombs, and as a result Desborough's conclusions have been challenged by Deshayes, *EP* 4: 249-250; Carl G. Styrenius, *Submycenaean Studies* (Lund, 1967) 161-163; and Snodgrass, *DAG*, 177-184. A Mycenaean cist tomb is reported in *AD* 19 (1964) 126, and in *AR* (1964-65) 11-12, but it contained several burials.

71. See *BCH* 82 (1958) 268-313 and his more complete *EP* 3. A few remains from other sites in the plain were studied by Carl M. Fürst, "Zur Anthropologie der Prähistorischen Griechen in Argolis," *Acta Universitatis Lundensis* 26 (1930) 1-130, and J. Lawrence Angel, *Lerna: A Preclassical Site in the Argolid* 2:*The People* (Princeton and Washington, D.C., 1971) has recently examined the material from Lerna.

72. Charles, *EP* 3:72-73, and see also the useful discussion of Snodgrass, *DAG*, 184-187.

73. The course of the Dorian conquest of Greece has been much debated. Most scholars believe they moved south into Greece by land, but Franz Miltner, "Die dorischen Wanderung," *Klio* 27 (1934) 54-68, has argued that the invasion

was primarily a naval movement; Crete, he believes, was captured first, and only then did the Dorians move from there into the Peloponnesus.

74. Thucydides 1.12.3. Greek tradition offers a wide range of dates for the fall of Troy and modern scholars have been equally unable to reach agreement about when it might have occurred. Carl W. Blegen, "The Mycenaean Age, the Trojan War, the Dorian Invasion and Other Problems," *Lectures in Memory of Louise Taft Semple* (Princeton, 1967) 5-41, discusses the problem on pp. 29-32 and on p. 32, n. 9, gives a list of modern speculation on the subject. Generally speaking, a date in the latter half of the thirteenth century has perhaps been more widely accepted than any other.

Chapter II

1. Two excellent works treat this period at some length: Chester G. Starr, *The Origins of Greek Civilization 1100-650 B.C.* (New York, 1961), and Antony M. Snodgrass, *DAG*, who discusses the literary evidence (pp. 1-21) and concludes that later Greek writers really knew nothing about the period. V. R. d'A. Desborough, *The Greek Dark Ages* (London, 1972), covers only the period 1125-900 B.C.

2. See the discussions of Wilhelm Kraiker and Karl Kübler, *Kerameikos: Ergebnisse der Ausgrabungen* 1 (Berlin, 1939); Carl G. Styrenius, "The Vases from the Submycenaean Cemetery on Salamis," *Opusc. Ath.* 4 (1962) 103-123; Furumark, *Mycenaean Pottery*, 576-582; Starr, *OGC*, 89-92; and Snodgrass, *DAG*, 34-40.

3. Desborough, *LMS*, 17-20; his arguments have been accepted by Snodgrass, *DAG*, 28-34.

4. Desborough, *GDA*, 33, 68-73; Deshayes, *EP* 4:39-46, 64-69, 98-101.

5. Styrenius, *SS*, 160-161; Deshayes, *EP* 4:195, 247.

6. Styrenius, *SS*, 127-136, where the pertinent archaeological publications are cited. V. R. d'A. Desborough, "Late Burials from Mycenae," *BSA* 68 (1973) 94-98. The material from Nauplia and Tiryns is known to me only from the discussion of Robin Hägg, *Die Gräber der Argolis in submykenischer, protogeometrischer, und geometrischer Zeit* (Uppsala, 1974) 71-72, 79-82.

7. The contents of these tombs have been published by Deshayes, *EP* 4:39-46, 50-56, 64-69, 98-101, and see also Styrenius, *SS*, 123, and Hägg, *GA*, 26.

8. On the material from these tombs see Paul Courbin, "Stratigraphie et stratigraphie: methodes et perspectives," *Études Archéologiques* 1 (1963) 70-73; *BCH* 78 (1954) 177; *BCH* 80 (1956) 376; and *BCH* 79 (1955) 312, where the containers were originally labeled Protogeometric but are now identified as Submycenaean; cf. Hägg, *GA*, 27. The Tripolis Street tombs are reported by O. Alexandri, *AD* 18 (1963) 62, and briefly discussed by Styrenius, *SS*, 132-133. For an excellent discussion of the Submycenaean material found at Argos and the other sites in the Argive plain see Hägg, *GA*, 23-27, 47-51, 65-66, 72, 79-82, in which there are full references to the published material as well as private correspondence with the author regarding unpublished material.

9. *BCH* 81 (1957) 677, 680; *BCH* 83 (1959) 768, and see also Courbin, *EA* 1 (1963) 63, 72.

10. Styrenius, *SS* 132-133, 157. It is worth noting, too, that Hägg, *GA*, 80-82,

88, reports that Submycenaean burials have been found in chamber tòmbs at Tiryns as well as at Argos; he believes the burials represent an unbroken Mycenaean tradition; cf. pp. 97-98.

11. Deshayes, *EP* 4, emphasizes that true cist tombs are not found in this cemetery, but he refers to Tomb 7, which dates from the LH IIIB period, as a "sorte de ciste assez rudimentaire" (p. 241).

12. On Submycenaean remains above virgin soil, see *BCH* 81 (1957) 677-678; *BCH* 83 (1959) 768; and cf. Desborough, *LMS*, 82, and *GDA*, 72.

13. This has been suggested by Desborough, *LMS*, 19-20; see also *CAH*[3] 2: Pt. 2, 663-669.

14. The amphora from Tomb XXIV is depicted in Deshayes, *EP* 4, plate LXVII, 3 and 4. Desborough, *LMS*, 19, 81, believes that if the vase had been found at Athens it would be considered Protogeometric or perhaps transitional between Submycenaean and Protogeometric. The amphora from the earth-cut tomb is depicted in *BCH* 80 (1956) 374, fig. 22. Desborough, *LMS*, 81, notes that the metal objects from the Argive chamber tombs are similar to those of the Athenian cist tombs. On the continuity from Mycenaean to post-Mycenaean pottery styles, see also Jan Bouzek,"The Beginning of Protogeometric Pottery and the 'Dorian Ware,' " *Opusc. Ath.* 9 (1969) 41-57.

15. Starr, *OGC*, 102-106; T. B. L. Webster, *From Mycenae to Homer* (New York, 1959) 292-294; Snodgrass, *DAG*, 34-40, but he also points out that the picture derived from ceramic remains alone may be misleading. See also V. R. d'A. Desborough, "The Greek Mainland, c. 1150-1000 B.C.," *Proceedings of the Prehistoric Society* 31 (1965) 213-228.

16. For examples of finer work from Argos see the vases referred to in n. 14 above, and see also *BCH* 81 (1957) 681, fig. 32.

17. The metal objects from the chamber tombs are discussed by Deshayes, *EP* 4:201-209, 249. At least two of the Submycenaean earth-cut and cist tombs contained metal objects. Two fibulae and two rings are reported from one in *BCH* 78 (1954) 177, and two pins from the Tripolis Street graves are reported in *AD* 18 (1963) 62. A convenient summary of the metal objects from sites in the plain is given by Styrenius, *SS*, 136.

18. This furnace is reported in *BCH* 81 (1957) 680; *BCH* 83 (1959) 768; Courbin, *EA* 1 (1963) 71-72, 98-100, and also Miltis Paraskevaidis, "Von den Ausgrabungen in Argos," *Das Altertum* 6 (1960) 33. On cupellation see Robert J. Forbes, *Metallurgy in Antiquity: A Notebook for Archaeologists and Technologists* (Leiden, 1950) 206-215. Unfortunately, the source of the raw ore used at Argos is not known, but the suggestion of O. Davies, "Bronze Age Mining round the Aegean," *Nature: A Weekly Journal of Science* 130 (1932) 985-987, that the Greeks "seem to have used small local deposits which they completely exhausted," seems reasonable.

19. The contents from the tomb at Tiryns have been published by Nicholas M. Verdelis, "Neue geometrische Gräber in Tiryns," *AM* 78 (1963) 10-14.

20. On the origin of and foreign influences detectable in the metal objects from Argos, see Deshayes, *EP* 4:249. Verdelis, *AM* 78 (1963) 14-24, 61-62, does the same for the objects from Tiryns, and Snodgrass, *DAG*, 305-309, 317-322, for those from the whole of Greece. All three authors believe they can detect influ-

ences from northern Europe, Italy, and the Orient. On the similiarity of ceramic development at Athens and Argos in this period, see Styrenius, *SS*, 129-135, and Kraiker, *Kerameikos* 1:59, where it is suggested that some Submycenaean vases found in the Kerameikos are so similar to pottery from the Argolid that they may have been the work of potters whose families, driven from the Argolid, migrated to Athens.

21. This subject will be treated more fully in the next chapter.

22. The most recent discussions of the chronology of the period are those of Styrenius, *SS*, 163-164, and Snodgrass, *DAG*, 123. Both would date the period approximately 1125-1040 B.C. On the importance of the Submycenaean period and the emergence of Protogeometric pottery, see Starr, *OGC*, 102-106.

23. V. R. d'A. Desborough, *Protogeometric Pottery* (Oxford, 1952). Kraiker, *Kerameikos* 1, provides a detailed study of the Attic style, and Snodgrass, *DAG*, 43-94, provides a convenient summary.

24. For Protogeometric pottery found in the Argive plain see the following: Asine: Frödin and Persson, *Asine*, 312-314, and Inga and Robin Hägg, *Excavations in the Barbouna Area at Asine* (Uppsala, 1973) 25, 38-39, 72-74, 79-80; Tiryns: August Frickenhaus, Walter Müller, and Franz Oelmann, *Tiryns* 1: *Die Ergebnisse der Ausgrabungen des Instituts* (Athens, 1912) 127-164 *passim*, and Verdelis, *AM* 78 (1963) 1-62; Mycenae: V. R. d'A. Desborough, "Four Tombs," *BSA* 49 (1954) 259-260, and "Late Burials from Mycenae," *BSA* 68 (1973) 87-101; I. Papadimitriou, " 'Ανασκαφαὶ ἐν Μυκήναι," *Praktika* (1952) 209; Midea: Axel W. Persson, *The Royal Tombs at Dendra near Midea*, 11, 41, 66-67; Prosymna: Charles Waldstein, *The Argive Heraeum* 2 (New York, 1905) plate LVI, and p. 72, where a single sherd is included with the Mycenaean pottery; Nauplia: Seraphim Charitonidis, " 'Ανασκαφαὶ ἐν Ναυπλία," *Praktika* (1955) 233-234, and Robin Hägg, "Protogeometrische und Geometrische Keramik in Nauplion," *Opusc. Ath.* 10 (1971) 41-52, and *BCH* 95 (1971) 874. Lerna: John L. Caskey, "The Ancient Settlement at Lerna in the Argolid," *Geras Antoniou Keramopoullou* (Athens, 1953) 24-28. The material found at Argos has been provisionally reported in "Chronique des fouilles," *BCH* 76 (1953) and following; see also Courbin, *EA* 1 (1963) 59-102. Specific references to this material will be made in the notes that follow. The discussion of Desborough, *PGP*, 204-212, remains vital; see also his *GDA*, 161-170.

25. Desborough, *PGP*, 119-126, 291-292, argues that the style originated in Attica; he reaffirms this view in *LMS*, 258-263, and in *GDA*, 145-147. Snodgrass, *DAG*, 43-48, accepts it as do many others. Nicholas M. Verdelis, 'Ο Πρωτογεομετρικὸς 'Ρυθμὸς τῆς Θεσσαλίας (Athens, 1958) 49-70, has argued, however, that the Protogeometric pottery of Thessaly is indigenous to that area, and other scholars have sought to place the origins of the style elsewhere; see the discussion of Starr, *OGC*, 89-98, especially 97, n. 8.

26. Protogeometric strata at Argos are reported in *BCH* 79 (1955) 314; *BCH* 81 (1957) 677; *BCH* 83 (1959) 766-768; and *EA* 1 (1963) 72-73, 79.

27. On experimental stages see Courbin, *EA* 1 (1963) 73.

28. On this handmade pottery and its origins, see Snodgrass, *DAG*, 94-97, which has a full bibliography in n. 69, pp. 104-105.

29. For the occurrence of these shapes at Argos, see the following: high-han-

dled pyxis: *BCH* 81 (1957) 654, figs. 29-30; lekythos: *BCH* 83 (1959) 756, fig. 4; high-footed cup: *BCH* 77 (1954) 176, fig. 34. There is an unpublished hydra (C 199), which I know only from a photograph in L'école français d'Athènes.

30. Desborough, *PGP*, 45-66, 211.

31. Desborough, *PGP*, 6-37.

32. A neck-handled amphora was found in Chamber Tomb 502 at Mycenae, and it is reported by Alan J. B. Wace, *Chamber Tombs at Mycenae* (Oxford, 1932) plate XII, 5. At Argos there is a neck-handled amphora from a Submycenaean chamber tomb (Tomb XXIV) and another from a Submycenaean earth-cut tomb; see Deshayes, *EP* 4, plate LXVII, 3 and 4, and *BCH* 80 (1956) 374 and 372, fig. 22. There is also a neck-handled amphora from a Protogeometric tomb; see *BCH* 81 (1957) 655, fig. 33. Tomb XXXIII contained a belly-handled amphora (Deshayes, *EP* 4, plate XCI, 1) from the Submycenaean period, but the only Protogeometric example I know of (*BCH* 83 [1959] 763, fig. 19) belongs to the fairly well developed style. It is none too elegant in shape or decoration and would seem to have no precise Attic parallel. It is more elongated than Attic examples, and the handles are placed higher up on the belly.

33. Paul Courbin, *La céramique géométrique de l'Argolide* (Paris, 1966), who conveniently summarizes his comments on stylistic development on pp. 557-566, and J. N. Coldstream, *Greek Geometric Pottery* (London, 1968) 112-147. Reports on the French excavations at Argos have appeared almost annually in "Chronique des fouilles," in *BCH* since 1954, and the tombs excavated between 1952 and 1958 have been published by Paul Courbin, *Études Péloponnésiennes* 7: *Tombes géométrique d'Argos*, 1 (Paris, 1974). Excavations undertaken by the Greek Archaeological Service have been reported in Ἀρχαιολογικὸν Δελτίον since 1963.

34. Courbin, *CGA*, 558-559, though Coldstream, *GGP*, 115-117, sees a sharper distinction between the two phases than does Courbin.

35. Instructive in this respect is a minute comparison of the pottery from an Early Geometric tomb at Mycenae with the contents from an Early Geometric tomb from the Athenian Agora. The Athenian material was published by Rodney S. Young, "An Early Geometric Grave near the Athenian Agora," *Hesperia* 18 (1949) 275-297; the tomb from Mycenae was published and the comparison made by V. R. d'A. Desborough, "Three Geometric Tombs," *BSA* 50 (1955) 239-247, who notes differences as well as similarities.

36. This suggestion has been made by Snodgrass, *DAG*, 57.

37. Courbin, *CGA*, 505-515.

38. On burial practices in this period, see Donna C. Kurtz and John Boardman, *Greek Burial Customs* (London, 1971) 28-67, 171-187. Hägg, *GA*, 100-161, has carefully studied the various types of tombs employed in the Argive plain; he notes that there are no pithos burials absolutely datable to the Protogeometric period at Argos. See also Snodgrass, *DAG*, 140-197, and Courbin, *EP* 7:107-123.

39. Antony M. Snodgrass, "Barbarian Europe and Early Iron Age Greece," *Proceedings of the Prehistoric Society* 31 (1965) 229-240, especially 229-234, and *DAG*, 213-286, from which my discussion is largely derived. He considers the material from the Argive plain on pp. 233-236, 265-270. It should be noted, however, that Radomir Pleiner, *Iron Working In Ancient Greece* (Prague, 1969) 13-15,

would date the beginnings of the Iron Age a bit later, perhaps about the middle of the ninth century.

40. A skeleton in Tomb XXIII at Tiryns, for example, wore nine bronze rings, six on the right hand and three on the left; see Verdelis, *AM* 78 (1963) 35. Rings at Argos are reported in *BCH* 79 (1955) 314 and *BCH* 81 (1957) 651, 663, and see Courbin, *EP* 7:21, 31, 33, 39, 57, 96, and generally 132-133. Fibulae are reported from Tiryns in *AM* 78 (1963) 6, 8, 11; and from Mycenae in *BSA* 49 (1954) 259; *BSA* 51 (1956) 129; *AD* 20 (1965) 165.

41. Verdelis, *AM* 78 (1963) 35-40, and Courbin, *EP* 7:20-22, 32-34.

42. Only two weapons have been reported from Protogeometric tombs at Argos. Tomb 184 contained an iron dagger, see *BCH* 83 (1959) 755. A bronze spear tip is reported from another tomb which is dated to the Protogeometric period, but it contained no vases and could not be dated precisely; see *BCH* 91 (1967) 840. Courbin, *EP* 7, reports iron weapons from Early Geometric Tomb 106/1 (p. 57), and from Tomb 14/2 from the Middle Geometric period (pp. 31-32).

43. Tombs 16, 37, and 106/1, all from the Early Geometric period, contained gold objects; see Courbin, *EP* 7:34, 39, 58. Tiryns: Tombs VII and XV, see Verdelis, *AM* 78 (1963) 28-32. Tomb 2 (*Tiryns* 1:128) also contained a gold object.

44. Tomb XXIII at Tiryns see Verdelis, *AM* 78 (1963) 35-40. Bronze bowls at Argos are reported by Courbin, *EP* 7:20, 57.

45. On the excellent quality of Argive metal products see Desborough, *BSA* 50 (1955) 241-243; Snodgrass, *DAG*, 233-236, 264-265, 269-270. Paul Jacobsthal, *Greek Pins and Their Connexions with Europe and Asia* (Oxford, 1956) 15-16, suggests that Argos was the leading center of pin production; but his classification of some of the pins from the Argive Heraeum to the Protogeometric and Early Geometric periods cannot be accepted. As we shall see later, the temple was not founded before the latter half of the eighth century. On the importance of metalworking in the Argolid in this period see Verdelis, *AM* 78 (1963) 61-62.

46. Walls and house foundations from this period have long been known at Asine; see *Asine* 40, 64. Such remains are frequently mentioned in the preliminary reports from Argos; the most interesting are those of an apsidal house which was destroyed early in the Geometric period; see *BCH* 77 (1953) 263; *BCH* 78 (1954) 177; and also Courbin, *CGA*, 162.

47. The relationship between Argive and Athenian pottery has been discussed above. For Argive influence at Corinth see Courbin, *CGA*, 515-520, and at Cos in the Protogeometric period see Desborough, *PGP*, 224, Courbin *EA* 1 (1963) 71, and Snodgrass *DAG*, 75-76, 163-164, where he notes a similarity in funeral practices as well as in pottery.

48. Wilhelm Kraiker, *Aigina: Die Vasen des 10. bis 7. Jahrhunderts v. Chr.* (Berlin, 1951) 25, no. 24, and cf. Courbin, *CGA*, 65.

49. The material from Perachora has been published by Humfry G. G. Payne, *Perachora. The Sanctuaries of Hera Akraia and Limenia* 1: *Architecture, Bronzes, Terracottas* (Oxford, 1940), and T. J. Dunbabin, *Perachora: The Sanctuaries of Hera Akraia and Limenia* 2: *Pottery, Ivories, Scarabs, and Other Objects from the Deposit of Hera Limenia* (Oxford, 1962). Payne, *Perachora* 1:27-77, discusses the pottery he believed to be of Argive origin and dates the original temple to about

850 B.C., but Coldstream, *GGP*, 352, and Snodgrass, *DAG*, 277, note that none of the material need date earlier than about 800 B.C.

50. Courbin, *CGA*, 550-551; the material has recently been more thoroughly examined by John Salmon, "The Heraeum at Perachora and the Early History of Corinth and Megara," *BSA* 67 (1972) 159-204, who agrees with Courbin's conclusions. Salmon also effectively refutes the argument of N. G. L. Hammond, "The Heraeum at Perachora and Corinthian Encroachment," *BSA* 49 (1954) 93-102, that the temple of Hera Akraia was founded by the Megarians.

51. On the lack of Argive Geometric pottery at Athens see Courbin, *CGA*, 551, though there are a few pieces from the late Geometric period. Corinth: Courbin, *CGA*, 63-64, 550.

52. The vases from a tomb at Cleonae were originally considered Argive, but Courbin, *CGA*, 550, n. 2, doubts this. He does, however, consider a handmade aryballos from the site to be of Argive manufacture.

53. G. Donatas, *AD* 18 (1963) 182-183, and Coldstream, *GGP*, 364.

54. Corinthian Geometric pottery is discussed by Coldstream, *GGP*, 90-111, and on the quantity and extent of its export see pp. 90, 352-354. This pottery was not wholly lacking in merit; its defects have on occasion been exaggerated, as for example, by Edouard Will, *Korinthiaka recherches sur l'histoire et la civilisation de Corinthe des origines aux guerres médiques* (Paris, 1955) 33 and n. 3.

55. Obsidian: *AM* 78 (1963) 41-42. On the Attic Protogeometric vase see Courbin, *CGA*, 65, and *EP* 7:30.

56. The statuette is reported in *BCH* 79 (1955) 312 and fig. 9, p. 313; see also Courbin, *Archaeology* 9 (1956) 171. Snodgrass, *DAG*, 382-383, considers it to be an heirloom or keepsake from an earlier period.

57. The evidence of vases of non-Argive manufacture found in the Argolid has been assembled by Courbin, *CGA*, 553-555. Most of these vases date from the Late Geometric period, however, and have not been included in my discussion. On the Corinthian vase found at Mycenae see Desborough, *BSA* 50 (1955) 243-245.

58. *Tiryns* 1:128, and on dating this tomb to the Early Geometric period see Desborough, *PGP*, 208; on the faience necklace see Verdelis, *AM* 78 (1963) 36-37, and Courbin, *EP* 7:37.

59. An Egyptian scarab found many years ago on the Larissa should be mentioned here. It is reported by Wilhelm Vollgraff, *MKAW* 72 (1932) 75, where it is dated to the period 950-750 B.C. It is virtually certain, however, that the scarab was part of a discarded votive deposit dating from the end of the eighth and the beginning of the seventh century, and in all probability ought to be dated to the same period.

60. For the general points suggested in this paragraph see Starr, *OGC*, 77-186, and Snodgrass, *DAG*, 296-436.

61. On the continuous use of this burial ground see Hägg, *GA*, 47, 95.

62. For sections of the city that seem to have been inhabited only during this period see *BCH* 83 (1959) 768, and Seraphim Charitonidis, "Recherches dans le quartier est d'Argos," *BCH* 78 (1954) 421. However, J. F. Bommelaer and Y. Grandjean, *BCH* 96 (1972) 157-163, report no trace of habitation in the south quarter from the Middle Helladic period to the Late Geometric period. Neither

Protogeometric nor Early or Middle Geometric material has been found on either acropolis. Vollgraff, *Mnem*. 56 (1928) 319, seems to hint at the discovery of Protogeometric pottery on the Larissa as Charitonidis *BCH* 78 (1954) 426, n. 6, points out; but Charitonidis's identification as Protogeometric of the potsherd depicted "en bas à droit" on plate XV accompanying Vollgraff's article seems unlikely.

63. Most of the pertinent publications of material from Argos, Mycenae, Tiryns, and Asine have been cited in the preceding notes. The material from Berbati is reported by Gösta Säflund, *Berbati* 81-90. The tombs from Lerna are reported by John L Caskey, "Excavations at Lerna, 1955," *Hesperia* 25 (1956) 171-172. Miscellaneous vases from various sites in the plain have recently been published by Robin Hägg, *Opusc. Ath.* 10 (1971) 41-52.

64. This point has been fully understood by Tomlinson, *Argos*, 64-73, though I see no reason to accept his contention (pp. 67-68) that the Dorian element of the city owned all the land and formed a separate warrior caste.

65. This is the conclusion of Charles, *EP* 3:74-76.

66. The clearest evidence of this sort concerns the destruction of the apsidal house early in the Geometric period; cf. Courbin, *CGA*, 162, n. 1.

67. Charles, *BCH* 82 (1958) 310; for other examples of trepanned skulls at Argos see Charles, *EP* 3:67-69, where he suggests that the practice may have been connected with some religious rite.

68. As noted above, the Protogeometric pottery of the island of Cos closely resembles the Protogeometric pottery of Argos, and there has been some speculation that this similarity is to be explained by a movement of people from the Argolid to Cos in the Protogeometric period. They may or may not, however, have come from the city of Argos. Snodgrass, *DAG*, 330, believes that it may have been emigrants from Asine who settled there, and Herodotus 7.99 reports that "Argives from Epidaurus" founded a colony on the island.

69. There were no especially rich grave offerings in any of the Middle Geometric tombs excavated by the French at Argos. Courbin, *EP* 7:126, notes that the largest number of vases in any MG grave was eight, in Tombs 191 and 6/1; EG Tomb 106/1 also contained eight vases. Tomb Makris 1 at Argos, however, which dates from MG 2, contained eighteen vases; see *AD* 18 (1963) 57-58. The single Geometric tomb from Berbati, which dates from MG 1, contained thirty-six vases; see Säflund, *Berbati*, 81-90. E. Protonotariou-Deïlaki, "Πρώιμος γεομετρικὸς τάφος ἐξ Ἀργους," *AAA* 3 (1970) 180-183, reports an Early Geometric tomb containing forty vases as well as several items of jewelry.

Chapter III

1. *Iliad*, 2.559-568.

2. See, for example, Denys Page, *History and the Homeric Iliad* (Berkeley and Los Angeles, 1959) 118-154; Viktor Burr, Νεῶν Κατάλογος: *Untersuchungen zum homerischen Schiffskatalog* (Leipzig, 1944); and George L. Huxley, "Mycenaean Decline and the Homeric Catalogue of Ships," *BICS* 3 (1956) 19-31. Günther Jachmann, *Der homerischen Schiffskatalog und die Ilias* (Cologne, 1958) and more recently A. Giovannini, *Étude historique sur les origines du catalogue*

des vaisseaux (Bern, 1969) have argued against this view and have sought to date it much later.

3. Burr, Νεῶν Κατάλογος, 44.

4. Herodotus 1.82, and cf. Karl J. Beloch, *Griechische Geschichte*[2] (Strassburg, 1912) 1:Pt. 1, 204, n. 1.

5. The fragments of Acusilaus and Hellanicus have been assembled by Felix Jacoby, *Die Fragmente der griechischen Historiker* (Berlin and Leiden, 1922-) 1: 47-58, 104-152. He suggests that the *Argolica* was a local history of Argos in which events were dated by the reigning king of the city, but Lionel Pearson, *Early Ionian Historians* (Oxford, 1939) 160-162, is not convinced that Hellanicus ever composed such a work. It is mentioned only once, in a scholia on Homer; see *FGrH* 4 F 36.

6. The few extant fragments of these plays have been assembled by A. Nauck, *Tragicorum Graecorum fragmenta*[2] (Leipzig, 1889) frags. 728-751.

7. Hellanicus, *FGrH* 4 F 79a, 79b, and Jacoby's commentary.

8. Apollodorus, *Bibliotheca* 2.8.4-5; Ephorus, *FGrH* 70 F 115; Strabo 8.3.33; Pausanias 4.3.45; see Tomlinson, *Argos*, 58-66.

9. This has often been suggested. Gilbert Murray, *Euripides* 3 (London, 1902) 348-350, has suggested that Pausanias's version of the story retains the substance of Euripides's *Temenidae*; W. Schmid and O. Stählin, *Geschichte der griechischen Literatur* 1 (Munich, 1940) 630, suggest that Ephorus relied on the plays of Euripides.

10. Troezen: Pausanias 2.30.10; Ephorus, *FGrH* 70 F 115; Nicolaus of Damascus, *FGrH* 90 F 30. On the basis of evidence such as this, Filippo Cassola, *La Ionia nel mondo miceneo*, 22, n. 19 has concluded that "Trezene fu sempre nell' orbita politica di Argo, prima e dopo l'invasione dorica." Epidaurus: Pausanias 2. 26.1-2. Aegina: Pausanias 2.29.5, and on the relations between Aegina and Epidaurus see Herodotus 5.83 and 8.46.

11. Phlius: Pausanias 2.13.1; Sicyon: Pausanias 2.6.7, 2.7.1. Pausanias's account is accepted by Charles H. Skalet, *Ancient Sicyon* (Baltimore, 1928) 48-49.

12. On the shortcomings of Pausanias as a source for Argive history generally see Jacoby, *FGrH* Part 3B 60-62.

13. Otto Gruppe, *Griechische Mythologie und Religionsgeschichte* 1 (Munich, 1906) 172-177.

14. Wilhelm Vollgraff, "Inscriptions d'Argos," *BCH* 33 (1909) 189-200, and "Rhodos order Argos?" *Neue Jahrbucher* 1 (1910) 305-317. Thomas Lenschau, "Forschungen zur griechischen Geschichte im VII. und VI. Jahrhundert v. Chr.," *Philologus* 91 (1936-37) 386-389. Hermann Bengtson, *Griechische Geschichte*[2] (Munich, 1960) 81, rightly dismisses an Argive empire based on such questionable evidence as "nur ein Phantasiegebilde."

15. See, for example, H. T. Wade-Gery, *CAH*[1] 3:527, where he credits Argos with ruling "the eastern Peloponnesus and the adjacent islands" during the Dark Age; N. G. L. Hammond, *A History of Greece to 323 B.C.* (Oxford, 1959) 77-78; Fritz Gschnitzer, *Abhängige Orte im griechischen Altertum. Zetemata* 17 (Munich, 1958) 79-80, and many others.

16. Desborough, *PGP*, 204-212, in his discussion of the Protogeometric pot-

tery from Corinthia and the Argolid mentions none from any of these sites except Aegina. So far as I am aware, none has been found since that work was published. Ålin, *SMA* 1: 50-52, 57, discusses the latest Mycenaean and earliest post-Mycenaean remains from these areas and provides full references to the pertinent archaeological publications.

17. On this epigraphical evidence see Lilian H. Jeffery, *The Local Scripts of Archaic Greece: A Study of the Origin of the Greek Alphabet and Its Development from the Eighth to Fifth Centuries B.C.* (Oxford, 1961) 139-142, 145-149, 174-175, 185.

18. On the early relationship between Corinth and Argos see Will, *Korinthiaka*, 288-292, 339-344. On the relationship between Argos and Megara see Krister Hanell, *Megarische Studien* (Lund, 1934) 69-71, and John Salmon, *BSA* 67 (1972) 192-195.

19. It now seems clear that a common alphabet was employed throughout the Argive plain. Jeffery, *LSAG*, 145-149, argued that the script employed at Tiryns differed from the script employed at Argos and that the Tirynthian script was probably derived from Corinth. This view must now be modified in the light of new information published by Michael H. Jameson and Ioannis Papachristodoulou, "Die archaischen Inschriften von Tiryns," *Akten des VI. Internationalen Kongress für Geschichte und Lateinische Epigraphik München 1972* (Munich, 1973) 421-425.

20. The pertinent passages are Strabo 8.6.10-11 (372-373) and 8.6.19 (377); Pausanias 2.17.5, 2.25.8, and 8.27.1; see also Diodorus 11.65. Gschnitzer, *Abhängige Orte*, 68-81, makes some observations on the literary reports that are pertinent to the problems discussed here.

21. The literary references for Argive colonization have been assembled by I. Kophiniotou, *IA*, 322-357, who spreads Argive colonization over a millennium or more beginning in 1866 B.C.

22. On colonization see Aubrey Gwynn, "The Character of Greek Colonization," *JHS* 38 (1918) 88-123; Johannes Hasebroek, *Trade and Politics in Ancient Greece* (London, 1933) 108-110; and John Boardman, *The Greeks Overseas* (Harmondsworth, 1964) 176-179. In later Greek history the factors of social discontent and adventure were added, but these can hardly have been involved during the Dark Age.

23. Herodotus 5.113 and Strabo 14.6.3 (682) both say that Curium was settled by Argive colonists. John F. Daniel, "Late Cypriot III Tombs from Kourion," *AJA* 41 (1937) 72-88, and "Excavations at Kourion," *AJA* 42 (1938) 261-275, suggests that any Greek colonization at Curium must have taken place before the fall of Mycenae. The literary evidence is fully examined by Einar Gjerstad, "The Colonization of Cyprus in Greek Legend," *Opusc. Arch.* 3 (1944) 107-123, who believes that colonists left Asine and Epidaurus for Cyprus late in the Cypriot III B period about 1100 B.C. H. W. Catling, *Cypriot Bronzework in the Mycenaean World*, 50-53, detects two different migrations into the island, but on pp. 36-49 argues against the colonization of Cyprus by Mycenaean Greeks and on pp. 300-302 notes that Cyprus was virtually cut off from the mainland during the Dark Age.

24. On Argive colonization in this area see Strabo 14.4.2 and 14.8.2 (673);

Pomponius Mela 1.13. On Argive colonization at Argeia see Wilhelm Vollgraff, "Inscriptions d'Argos," *BCH* 28 (1904) 421-424. On the basis of the literary evidence alone scholars have usually seen some justification for Argive colonization in this area; see, for example, Josef Keil, "Das Problem der ältesten griechischen Kolonisation Kilikiens," *Mitteilungen des Vereines Klassischer Philologen in Wien* 3 (1926) 9-18, W. Ruge, "Pamphylia," *RE* (Stuttgart, 1949) 363, Afif Erzen, *Kilikien bis zum Ende der Perserherrschaft* (Leipzig, 1940) 38-54, and also "Das Besiedlungsproblem Pamphyliens in Altertum," *AA* 88 (1973) 388-401.

25. A handful of Protogeometric and Geometric sherds have been found at Tarsus and Mersin, but large-scale contact with the Greek mainland does not seem to have existed before the middle of the eighth century. The evidence is summarized by Desborough, *LMS*, 22-26, 205-206, and see also G. M. A. Hanfmann, "On Some Eastern Wares Found at Tarsus," *Studies Presented to Hetty Goldman*, 165-184.

26. Michel B. Sakellariou, *La migration grecque en Ionie*, 169-172, 181-185, 209, 492, believes that settlers from the Argolid eventually made their way to Teos, Chios, Colophon, Ephesus, and Smyrna after fleeing the Dorian invaders. Later literary tradition credits the Argives with introducing the worship of Hera to the island of Samos; see Pausanias 7.4.4 and Athenaeus 4.11-15 (672a). Other references have been assembled by Martin P. Nilsson, *Griechische Feste von religiöser Bedeutung* (Leipzig, 1906) 46-49. These claims have not been supported by the archaeological evidence, however. Werner Technau, "Griechische Keramik im samischen Heraion," *AM* 55 (1929) 6-64, and see especially p. 8 where he says "die Scherben zeigen keine Beziehung zu Argos." In fact, the only Argive object found at the site of which I am aware is a griffin protome from the seventh century; see Ulf Jantzen, "Greifenprotomen von Samos: Ein Nachtrag," *AM* 73 (1958) number 53a, pp. 31-32.

27. Strabo 14.2.6 (653), 10.4.15 (470), 10.4.18 (481). quoting Ephorus, says that the Argive Althamenes founded ten colonies on the island, but he does not name any of them. Other references to Argive colonization on the island have been assembled by Wilhelm Vollgraff, "Le décret d'Argos relatif à une pacte entre Knossos et Tylissos," *Verhandeling der Koninklijke Nederlandsche Akademie van Wetenschappen, Afdeeling Letterkunde* 51 (1948) 91-102.

28. The remains from Cnossus have been published by J. K. Brock, *Fortetsa: Early Greek Tombs near Knossos* (Cambridge, 1957); John Boardman, "Protogeometric Graves at Agios Ioannis near Knossos," *BSA* 55 (1960) 128-148, and J. N. Coldstream, "A Geometric Well at Knossos," *BSA* 55 (1960) 159-171.

29. See, for example, R. W. Hutchinson, *Prehistoric Crete* (Harmondsworth, 1962) 319; Gschnitzer, *Abhängige Orte*, 44-48; A. J. Graham, *Colony and Mother City in Ancient Greece* (New York, 1964) 156-157, 212, 214, though he notes that such colonization cannot be definitively proven, nonetheless accepts it.

30. The inscription (*SEG* 11.316) has been published many times, but see especially the work of Vollgraff cited above in n. 27. Even if his restoration is correct, we need not take a fifth-century Argive claim seriously. It undoubtedly tells us more about Argive aims in the fifth century than about Argive history in the Dark Age. Ulrich Kahrstedt, "Zwei Urkunden zur Geschichte von Argos und

Kreta in der Pentekontaëtie," *Klio* 34 (1941-42) 72-91, has questioned Vollgraff's reading of the inscription as well as the belief that Argos colonized Cnossus. Brock, *Fortetsa*, 197, 217, disputes the claim on the basis of the archaeological material from Cnossus.

31. Herodotus 7.99, followed by Strabo 14.2.16 (656) and Pausanias 2.30.9, said that Halicarnassus was founded from Troezen; but P. Mela 1.85 believed it was colonized by Argives and Vitruvius 2.18.12 believed it was founded by settlers from both Troezen and Argos. The smaller cities of Tabai (Steph. Byz., *s.v.* "Tabai,") and Tralles (Strabo 14.1.12, 655) also claimed Argive ancestry. The archaeological evidence would seem to suggest that although a few Greeks might have resided in this general area in the Dark Age, their cultural background differed somewhat from those inhabiting the offshore islands. Their pottery closely resembled the pottery of Attica, and they practiced cremation burial. On this see W. R. Paton, "Excavations in Caria," *JHS* 9 (1887) 64-82; George F. Bass, "Mycenaean and Protogeometric Tombs in the Halicarnassus Peninsula," *AJA* 67 (1963) 353-361; G. E. Bean and J. M. Cook, "The Halicarnassus Peninsula," *BSA* 50 (1955) 85-171; Desborough, *PGP*, 218-221.

32. Cnidus was known to Herodotus 1.174, as a Laconian colony but Strabo 14.2.6 (653) refers to it as an Argive colony.

33. Thucydides 8.57.6; Pindar, *Ol.* 7.19, and see also R. Hope Simpson and J. F. Lazenby, "Notes from the Dodecanese III," *BSA* 68 (1973) 131-133. F. Hiller von Gaertringen, *s.v.* "Rhodos," *RE*, 819-827, discusses literary reports crediting other cities with colonizing the island.

34. The archaeological evidence has been summarized by Desborough, *LMS*, 152-158. The Protogeometric material has been published in *Clara Rhodos* 3.146-147, 6.119-130, 7.360-363, 8.161-166. On the relation of this pottery to other styles see Desborough, *PGP*, 225-233, and Snodgrass, *DAG*, 75-78, who also discusses burial practices on the island, pp. 163-164.

35. Alfred Laumonier, *Les cultes indigenes en Carie* (Paris, 1958) 676-685, has assembled the information for Rhodian cults. Jeffery, *LSAG* 42, 153-154, 353-354, traces the origin of the Argive script to this section.

36. The name of the phyle and deme are known from inscriptions that date from the second century B.C.; see Christian Blinkenberg, *Lindos; Fouilles et recherches, 1902-1914* (Copenhagen, 1941) 2:470-471, 1012-1014.

37. Wilhelm Vollgraff, "Novae Inscriptiones Argivae," *Mnem.*, 44 (1916) 221.

38. Pausanias 3.2.2-3. The war is accepted as fact by Pierre Roussel, *Sparte* (Paris, 1939) 27-28, and Leo Heidemann, *Die territoriale Entwicklung Lacedämons und Messeniens bis auf Alexander* (Berlin, 1904) 77-78, but see my discussion in "The Traditional Enmity between Sparta and Argos: The Birth and Development of a Myth," *AHR* 75 (1970) 993-1000.

39. 5.41.2.

40. On the geographical features of Cynouria see Philippson and Kirsten, *Die griechischen Landschaften* 3:Pt. 2, 480-488, and see also K. A. Rhomaios, "Κυνουρία καὶ Κυνούριοι," *Peloponnesiaka* 1 (1956) 1-22. A summary of the archaeological remains found in the area is given by Israel Walker, *Kynouria: Its History in the Light of Existing Remains* (Williamsport, Pa., 1936).

Chapter IV

1. On the many significant changes that were taking place in this period see Starr, *OGC*, 189ff., and Snodgrass, *DAG*, 336-352.

2. A convenient summary of the Geometric pottery found at each of these sites is given by Coldstream, *GGP*, 405-407, and see also Hägg, *GA* 53-55, 62-64, 68-70, 72-74, 84-86. Both works contain complete bibliographical references to the pertinent archaeological publications. On burial grounds at Argos see Hägg, *GA*, 30-35, 42, 46, and Courbin, *EP* 7:101-107.

3. Reference to much of the Geometric material at Argos has been cited in the previous chapter. More recent finds are briefly noted in *BCH* 91 (1967) 808, 841-846; *BCH* 92 (1968) 1020; *BCH* 93 (1969) 976; *BCH* 94 (1970) 798; *BCH* 95 (1971) 738, 748; *BCH* 96 (1972) 161-167; and in *AD* 17 (1961-62) 55-56; *AD* 18 (1963) 57-63; *AD* 21 (1966) 126-127; *AD* 22 (1967) 169-170; *AD* 23 (1968) 127-128; *AD* 24 (1969) 106-109. On remains from the Deiras see Vollgraff, *BCH* 28 (1904) 364-366. On the extent of the settlement in this period see Seraphim Charitonidis, " 'Ανασκαφαὶ ἐν 'Αργεία," *Praktika* (1952) 413-426; *BCH* 78 (1954) 422-423; and *BCH* 83 (1959) 755-762. On urbanization at Argos in this period see Hägg, *GA*, 90-91. On the city as it existed in the time of Pausanias see Axel Boëthius, "Zur Topographie des dorischen Argos, "*Strena Philologica Upsaliensis Festskrift Per Persson* (Uppsala, 1922) 248-288.

4. On the remains from the Aspis and Larissa see Wilhelm Vollgraff, *Études Péloponnésiennes* 1: *Le sanctuaire d'Apollon Pythéen à Argos* (Paris, 1956) 29, and *MKAW* 66 (1928) 92; Deshayes, *EP* 4:2-3, 8-9, 13-14; Anne Roes, "Fragments de poterie géométrique trouvés sur les citadelles d'Argos," *BCH* 77 (1953) 90-104.

5. The architectural remains are published in Charles Waldstein, *The Argive Heraeum*; see *AH* 1:108-136; they have been restudied by Pierre Amandry, "Observations sur les monuments de l'heráion d'Argos," *Hesperia* 21 (1952) 222-274. We can ignore the fantastic date ("ca. 1910-1830 B.C.") proposed for the walls and early temple in *AH* 1:29.

6. On the earliest material found at the site see Courbin, *CGA*, 565. Blegen reports his findings in *Prosymna* 1:19-20 and *AJA* 43 (1939) 432. A. Frickenhaus and W. Müller, "Aus der Argolis: Bericht über eine Reise von Herbst 1909," *AM* 36 (1911) 26-27, found some Protocorinthian pottery between the blocks of the Old Temple Terrace Wall and suggested that the pottery had been deposited there during the course of construction; but Blegen's findings suggest they were in error.

7. The abundance of Late Geometric pottery is emphasized in *BCH* 83 (1959) 755-762 and by Courbin, *CGA*, *passim* but especially 1-2 and his discussion 172-177. The finds from a remarkably rich tomb (Tomb 45) from this period have been published by Paul Courbin, "Une tombe géométrique d'Argos," *BCH* 81 (1957) 322-386; see also *EP* 7:40-41.

8. The excellent quality of Argive Geometric pottery only became apparent with the excavations begun there by l'école française d'Athènes in the 1950s; see Georges Daux, "Les fouilles de l'école française d'Athènes à Argos, "*CRAI* (1953) 455-463. Courbin, *CGA*, 561-564, summarizes his remarks on the Argive Late Geometric style; and see also Coldstream, *GGP*, 125-147.

9. The most severe critic of Argive Late Geometric pottery is Anne Roes, *BCH* 77 (1953) 90-104. Charitonidis, *BCH* 78 (1954) 418, has suggested that sloppily painted Argive vases might be the product of one particular workshop, or perhaps of one particular potter, and this seems to be borne out by the work of Courbin and Coldstream who have been able to identify the products of individual potters; see Courbin, *CGA*, 447-452, and Coldstream, *GGP*, 132-141. Robin Hägg, "Research at Dendra 1961." *Opusc. Ath.* 4 (1962) 102, notes that sloppy painting is usually confined to small vases and that larger ones are usually carefully done. This is generally, but not universally, true.

10. The relationship of Argive Geometric pottery to other Geometric schools has been exhaustively examined by Courbin, *CGA*, 500-544, whose conclusions I summarize here; see also Coldstream, *GGP*, 125-144. Interestingly enough, Attic influence seems to have been more pronounced at Asine than at Argos; see Coldstream, *GGP*, 132-133, and Robin Hägg, "Geometrische Gräber von Asine," *Opusc. Ath.* 6 (1965) 117-138.

11. Several excellent terra-cotta figurines have recently been published by Haiganuch Sarian, "Terres cuites géométriques d'Argos," *BCH* 93 (1969) 651-678.

12. Courbin, *CGA*, 547-549.

13. Imitation of Corinthian Geometric: *BCH* 83 (1959) 757; of Protocorinthian: *BCH* 78 (1954) 160.

14. On the decline in Argive Late Geometric pottery see Courbin, *CGA*, 563-564; Argive Subgeometric pottery will be discussed in the following chapter.

15. See, for example, Fritz M. Heichelheim, *An Ancient Economic History* 1 (Leiden, 1958) 241, where he states that Argive vases have been found in Egypt, Asia Minor, Italy, and southern France.

16. Courbin, *CGA*, 450, 549-553, has examined all of the allegedly Argive Geometric pottery found beyond the Argive plain, and this paragraph is largely a summary of his conclusions. The allegedly Argive material from Perachora has also recently been reexamined by Salmon, *BSA* 67 (1972) 179-192. Coldstream, *GGP*, 363-364, recognizes the small-scale exportation of Argive Late Geometric pottery but seems nonetheless to overestimate its significance. He would add a single fragment found at Cnossus to Courbin's list.

17. Foreign importations into the Argive plain have been discussed by Courbin, *CGA*, 553-555.

18. The key passages are Herodotus 4.152; Athenaeus 1.28e; Pindar, *Ol.* 7.83, and see Hugo Blümner, *Die gewerbliche Thätigkeit der Völker des klassischen Altertums* (Leipzig, 1869) 78-79. Jean Charbonneaux, *Les bronzes grecs* (Paris, 1961) 74, believes that Argos was the most active center in the manufacture of bronze objects.

19. This, at least, in the conclusion of Snodgrass, *DAG*, 269-270.

20. On this find see Courbin, *BCH* 81 (1957) 322-386. This armor has been much discussed; see, for example, Antony M. Snodgrass, *Early Greek Armour and Weapons from the End of the Bronze Age to 600 B.C.* (Edinburgh, 1964) 72-77, 81-84.

21. From the original excavation, 5,738 pieces were catalogued in *AH* 2:191-339, but subsequent excavation has added many more. They are reported by Blegen, *AJA* 43 (1939) 410-444, and John L. Caskey, "Investigations at the

Heraion of Argos, 1949," *Hesperia* 21 (1952) 176-183. In addition many others have been found in tombs and deposits in the city of Argos; see *BCH* 79 (1955) 314; *BCH* 81 (1957) 322-386; *AD* 18 (1963) 62-63; and see also Anne Roes, "Les ex-voto de bronze de l'époque géométrique," *RA* (1970) 195-208. Although the catalogue in *AH* 2 is exhaustive, the dating and classification is inaccurate; the material from Perachora (*Perachora* 1:72-74, 168-174) is similar and much more carefully and accurately classified and dated. In contrast to the many metal objects found at the Heraeum, the votive deposit from the temple of Hera at Tiryns produced only thirty-three metal objects; see *Tiryns* 1:107. However, the graves recently excavated at Tiryns by Verdelis contained numerous metal objects as reported in *AM* 78 (1963) 61-62.

22. On this see Snodgrass, *DAG*, 271-272, 345.

23. John Boardman, *Island Gems: A Study of Greek Seals in the Geometric and Early Archaic Periods* (London, 1963) 163-165.

24. On the few artists involved in cutting seal stones see Boardman, *Island Gems*, 85-88.

25. This is the conclusion of Courbin, *Archaeology* 9 (1956) 171; R. M. Cook, *Greek Painted Pottery* (Chicago, 1960) 22; and Hägg, *Opusc. Ath.* (1962) 90,102.

26. Martin P. Nilsson, *Geschichte der griechischen Religion* 1 (Munich, 1955) 478; L. R. Farnell, *The Cults of the Greek States* 1 (Oxford, 1896) 188-189; see also Sam Wide, *Lakonische Kulte* (Leipzig, 1893) 24, 186, and Hannell, *Megarische Studien*, 75-79. The similarities between the worship of Hera at Samos and at Argos are pointed out by Nilsson, *Griechische Feste*, 46-49, and S. Eitrem, *s.v.* "Hera," *RE*, 370-382, but as noted above (Chapter III n. 26), the archaeological evidence from Samos shows virtually no contact with Argos. There were also cults of Hera scattered throughout Italy, but these clearly had no connection with Argos; the whole problem has been most recently discussed by G. Maddoli, "Il rito degli Argei e le origini del culto di Hera a Roma," *La parola del passato* 26 (1971) 153-166.

27. Homer, *Iliad* 4.51, where the poet states that three cities, Argos, Sparta, and Mycenae, are Hera's favorite cities. At 5.908 Hera is referred to as Hera Argeia, but in this passage Homer may be using the term to mean more than the city of Argos.

28. Pausanias 2.24.1 Volgraff, *BCH* 31 (1907) 160-161, and *EP* 1:7, has argued that this temple was probably located on the site now occupied by the convent Παναγία τοῦ βράχου, but no ancient remains have ever been found there.

29. The earliest temple remains at the site date only from the early half of the seventh century, but some idea of what the original temple may have looked like can perhaps be gotten from the so-called temple models that were found in the votive deposit there. On these see Kurt Müller, "Gebaudemodelle spätgeometrischer Zeit," *AM* 48 (1923) 52-68, and G. Oikonomou, " 'Ο ἐκ τοῦ Ἀργείου Ἡραίου πήλινος οἰκίσκος κατὰ νέαν συμπλήρωσιν," *Arch. Eph.* (1931) 1-53. Similar models have been found at Perachora (*Perachora* 1:34-51), and see generally Heinrich Drerup, *Griechische Baukunst in geometrischer Zeit* (Göttingen, 1969) 69-74.

30. On various aspects of religion in this period see Starr, *OGC*, 277-283, and Nilsson, *GGR*, 1:378-384.

31. Religious scenes on Argive vases: Courbin, *CGA*, 492-494. Cremation at Argos: *BCH* 78 (1954) 410 and *Praktika* (1952) 413-414. Nauplia: *Praktika* (1953) 194-195. Several graves from Asine were originally identified as cremation burials, but this claim has been disputed by Hägg, *Opusc. Ath.* 6 (1965) 117-138, who does, however, recognize (pp. 127-128) a single burial from the site as a cremation. See also the comments of Verdelis, *AM* 78 (1963) 54-55, and Courbin, *EP* 7:115-116.

32. Mycenae: A. J. B. Wace, "Excavations at Mycenae," *BSA* 25 (1921-23) 329, 364-366. Argos: *BCH* 79 (1955) 312 and Deshayes, *EP* 4:215-219. Heraeum: Blegen, *Prosymna* 1:262-263, and "Post-Mycenaean Deposits in Chamber Tombs," *Arch. Eph.* (1937) 377-390. Snodgrass, *DAG*, 192-194, discusses the evidence for the emergence of this practice throughout the Greek world in this period.

33. Aspis: Vollgraff, *EP* 1:11, 29; Larissa: Vollgraff, *MKAW* 66 (1928) 91-92, and *MKAW* 72 (1932) 72; see also *BCH* 77 (1955) 314 and *AR* (1955) 9. Tiryns: *Tiryns* 1:42-46 and Karo, "Tiryns," *RE*, 1465-1466.

34. J. M. Cook, "The Agamemnoneion," *BSA* 48 (1953) 30-68, and "The Cult of Agamemnon at Mycenae," *Geras Antoniou Keramopoullou* (Athens, 1953) 112-118.

35. There are perhaps a few Protogeometric fragments from the site. The fragment depicted on plate LVI, no. 1, *AH* 2, although labeled Geometric, would seem rather to be Protogeometric, and the excavators report (p. 105) finding several similar fragments. Courbin, *CGA*, 565, n. 3 dates the earliest post-Mycenaean pottery from the site slightly before 750 B.C. It must be noted here that Jacobsthal, *Greek Pins*, 3, suggests that some pins found at the site "have a Protogeometric look," and he seems to suggest on p. 5 that others date from fairly early in the Geometric period.

36. In the fifth century B.C. Hellanicus drew up a list of priestesses of Hera that extended back to Mycenaean times, see *FGrH* 4 F 74-84 with Jacoby's commentary. N. G. L. Hammond, *CAH*³ 2:Pt. 2, 678-679, suggests that traditions concerning the Dorian invasion and Pre-Dorian Greece were preserved at the site throughout the Dark Age. Paul Friedländer, "Zur Frühgeschichte des Argivischen Heraions," *AM* 34 (1909) 69-79, recognized that the site was a center of habitation in the Bronze Age, but believed it became an important religious center immediately after the Bronze Age settlement was destroyed. Tomlinson, *Argos*, 33-34, refuses to rule out continuous worship from the Bronze Age at the site, but on the subject of continuity of worship at the major sites in Greece see Snodgrass, *DAG*, 277-285, 394-399.

37. Nilsson, *GGR* 1:73-74, and see also R. E. Wycherley, *How the Greeks Built Cities*² (London, 1962) 87-89.

38. Strabo 8.6.10 (372) is, so far as I know, the only ancient author to comment on the central location of the temple. It has, however, been recognized by many modern scholars; see, for example, Tomlinson, *Argos*, 203-204; Friedländer, *AM* 34 (1909) 69-79, and Waldstein, *AH* 1:10-25, who greatly exaggerates the role of Tiryns in founding the temple.

39. Mycenae: *Iliad* 4.51, and an inscription published by A. G. Woodhead, "The Boundary Stone from the Persia Fountain House," *BSA* 48 (1953) 27-29.

Nauplia: Pausanias 2.38.2, and see S. Casson, "Hera of Kanathos and the Ludovisi Throne," *JHS* 40 (1920) 137-142. Tiryns: *Tiryns* 1:42-46; *Tiryns* 3:213-214, and Karo, "Tiryns," *RE*, 1465-1466.

40. This or a very similar suggestion has been made before by Charles Waldstein, "The Argive Heraeum and Bacchylides XI. 43-84," *Classical Review* 14 (1900) 473-474, who believes that the temple "was once the civic (as well as the religious) centre of Argos the country." However, he supported his view by a strained interpretation of Bacchylides. Friedländer, *AM* 34 (1909) 78, considered the possibility but refused to assert it dogmatically.

41. Victor Ehrenberg, *The Greek State* (Oxford, 1960) 19. On religion and foreign policy generally in Greece see Martin P. Nilsson, *Cults, Myths, Oracles, and Politics in Ancient Greece* (Lund, 1951) 41-48, and F. E. Adcock, "The Development of Ancient Greek Diplomacy," *AC* 17 (1948) 1-12.

42. Blegen, *AJA* 43 (1939) 427-430. It may also be worth noting that traces of a roadway that ran from the Heraeum toward Midea and Tiryns have been found, but there is no way to determine when it might have been constructed.

43. Theopompus, *FGrH* 115 F 383, would seem to be the earliest mention of the event, but the text as preserved by Strabo, 8.6.11 (373), is not complete. Most of our information comes, however, from Pausanias 2.36.4-5; 3.7.4; 4.8.3; and 4.34.6. On the archaeological evidence see Frödin and Persson, *Asine*, 148-151, 437.

44. See "The Argive Destruction of Asine," *Historia* (1967) 422-431; much of that argument is repeated here. Arnold J. Toynbee, *Some Problems of Greek History* (Oxford, 1969) 184-185, has also recently rejected Pausanias's reasons for the Argive destruction of the site.

45. Desborough, *PGP*, 204-205, 211-212, on the Protogeometric pottery found at the site; on the Geometric material see n. 10 above. On the Dryopian heritage of the inhabitants of Asine see Herodotus 8.73; on the connection between Dryopes and Apollo see Pausanias 4.34.11. On the cult of Apollo at Asine see W. S. Barrett, "Bacchylides, Asine, and Apollo Pythaieus," *Hermes* 82 (1954), 438-441, where it is argued that this was perhaps the oldest cult of Apollo in the Peloponnesus.

46. Courbin, *CGA*, has exhaustively examined the scenes on Argive vases; see especially 418-428; see also Coldstream, *GGP*, 143, and Snodgrass, *EGAW*, 6-8. Courbin, *EP* 7:133-135, discusses military equipment found in tombs at Argos.

47. On the importance of the horse in Argive Late Geometric art see Courbin, *CGA*, 403-413. On the importance of the horse in late eighth-century warfare see Snodgrass, *EGAW*, 163-166, and *DAG* 414-415. On mounted-warrior figurines see *Asine*, 333, fig. 225, 6-7.

48. *AH* 2:plate LVII, 10 and Coldstream, *GGP*, 143. It is also interesting that several arrowheads have been found in a Geometric context in the Argolid. One at Asine (*Asine*, 333, fig. 225.2) is called "Scythian" by Snodgrass, *EGAW* 150. There is also one from a Geometric tomb at Argos; see *BCH* 80 (1956)376. Two obsidian examples were found in Tomb XXVI at Tiryns; see Verdelis, *AM* 78 (1963) 41-42.

49. On the first Messenian War see any general history of Sparta; on the war of the Lelantine Plain see John Boardman, "Early Euboean Pottery and History,"

BSA 52 (1957) 27-29, where he suggests that there was perhaps a series of wars between Eretria and Chalcis in the latter half of the eighth century. The ancient evidence for the war is discussed by Donald Bradeen, "The Lelantine War and Pheidon of Argos," *TAPA* 78 (1947) 223-241, though his connection of Pheidon with the war is excessively strained. Walter Donlan, "Archilochus, Strabo and the Lelantine War," *TAPA* 101 (1970) 131-142, would date the war after 700 but before 650 B.C. On the war between Corinth and Megara see Plutarch, *Greek Questions* 17 and Hammond, *BSA* 49 (1954) 93-102, who dates the war to the last quarter of the eighth century, though his identification of some of the pottery from Perachora as Megarian is hardly convincing.

50. See, for example, Karl Otfried Müller, *Die Dorier*. 2 vols. (Breslau, 1824) 1:154; Beloch, *GG*² 1:Pt. 1, 205, n. 1, and especially Georg Busolt, *Die Lakedaimonier und ihre Bundesgenossen* (Leipzig, 1878) 82-90.

51. Herodotus 6.92 is the chief source for the existence of such a league; but it may be worth noting that Plutarch, *Moralia* 306a, and Chrysermus, *FGrH* 287 F 2, report that it was an amphictionic council which decided that three hundred men from Argos and Sparta should fight in the Battle of Champions about the middle of the sixth century, and Pausanias 4.5.2 mentions an amphictionic council at Argos before the First Mesenian War. None of these reports inspire much confidence, however. On the inclusion of Sicyon and Aegina in the Peloponnesian League in the time of Cleomenes's invasion of the Argive plain see Konrad Wickert, *Der peloponnesische Bund von seiner Entstehung bis zum Ende des archidamischen Krieges* (Königsberg, 1961) 15-20, 23-33, and Luigi Moretti, *Ricerche sulle leghe greche* (Rome, 1962) 72-73.

52. Pausanias 2.35.2, quoting the Argive poetess Telesilla, reports that Pythaeus, Apollo's son, visited the Argives before any other Greeks, and at 2.24.1 he credits Pythaeus with founding a temple of Apollo in the city. Apollo was apparently worshiped on the Aspis from the eighth century (Vollgraff, *EP* 1:11, 29), but the earliest temple remains date from much later. Vollgraff, *EP* 1:13-33, dates them to the early sixth century, but Georges Roux, "Le sanctuaire argien d'Apollo Pythéen," *REG* 70 (1957) 474-487, argues convincingly for a fourth-century date.

53. The view that there was an amphictiony centered around a temple of Apollo rests upon Thucydides 5.53, where it is related that in 419 Argos went to war against Epidaurus because the people of that city had not sent an offering to Pythian Apollo whose temple was under the management of the Argives. Karl Müller, *Die Dorier* 1:154, and Georg Busolt, *Die Lakedaimonier und ihre Bundesgenossen*, 82-90, have argued that the amphictiony centered around the Apollo temple on the Aspis. Barrett, *Hermes* 82, (1954) 438-442, and L. R. Farnell, *The Cults of the Greek City States* 4 (Oxford, 1906) 215, suggest the temple of Apollo at Asine was the league's center, but the archaeological evidence does not support this conclusion. The excavators report (*Asine*, 148-151) finding Geometric and Protocorinthian pottery and archaic and Hellenistic roof tiles around the temple, but they do not mention classical remains. There is no proof, therefore, that the temple was in use in 419 B.C. Vollgraff, *EP* 1:31-33, argues that the center of the amphictiony was a temple of Apollo between Nauplia and Epidaurus,

but there is absolutely nothing to prove that the temple that once stood on that site was a temple of Apollo.

54. This suggestion was advanced long ago by Guilelmus Lilie, *Quae ratio intercessit inter singulas Argolidis civitates*, 35-36. It is also the opinion of Beloch, *GG*[2] 1: Pt. 1, 205, n. 1, and N. G. L. Hammond, *A History of Greece*, 166, 168, who bases his view on Chrysermus, *FGrH* 287 F 2.

55. On Dark Age kingship see Starr, *OGC*, 124-129, and "The Decline of the Early Greek Kings," *Historia* 10 (1961) 129-138.

56. Most scholars are convinced that this fourth phyle was created at an early date; see, for example, Josef Keil, "Die dorischen Phylen," *Mitteilungen des Vereines Klassischer Philologen in Wien* 6 (1929) 5-8, and Nilsson, *Cults, Myths, Oracles, and Politics*, 73-74, who synthesizes much current opinion on the subject. The earliest reference to the phylae at Argos come from *IG* 4.517, which Jeffery, *LSAG*, 170, dates ca. 460-450 B.C. The inscription lists, in addition to the customary three Dorian phylae, a fourth, the Hyrnathioi. N. G. L. Hammond, "An Early Inscription at Argos," *CQ* 54 (1960) 33-36, has argued that this phyle was added only after the Battle of Sepeia in 494 B.C. This date may be somewhat too late, but Hammond has shown that it must have been added after about 550 B.C. His argument is based on two other Argive inscriptions (*IG* 4.614 and *SEG* 11.314) which date from the first half of the sixth century. Neither inscription mentions the phylae, but one speaks of six demiourgoi and the other of nine demiourgoi. Hammond assumes that these demiourgoi held office in a single year, and he notes that although both numbers are divisible by three, neither is divisible by four. Hammond's argument seems generally sound even though Wilhelm Vollgraff, "Inscriptio in arce Argorum reperta," *Mnem.* 57 (1929) 206-234, who rediscovered and republished *IG* 4.614, argued that the nine demiourgoi mentioned there held office in nine consecutive years rather than in a single year. The evidence for the phylae at Argos has been discussed by Michael Wörrle, *Untersuchungen zur Verfassungsgeschichte von Argos im 5. Jahrhundert vor Christus* (Munich, 1964) 11-18.

57. On the Argive phratries see Wilhelm Vollgraff, "Inscriptions d'Argos," *BCH* 30 (1909) 175-200, and *Mnem.* 44 (1916) 51-56. More recent epigraphical discoveries necessitate some additions to earlier lists of the Argive phratries; see especially Pierre Charneaux, "Inscriptions d'Argos," *BCH* 82 (1958) 1-15. The evidence is fully discussed by Wörrle, *UVA*, 18-27; Wilhelm Vollgraff, "Observations sur les noms de trois phratries argiennes," *BCH* 83 (1959) 254-257, and Margherita Guarducci, "L'istituzione della fratria nella grecia antica e nelle colonie greche d'Italia," *Atti della Reale Accademia Nazionale dei Lincei: Memorie della classe di scienze morali, storiche e filologiche* 8 (1938-39) 86-89.

58. See above Chapter III.

59. Carlo Gallovotti, "Le origini micenee dell' istituto fraterica," *La parola del passato* 16 (1961) 20-39, believes that phratries originated in Mycenaean times, but the argument of A. Andrewes, "Phratries in Homer," *Hermes* 89 (1961) 129-140, that they came into existence toward the end of the Dark Age seems more likely.

60. For what it is worth, Pausanias 2.36.4 tells us that Eratus was king

of the city when Asine was attacked and destroyed late in the eighth century.

61. On the size of tombs generally in this period see Courbin, *EP* 7:108-109; on large tombs see Hägg, *GA*, 119-120, 129; and see also *BCH* 77 (1953) 260. On grave offerings generally see Courbin, *EP* 7:125-126. On the contents of Tomb 1 see Courbin, *EP* 7:10-13. A tomb containing thirty vases is briefly noted in *BCH* 91 (1967) 846.

62. The contents of this tomb (Tomb 45) have been fully described by Courbin, *BCH* 81 (1957) 322-386, and see also Waldemar Deonna, "Haches, broches et chenets dans une tombe géométrique d'Argos," *BCH* 83 (1959) 247-252.

63. On the crater (Tomb 43) see Courbin, *EP* 7:40; on the pyxis (Tomb 23) see *EP* 7:34-35.

64. Charitonidis, *Praktika* (1953) 194-195, reports finding at Nauplia a pyxis similar in size and decoration to the pyxis found at Argos. At Tiryns, Tomb 26 (*Tiryns* 1:131-132) contained fourteen fine Late Geometric vases.

65. On the agricultural orientation of the economy and the basis of aristocratic wealth in this early period see Heichelheim, *AEH* 1:273-280; Moses I. Finley, *The World of Odysseus* (London, 1962) 68-69; and Starr, *OGC*, 357-359.

66. Our knowledge of landholding in early Greece is far from satisfactory and opinions vary widely. There is more information for Athens than for any other Greek city, but even here the evidence has led to varying conclusions. Jan Pecirka, "Land Tenure and the Development of the Athenian Polis," *Studies Presented to George Thomson on the Occasion of His 60th Birthday* (Prague, 1963) 183-201, gives a good annotated bibliography on the subject.

67. Such scenes are frequently found on Argive Late Geometric vases; see *BCH* 78 (1954) 480 and plate VI; *AH* 2:112-114 and plates LVII and LVIII; and Courbin, *CGA* 446-447, 490-495.

68. The motive most frequently seen on Argive Late Geometric pottery is the horse. See *AH* 2:109-111, and Courbin, *CGA*, 403-413, and n. 47 above.

69. That the warrior who lay buried with the armor in Tomb 45 was a man of means seems clear from the offerings found in the tomb; see Snodgrass *EGAW*, 83-84, and also the penetrating remarks of H. Drerup, *Griechische Baukunst in geometrischer Zeit*, 127. On the expense of hoplite armor and its use, initially, on a limited rather than general scale see A. M. Snodgrass, "The Hoplite Reform and History," *JHS* 85 (1965) 110-122.

70. It should be noted that my account of Argive history in the latter half of the eighth century differs substantially from Tomlinson's *Argos*, 67-78. Tomlinson rightly recognizes that the position of Argos within the Argive plain was enhanced in this period, but his notion that Sparta and Argos were enemies at this early date is, as will be discussed further below, not likely. I would, moreover, reject his notion that internal affairs at Argos can be explained on the basis of natural antagonism between the Dorian and non-Dorian inhabitants of the city.

Chapter V

1. See my article "The Traditional Enmity between Sparta and Argos: The Birth and Development of a Myth," *AHR* 75 (1970) 971-1003. Much of my discussion in several of the paragraphs that follow has been derived from that article where more complete bibliographical information is cited.

2. On the absence of the ship as a motive at Argos see Courbin, *CGA*, 445 n. 3. The evidence for Argive trade and colonization will be discussed later in this chapter. It is worth noting here, however, that the only known Argive object from this period that has been found at Cythera is a Subgeometric crater similar to those found at Fusco. It is called Argive by J. N. Coldstream, *Kythera: Excavations and Studies Conducted by the University of Pennsylvania Museum and the British School at Athens* (Park Ridge, N.J., 1973) 201, but Courbin, *CGA*, 550 n. 1, refers to it as "apparemment Argien."

3. Strabo 8.6.14 (374) is our only evidence for the early existence of this league, but see also *IG* 4.842 which dates from the Hellenistic period. I have argued in "The Calaurian Amphictiony," *AJA* 70 (1966) 113-121, that the league came into existence only about the middle of the seventh century. My argument supporting this date remains valid, but my belief that the purpose of the league was to present a united front against Pheidon will not stand. It rested on the mistaken notion that the Argive tyrant lived and ruled in the seventh century. In fact, we do not know why the league was founded, though the argument of J. P. Harland, "The Calaurian Amphictiony," *AJA* 29 (1925) 160-171, that it came into existence to promote commerce has been almost universally accepted.

4. Strabo 8.6.14 (374) says that the Spartans paid the dues for Prasiae and it is generally assumed that they began to do so shortly after they defeated the Argives in the Battle of Champions; see, for example, George L. Huxley, *Early Sparta* (Cambridge, Mass., 1962) 73.

5. On the ancient routes between Argos and Sparta see J. G. Frazer, *Pausanias's Description of Greece* (London, 1913) 3:305-309; William Loring, "Some Ancient Routes in the Peloponnese," *JHS* 15 (1895) 51-66, 78-80; and Philippson and Kirsten, *Die griechischen Landschaften*, 3: Pt. 3, 467-471.

6. 5.49, and see my discussion in *AHR* 75 (1970) 974-976.

7. Spartan expansion has been discussed many times, most recently by Huxley, *ES*, 13-36, 53-57; W. G. Forrest, *A History of Sparta 950-192 B.C.* (London, 1958) 35-39, 69-77; and Toynbee, *Some Problems of Greek History*, 163-185. These discussions rest far too much on Pausanias, and all assume that Argos defeated Sparta at Hysiae in 669 B.C. The trustworthiness of Pausanias as a guide to early Argive history and the Battle of Hysiae will be discussed more fully later in this chapter.

8. Herodotus does not specifically mention this war, and most of our information comes from Pausanias 4.7.1-4.13.7. There is a lengthy bibliography on the usefulness of Pausanias's account; see, most recently, Franz Kiechle, *Messenische Studien* (Kallmünz Opf, 1959), who regards Pausanias as generally reliable, and Lionel Pearson, "The Pseudo History of Messenia and Its Authors," *Historia* 11 (1962) 397-426, who shows clearly how untrustworthy our information is. Toynbee, *Some Problems of Greek History*, 180-182, notes that the Spartans probably did not conquer all of Messenia in the first war.

9. On Spartan difficulties in the late eighth and early seventh centuries see Huxley, *ES* 33-39; Forrest, *A History of Sparta*, 40ff.; Toynbee, *Some Problems of Greek History*, 183-202; and Franz Kiechle, *Lakonien und Sparta* (Munich, 1963) 176-202.

10. Pausanias 3.7.5 and 2.24.7. H. T. Wade-Gery, "A Note on the Origin of the

Spartan Gymnopaidiai," *CQ* 43 (1949) 81, n. 1, has suggested that the Battle of Hysiae occurred during Theopompus's incursion into Cynouria.

11. See, for example, Huxley, *ES*, 53, and Tomlinson, *Argos*, 79-85, and many others.

12. Our evidence for this war also comes mainly from Pausanias 4.15.1-4.24.4, and see the bibliography cited in n. 9 above.

13. These events are described by Herodotus 1.65, 67-68. On Spartan-Arcadian relations in this period see Christian Callmer, *Studien zur Geschichte Arkadiens* (Lund, 1943) 41-77; Josef Hejnic, *Pausanias the Perieget and the Archaic History of Arcadia* (Prague, 1961); Angelo Brelich, *Guerre, agoni e culti nella grecia arcaica* (Bonn, 1961) 23-34; and Luigi Moretti, "Sparta alla metà del VI secolo: La guerre contro Tegea," *RFC* 24 (1946) 87-103.

14. The treaty between Sparta and Tegea is recorded only by Aristotle, fr. 592 (Rose); see also Felix Jacoby, "ΧΡΗΣΤΟΥΣ ΠΟΙΕΙΝ (Aristotle fr. 592R)," *CQ* 38 (1944) 15-16, and Hermann Bengtson, *Die Staatsverträge des Altertums* 2 (Munich and Berlin, 1962) Nr. 112.

15. I have treated the matters discussed in this paragraph more fully in *AHR* 75 (1970) 971-1003.

16. On this Subgeometric pottery see Cook, *BSA* 48 (1953) 34-41; Coldstream, *GGP*, 146-147; Deshayes, *EP* 4:215-219; and Jean-François Bommelaer, "Nouveau documents de céramique protoargienne," *BCH* 96 (1972) 229-251. It is worth noting here that although a number of seventh-century tombs have been excavated in the city, their contents have not yet been published.

17. The absence of a true orientalizing style at Argos is emphasized by Cook, *BSA* 43 (1953) 34-41. Karl Kübler, *Kerameikos* 5:174, n. 160, has compiled a modest list of Argive vases that show oriental influence.

18. The most complete discussion of this Protoargive style is Paul Courbin's "Un fragment de cratère protoargien," *BCH* 79 (1955) 1-49, where the Polyphemus fragment is published. Other examples of the style are rare but equally fine; cf. *BCH* 78 (1954) 180. Two fragments from the Athenian Agora were originally labeled Protoattic by Dorothy Burr, "A Geometric House and Protoattic Votive Deposit," *Hesperia* 2 (1933) 572-574, but are now correctly identified as Protoargive by Courbin, *BCH* 79 (1955) 12-13, and also by Eva T. H. Brann, *The Athenian Agora* 8: *Late Geometric and Protoattic Pottery* (Princeton, 1962) 105, n. 649. Brann also lists two other pieces (numbers 650, 651) as "Protoargive," but they are probably not of Argive manufacture. Courbin believes they are Protocorinthian. A crater found at Corinth and published by Theodore L. Shear, "Excavations in the North Cemetary at Corinth in 1930," *AJA* 34 (1930) 411-413, as Corinthian is now identified as Protoargive by Courbin, *BCH* 81 (1957) 337, n. 2. Bommelaer, *BCH* 96 (1972) 229-251, discusses several sherds recently found at Argos.

19. The Argive pottery found in the votive deposits of the temple of Hera Limenia at Perachora (*Perachora* 2:370-371), illustrates how little Argive pottery was produced after the early seventh century and how little is known about it. Nineteen pieces of Argive pottery were catalogued. Of these, ten are Geometric or Subgeometric and belong to the late eighth and early seventh century. The other nine pieces belong to the second half of the seventh century; but of these

nine, only six were certainly identified as Argive; the remaining three have been designated "perhaps Argive (?)." The best discussion of seventh-century Argive pottery is Cook's, *BSA* 48 (1953) 34-41.

20. Brief notice of the discovery of Argive Black Figure pottery is made by Cook, *BSA* 48 (1953) 57, and "Chronique des fouilles," *BCH* 77 (1953) 253, and 81 (1957) 674 There is no detailed discussion of the style. On black glazed ware see Cook, *BSA* 48 (1953) 42 and *BCH* 79 (1955) 312; Argive monochrome: Cook, *GPP*, 23, Caskey, *Hesperia* 21 (1952) 202-207, and especially *Perachora* 2:291, 314-315. This "Argive Monochrome" pottery may not all have been of Argive manufacture. Although some of it may have been manufactured at Argos, it seems just as likely that most of it came from Corinth. It enjoyed a rather wide distribution, which closely parallels the distribution of Corinthian pottery. Boardman, *The Greeks Overseas*, 72-74, believes that some of the seventh-century monochrome ware found at al-Mina was Argive.

21. About ten percent of the miniature vases found at Tiryns (*Tiryns* 1:103-105) were imported from Corinth. About five percent of the miniature vases found in the most recent excavation at the Argive Heraeum were imported from Corinth; see Caskey, *Hesperia* 21 (1952) 187-207. William R. Biers, "Excavations at Phlius, 1924, the Votive Deposit," *Hesperia* 40 (1971) 397-423, notes that Argive influence predominates among the seventh-century miniature vases at Phlius, but is superseded by Corinthian influence in the sixth century.

22. It ought to be noted here, however, that at both Corinth and Athens a Subgeometric tradition lingered beside the new orientalizing styles, but it was the exception rather than, as at Argos, the rule. On Corinth see Weinberg, *Corinth* 7: Pt. I, 72-73, and for Athens see Rodney S. Young, *Late Geometric Graves and a Seventh Century Well in the Agora* (Athens, 1939), especially 140-141, 150-155, 163-164, 169-171, 173-177, 212-213.

23. For figurines found in the city and on the Larissa see *BCH* 54 (1930) 480; *BCH* 79 (1955) 314; *BCH* 81 (1957) 673-677; *BCH* 83 (1959) 761; *BCH* 89 (1965) 896; *BCH* 92 (1968) 1028, where most are from the sixth and fifth centuries. Phlius: *Hesperia* 40 (1971) 416-423. Anne Roes, "Les souris d'Argos aux yeux bandés," *BCH* 93 (1969) 333-336, discusses several seventh-century pieces found many years ago on the Larissa.

24. *AH* 2:3-44, where the classification and dating are not sound; *Tiryns* 1:50-93, where the dating is rather too early. Gertrud Baumgart, "Aus der heidelberger Sammlung II," *AA* 36 (1921) 288-297, stresses the provincial nature of the Tirynthian material. Some seven hundred figurines were found many years ago at Phlius and recently published in *Hesperia* 40 (1971) 416-423.

25. R. J. H. Jenkins, "Archaic Argive Terracotta Figurines to 525 B.C.," *BSA* 32 (1931-32) 23-40, and see also his *Dedalica: A Study of Dorian Plastic Art in the Seventh Century B.C.* (Cambridge, 1936) 24, 36-37, and also his discussion in *Perachora* 2:102, 241-248.

26. Georg Kaulen, *Daidalika: Wekstätten griechischer Kleinplastik des 7. Jahrhunderts v. Chr.* (Munich, 1967) 39-40, and also 18-22, where he discusses several bronze figurines which he identifies as Argive. Their actual place of origin is, however, far from certain

27. Boardman, *Island Gems*, 163-164, although on pp. 152-153 he notes

that the ivory seals may have been made either at Corinth or at Argos.

28. On the metal objects found at the Heraeum see *AH* 2:191-339, and the further bibliography cited in n. 21 Chapter IV above. Jacobsthal, *Greek Pins*, 3-15, 20-24, has reclassified and redated the pins and spits.

29. Many scholars, as for example, Charbonneaux, *Les bronzes grecs*, 39, following Herodotus 4.152, postulate an Argive origin for the griffin protome; but none have ever been found in the city and only one has been found at the Argive Heraeum; see Blegen, *AJA* 43 (1939) 428-430. Ulf Jantzen, *Griechische Geifenkessel* (Berlin, 1955) 41-52, leaves open the place of their origin.

30. Several of these objects would seem, however, to be imports; see below n. 38 and 39.

31. *AH* 1:110-111; Amandry, *Hesperia* 21 (1952) 223-226, dates the temple to the first half of the seventh century and suggests that it may be the oldest peripteral temple in the Peloponnesus. P. de la Coste Messelière, "Chapiteaux doriques du haut archaïsme," *BCH* 87 (1963) 639-652, dates one of the capitals from the temple later than 675 but earlier than 630 B.C. Recently, however, B. Berquist, *The Archaic Greek Temenos* (Lund, 1967) 19-21, has argued that the temple was constructed about the middle of the sixth century. Tilton, in *AH* 1:111, calculated that the temple was 36.3 meters long and 8.5 meters wide. This may be an exaggeration, but in any case the stylobate is preserved for a length of approximately 14 meters. The remains in the south quarter are reported in *BCH* 96 (1972) 168-177, 226-228.

32. On the Corinthian origin of these fragments see Jenkins, *Dedalica*, 45, and Humfry G. G. Payne, *Necrocorinthia: A Study of Corinthian Art in the Archaic Period* (Oxford, 1931) 233. They have been fully discussed by Gerhart Rodenwalt, "Metope aus Mykenai," *Corolla Ludwig Curtius* (Stuttgart, 1937) 63-66, and most recently by F. Harl-Schaller, "Die archaischen 'Metope' aus Mykene," *JdAOI* 50 (1972-73) 94-116, who questions many earlier assumptions about them.

33. On the temple of Enyalius see *BCH* 90 (1966) 782; on the temple of Aphrodite see *BCH* 93 (1969) 986-1002.

34. In this connection it may be worth noting that Jenkins, *Dedalica*, 10-24, has argued that the introduction of the Dedalic style in the seventh century embodied far more than merely the use of new techniques. He believes it reflected a complete change in man's intellectual attitude and his whole outlook on life. C. A. Robinson Jr., "The Development of Archaic Greek Sculpture," *AJA* 42 (1938) 451-455, and *AJA* 48 (1944) 132-134, surely goes too far when he connects the emergence of the new style with the rise of tyrants.

35. On ivory see *AH* 2:351-354, *Perachora* 2:403-451, and R. M. Dawkins, *The Sanctuary of Artemis Orthia at Sparta* (London, 1929) 203-248. On the chronology of the Spartan ivory see John Boardman, "Artemis Orthia and Chronology," *BSA* 58 (1963) 1-7.

36. *AH* 2:351-354; discs of this type were not manufactured after the first half of the seventh century, however; see *Perachora* 2:403, and also Boardman, *Island Gems*, 145-153.

37. *AH* 2:367-374, and see J. D. S. Pendlebury, *Aegyptiaca: A Catalogue of*

Egyptian Objects in the Aegean Area (Cambridge, 1930) 58-61, where they are dated to the last half of the seventh and first half of the sixth century. But this date must now be revised in view of the material from Perachora (*Perachora* 1 :461-516) where most are dated 750-650 B.C.

38. A few fibulae would seem to be imports see Christian Blinkenberg, *Fibules grecques et orientales* (Copenhagen, 1926) 204-230, *passim*. For vase attachments and other objects see Emil Kunze, "Verkännter orientalischer Kesselschmuck aus dem argivischen Heraion," *Reinecke Festschrift* (Mainz, 1950) 96-101, and Pierre Amandry, "Chaudrons à protomes de taureau en orient et en grèce," *Studies Presented to Hetty Goldman*, 239-261, especially 249-251, and Georg Karo, *Greek Personality in Archaic Sculpture* (Cambridge, Mass., 1948) 66-67, cites a number of other imports from Asia Minor. On the griffin protome found at Samos see Jantzen, *AM* 73 (1958) 31-32.

39. For a list of Cretan objects at the Argive Heraeum see John Boardman, *The Cretan Collection in Oxford: The Dictaean Cave and Iron Age Crete* (Oxford, 1961) 154, n. 6.

40. Attic Pottery at Argos see *AH* 1 :173-174; Caskey, *Hesperia* 21 (1952) 188; *Tiryns* 1 :106. The small amount of Attic pottery found here is recognized by Courbin, *Archaeology* 9 (1956) 173, and T. J. Dunbabin, "'Εχθρη παλαίη," *BSA* 37 (1936-37) 83-91, especially 84. Karo, *Greek Personality*, 66-67, greatly overestimates the Attic influence at Argos, for the vase fragments that serve as the basis of his discussion are probably not Argive; see Courbin, *BCH* 79 (1955) 10-12, n. 7. At Aegina there is a single terra-cotta figurine which Jenkins, *Dedalica*, 24, considers Argive. Kaulen, *Daidalika*, 18-22, considers several bronze figurines found at Olympia as Argive, but this designation is far from certain. The problem of their origin is discussed by Kaulen who refers to the earlier literature.

41. On the Protoargive fragments at Athens see above n. 9.

42. The phrase is Humfry G. G. Payne's, *Protokorinthische Vasenmalerei* (Berlin, 1933) 11, and see also *Perachora* 1 :32-33.

43. Protocorinthian pottery was found in abundance at Argos; see Courbin, *Archaeology* 9 (1956) 171; *BCH* 78 (1954) 180; *BCH* 79 (1955) 312, 314; *BCH* 83 (1959) 753-754, 762. It was also the most prevalent pottery at the Heraeum (*AH* 1 :50, 2 :119-155), and at Tiryns (*Tiryns* 1 :103-105). Caskey, *Hesperia* 21 (1952) 188, found Corinthian pottery in even greater quantity than Protocorinthian.

44. On terra-cottas see above pp. 79-80 and nn. 22 and 23. Pottery: *Perachora* 2 :368-371 and see above n. 19. Ivory: *Perachora* 1 :403, 426-428, where five seals are considered possibly Argive; see, too, Boardman, *Island Gems*, 153, who suggests that either Corinth or Argos was the main center for the production of ivory seals. Bronzes: *Perachora* 1 :123-184 where many parallels with the finds from the Argive Heraeum are noted.

45. Cythera: see above n. 2. Sparta: E. A. Lane, "Lakonian Vase-Painting," *BSA* 34 (1933-34) 122-123, 174, n. 4, notes several seventh- and sixth-century sherds of Spartan pottery found at the Argive Heraeum, and Olga Alexandri, "Une broche dédalique laconienne," *BCH* 88 (1964) 525-530, publishes a lead brooche of Spartan origin found at the site. Aegina: Jenkins, *Dedalica*, 24. Tegea:

Jenkins, *BSA* 32 (1931-32) 23-40, and R. A. Higgins, *Catalogue of the Terra-cottas in the Department of Greek and Roman Antiquities British Museum* (London, 1954) 272-276.

46. On this league see above nn. 3 and 4.

47. The inscription has not yet been published but see *BCH* 87 (1963) 755, *AJA* 67 (1963) 281, and the work of Jameson and Papachristodoulou in Chapter III, n. 19.

48. Emil Kunze, *Olympische Forschungen* 2: *Archaische Schildbänder: Ein Beitrage zur frühgriechischen Bildgeschichte und Sagenüberlieferung* (Berlin, 1950) 215-216, assembles the ancient evidence and concludes that the Argives invented the hoplite shield. Snodgrass, *EGAW*, 63-66, is unwilling to go that far, but in *Arms and Armour of the Greeks* (London, 1967) 66-67, he does suggest that the Argives played an important role in the development of the hoplite armor in the seventh century. A. Andrewes, *The Greek Tyrants* (London, 1956) 31-42, suggests that Pheidon was the first Greek to employ hoplite tactics.

49. Pindar, fr. 73; the evidence for the Heraea at Argos has been assembled by Irene C. Ringwood, *Agonistic Features of Local Greek Festivals Chiefly from Inscriptional Evidence* (Poughkeepsie, 1927) 67-69, and Irene R. Arnold, "The Shield of Argos," *AJA* 41 (1937) 436-440.

50. Pliny, *Natural History* 7.200; Apollodorus, *Bibliotheca* 2.2.1-2.

51. Pausanias, 2.25.7, and see also 8.50.1; *Ox. Papy.* 10.1241, especially col. 5, lines 1-36.

52. Pausanias 2.25.7. On this building and similar pyramid-shaped buildings in the Argolid see Louis E. Lord, "The 'Pyramids' of Argolis," *Hesperia* 7 (1938) 481-527, and "Blockhouses in the Argolid," *Hesperia* 10 (1941) 93-112. It is not at all clear, however, why such a building should have carried sculptured decoration as Pausanias reports.

53. This point is generally recognized by Snodgrass, *Arms and Armour of the Greeks*, 67-68. It is worth pointing out, too, that with the decline of painted pottery at Argos in the seventh century we do not even have pictorial representation as a guide.

54. These shield bands have been the subject of a careful study by Emil Kunze, *Olympische Forschungen* 2, who argues forcefully for an Argive origin. Additional discoveries at Olympia are reported and discussed by Emil Kunze, "Schildbeschläge," *Bericht über die Ausgrabungen in Olympia* 5 (Berlin, 1956) 51-58.

55. See *AHR* 75 (1970) 989-1000, and see below n. 58.

56. Pausanias 3.7.5 and 2.24.7, and see above n. 10.

57. The pertinent passages of Pausanias are 4.8.3, 4.10.1, and 4.11.1 on the First Messenian War, and 4.15.7-8 on the Second Messenian War. Apollodorus, *FGrH* 244 F 334, followed by Strabo 8.4.10 (362), also lists the Argives as allies of the Messenians in the Second War.

58. My remarks on the Battle of Hysiae in this paragraph are taken from my article, "Did the Argives Defeat the Spartans at Hysiae in 669 B.C.?," *AJP* 91 (1970) 31-42, where further bibliography has been cited.

59. I have discussed the unlikelihood that Argos participated in the Messenian wars more fully in *AHR* 75 (1970) 988-992, where additional bibliography has been cited.

60. Theopompus, *FGrH* 115 F 383; Pausanias 4.35.2.

61. There is no other evidence to help us date the event. An Argive king by the name of Damocratidas is otherwise unknown. Beloch, GG^2 1: Pt. 2, 194, long ago suggested that the name implied that he did not belong to the Temenid line of kings. Huxley, *ES*, 60, and "Argos et les derniers Téménides," *BCH* 82 (1958) 599, has suggested that Damocratidas must have been born at "a time when the *damos* was dominant at Argos." Huxley's argument is accepted by Wörrle, *UVA*, 87, n. 35, where he notes that this interpretation would necessitate dating the destruction of Nauplia well after the seventh century.

62. This point is stressed by Chester G. Starr, "The Early Greek City-State," *La parola del passato* 12 (1957) 97-108, and see also his *OGC*, 335-345.

63. Starr, *OGC*, 350-355, suggests that an "economic spirit" emerged in Greece in this century; see also Heichelheim, *AEH* 1:273-280.

64. The Egyptian objects found at the Heraeum have been discussed above, as have the ivory objects. Miniature vases at the Heraeum: *AH* 2:96-101, and Caskey, *Hesperia* 21 (1952) 193-207, and see especially 211 where he notes that they were probably a votive of poorer segments of the population. Tiryns: *Tiryns* 1:48, 94-106. Mycenae: Cook, *BSA* 48 (1953) 48-50. A number have recently been found in the city of Argos; see *BCH* 93 (1969) 996.

65. Snodgrass, *EGAW*, 197-199, and *Arms and Armour of the Greeks*, 48-77, traces the introduction and spread of hoplite armor throughout Greece and concludes that the phalanx formation did not make its appearance until the middle of the seventh century. In *JHS* 85 (1965) 110-112 he argues against the widely accepted notion that the new style of fighting had immediate and serious far-reaching social and political consequences.

66. On colonization see generally Aubrey Gwynn, *JHS* 38 (1918) 88-123; Starr, *OGC*, 365-378; J. Hasebroek, *Trade and Politics*, 105-110, points out that colonies were almost always founded by individuals, not states.

67. Hippys of Rhegion, *FGrH* 554 F 4 (Athenaeus 1.56, 3lb). The report is doubted by Jacoby in his commentary on this fragment and by T. J. Dunbabin, *The Western Greeks* (Oxford, 1948) 14-15, 93-94, and by Will, *Korinthiaka*, 342-343. Recently, however, René van Compernolle, "Syracuse, colonie d'Argos?," *Kokalos* 12 (1966) 75-101, has examined the whole problem of Argive colonization at Syracuse, including the evidence of myth, cult, and archaeology, and concluded that more work is needed on the history of Corinth and Argos in this period before a definitive decision might be reached.

68. The vases were published by Paolo Arias, "Geometrico insulare," *BCH* 60 (1936) 144-151, who believed they were Argive. This claim has been questioned many times but perhaps most effectively by Courbin, *CGA*, 34-38, who shows that they are of local manufacture and that they date to the early half of the seventh century. He acknowledges at the same time their striking resemblance to contemporary pieces at Argos and that they might have been the work of Argive painters resident at Syracuse.

69. These fragments have been discussed by Jeffery, *LSAG*, 154, 353-354, who believes it quite likely that Argive emigrants settled on the island; on pp. 153-154 she suggests that the well-known Euphorbus plate found at Camirus on Rhodes might be the work of the same craftsmen.

70. Bürchner, "Kalymna," *RE* (Stuttgart, 1919) 1768-1771.

71. Hesychius, *FGrH* 390 F. 1. The report is doubted by Jacoby in his commentary on this fragment and by Hanell, *Megarische Studien*, 123-129, 148. There are to be sure other traditions about the foundation of this colony which do not mention the Argives as participants; these traditions have been fully analyzed and discussed by Hanell.

72. Hanell, *Megarische Studien*, 194-195, but he assumes that this influence came indirectly through Megara, which he believes (pp. 69-91) was originally settled from Argos. He overlooks the fact that the Argive calendar came into existence not before the late eighth or early seventh century; on this see Martin P. Nilsson, *Die Entstehung und religiöse Bedeutung des griechischen Kalendars* (Lund, 1962) 31-32.

73. This date has not yet been confirmed by archaeological excavation. Boardman, *The Greeks Overseas*, 254-255, notes that the earliest finds from the site date from the late seventh century, but only limited investigation has thus far been conducted there.

Chapter VI

1. The ancient evidence will be discussed below. The following list of modern dates for Pheidon is representative, not exhaustive. G. L. Huxley, *ES*, 28-30, and *BCH* 82 (1958) 588-60, suggests 750-735; P. N. Ure, *The Origin of Tyranny* (Cambridge, 1922) 181-182, suggests 715-665; Beloch, *GG*² 1: Pt. 2, 196, suggests 660-630; Thomas Lenschau, *s.v.* "Pheidon," *RE* (Stuttgart, 1938) 1939-1945, suggests 660 or 650-613 B.C.; Conrad Trieber, *Pheidon von Argos* (Hannover, 1886), and Wilhelm Vollgraff, "Fouilles et sondages sur le flanc Oriental de la Larissa à Argos," *BCH* 82 (1958) 516-570, especially 536-537, have him living in the early decades of the sixth century. For additional bibliography on the dating of Pheidon see Willem Den Boer, *Laconian Studies* (Amsterdam, 1954) 55-64, and Markellos Th. Mitsos, Ἀργολική Πρωσοπογραφία (Athens, 1952) 180-182, *s.v.* "Φείδον."

2. This solution was offered long ago by Henricus Fischer, *Historiae Argivae Fragmenta* (Breslau, 1850) 43, and Müller, *Die Dorier* 1:104-105 n. 1. G. F. Unger carried this idea to its logical conclusion by writing biographies of both Pheidons; see "Die zeitverhältnisse Pheidons," *Philologus* 28 (1869) 399-424, and *Philologus* 29 (1870) 245-273. This theory was forsaken in the latter part of the nineteenth century only to be revived after the discovery of an inscription (*SEG* 11.290 and *SEG* 14.314) at Nemea bearing the name Pheidon but not referring to the Argive Pheidon; for additional bibliography on the inscription see Jeffery, *LSAG*, 150. Among recent scholars to believe that Herodotus confused the Argive tyrant with another man of the same name see Den Boer, *LS*, 60-61; Huxley, *BCH* 82 (1958) 601; Will, *Korinthiaka*, 317-318, n.5; Tomlinson, *Argos*, 81, and many others.

3. Herodotus 6.127; Ephorus, *FGrH* 70 F 115; Strabo 8.3.33 (358).

4. Pausanias 6.22.2.

5. On the primitive state of the Greek world in the early eighth century see Starr, *OGC*, 147-186.

6. The whole subject of the origin and development of the Olympic games deserves more judicious and considered treatment than it has received. Julius

Juethner's "Herkunft und Grundlegen der griechischen Nationalspiele," *Die Antike* 14 (1939) 231-264, is too much a product of its time, and Ludwig Drees, *Der Ursprung der olympischen Spiele* (Stuttgart, 1962), confidently relies on myth to place the origin of the games back in the sixteenth century B.C. Although A. Brinkmann, "Die olympische Chronik," *RhM* 70 (1915) 622-637, has shown that the names of the earliest recorded victors may well be authentic, there is no compelling reason to believe that the games were actually founded in 776 B.C. This is, nonetheless, the conclusion advanced by Augusta Hönle, *Olympia in der Politik der griechischen Staatenwelt (von 776 bis zum Ende des 5. Jahrhunderts)* (Tubingen, 1968) 5-13, 24-28. Thomas Lenschau, "Die Siegerliste von Olympia," *Philologus* 91 (1936-37) 396-411, has, for example, argued that the first Olympiad fell in the year 632/631 and that the games were held yearly thereafter until 584, after which they were held at four-year intervals. Albert Brouwers, "Lycurge et la date de la fondation des jeux olympiques," *Mélanges Georges Smets* (Brussels, 1952) 117-124, has also argued forcefully against the traditional date.

7. Eusebius preserves a report of Aristodemus of Elis to the effect that no records of victors were kept at Olympia until the twenty-eighth Olympiad, and a certain Polybius is credited with making the same claim. Jacoby, *FGrH* 414 F 1, comments on this passage and assigns Aristodemus to the early second century B.C., but this is far from certain. Although the first list of victors in the games seems to have been drawn up by Hippias probably late in the fifth century, Thucydides did not employ this means of dating and it became common only in the fourth century.

8. Aristotle, *Politics*, 1310b 26.

9. Plutarch, *Moralia*, 772d-773b; scholiast on Apollonius, 4.1212; both passages have been discussed by Will, *Korinthiaka*, 180-187, 344-346.

10. In addition to the works cited in nn. 1 and 2 above see Kophiniotou, *IA*, 224-231; J. H. Schneiderwirth, *Politische Geschichte des dorischen Argos* (Heiligenstadt, 1865). Even in this century, however, scholars continue to date Pheidon to the middle of the eighth century; see, for example, Felix Jacoby, *Das Marmor Parium* (Berlin, 1904) 158-162, and Gerhard Vitalis, *Die Entwicklung der Sage von der Rückkehr der Herakliden* (Greifswald, 1930) 15-16, but the main present-day advocates of the date are Huxley, *ES*, 28-30, and *BCH* 82 (1958) 588-601, and A. B. Dascalakis, *The Hellenism of the Ancient Macedonians* (Thessalonike, 1965) 127-130, and see also Helmut Berve, *Die Tyrannis bei den Griechen* (Munich, 1967) 1:6-7.

11. The ancient evidence for the Anolympiads has been assembled by Ludwig Ziehen, "Olympische (Spiele)," *RE* (Stuttgart, 1939) 2520-2536, and A. Andrewes, "The Corinthian Actaeon and Pheidon of Argos," *CQ* 43 (1949) 75-78.

12. Eusebius, *Chronica* 1:196, and see also Strabo 8.3.30 (355).

13. Pausanias 6.22.2.

14. Pausanias 2.24.7; I have not seen Falconer's edition of Strabo published at Oxford in 1807. This is still the most widely accepted date for Pheidon; see, for example, the works of Andrewes, Den Boer, Mitsos, Will, and Tomlinson cited in nn. 1, 2, and 11 and also H. T. Wade-Gery, *CAH* 3:761-762, and W. W. How and J. Wells, *A Commentary on Herodotus* 2, (Oxford, 1912), who say on p. 112

"Whether the emendation be justifiable or not, the date is most suitable. . . ."

15. Hönle, *Olympia der Politik der griechischen Staatenwelt*, 36, has recently argued that Pheidon must have usurped the games in the thirty-second Olympiad in 652. But the only evidence she presents is that two Megarians were victors in the games that year, and so far as we know as least, there were no Spartan victors. Oskar Viedebantt, "Forschungen zur altpeloponnesischen Geschichte I: Der Tyrann Pheidon von Argos," *Philologus* 81 (1925) 208-232, has argued that he usurped the games in the thirty-third Olympiad in 648, and Lenschau, *Philologus* 91 (1936-37) 395-411, has argued for a date of 625/624.

16. Ure. *The Origin of Tryanny*, 154-183, provides a good illustration of the problems involved in dating Pheidon and establishing his connection with coinage as these problems were understood a half century ago.

17. E. S. G. Robinson, "The Coins from the Ephesian Artemision Reconsidered," *JHS* 71 (1951) 156-167, and "The Date of the Earliest Coins," *NC* 16 (1956) 1-8.

18. The most effective arguments against the acceptance of the ancient reports that Pheidon was the inventor of coinage have been advanced by W. L. Brown, "Pheidon's Alleged Aeginetan Coinage," *NC* 10 (1950) 177-204. His argument has been challenged but not refuted by Donald Kagan, "Pheidon's Aeginetan Coinage," *TAPA* 91 (1960) 121-134, and see below n. 44.

19. This date has recently been suggested by R. Ross Holloway, "An Archaic Hoard from Crete and the Early Aeginetan Coinage," *The American Numismatic Society. Museum Notes* 17 (1971) 1-21.

20. See, for example, William Ridgeway, *The Origin of Metallic Currency and Weight Standards* (Cambridge, 1892) 211-215, 311-312; Percy Gardner, *A History of Ancient Coinage 700-300 B.C.* (Oxford, 1918) 110-116; W. Schwabacher, "Pheidonischer Münzfuss," *RE* (Stuttgart, 1938) 1946-1949, and most recently the articles of Brown and Kagan cited above in n. 18.

21. Ridgeway, *The Origin of Metallic Currency and Weight Standards*, 112-113, 169-194.

22. The most recent discussion of such measures is Mabel Lang's *The Athenian Agora 10: Weights, Measures, and Tokens* (Princeton, 1964) 39-48.

23. Herodotus 6.127 is precise and refers only to a Pheidonian system of μέτρα. This word is frequently translated into English as weights and measures, as for example, by A. D. Godley in his translation in the Loeb Classical Library (London, 1920) and in the Greek-English lexicon of Liddell-Scott. But this translation seems inappropriate here. Herodotus used the word μέτρα on ten other occasions in his work, and in none of these passages can it possibly have anything to do with weight. Ephorus, *FGrH* 70 F 115, says that Pheidon introduced μέτρα καὶ σταθμά, that is, weights and measures. The word σταθμός is used by Herodotus on nine different occasions when he wishes to say weight, but he does not use it in connection with Pheidon.

24. Ephorus, *FGrH* 70 F 115; Strabo 8.3.33 (358); Aristotle, *Ath. Pol.* 10.2 and fr. 480 (Rose); Pollux, *Onomasticon* 10.179; Theophrastus, *Characters* 30.11; Marmor Parium (*IG* 12.5) 106 1.30.

25. For its use at Athens see Aristotle, *Ath. Pol.* 10.2; this passage is extremely difficult to interpret and has given rise to a great deal of discussion; see most

recently, C. M. Kraay, "An Interpretation of Ath. Pol. Ch. 10.," *Essays in Greek Coinage Presented To Stanley Robinson* (Oxford, 1968) 1-9. For its use at Apollonia and the size of the Pheidonian medimnos in relation to the medimnos used at Delphi see *Fouilles de Delphes* 5, nr. 3, col. 2, lines 1-8, and Marcus N. Tod, *A Selection of Greek Historical Inscriptions to the End of the Fifth Century B.C.* (Oxford, 1948) 2.140. In all probablility the medimnos used at Delphi was the Aeginetan medimnos.

26. Pollux, *Onomasticon* 10.179, quoting Aristotle, see fr. 480 (Rose). Note too that Theophrastus, *Characters* 30.11, also speaks of the Pheidonian medimnos as a measure of grain.

27. Most attempts to determine the standard of linear measure supposedly introduced by Pheidon have taken their beginning from a bundle of spits found at the Argive Heraeum (*AH* 1:63). A fragment of Heracleides of Pontus (Wehrli, fr. 152) states that Pheidon dedicated spits at the Heraeum when he first began to issue coins. Many believe that these are the actual spits dedicated by Pheidon and that the length and weight of these spits provides a clue to his standards of linear and weight measure; see, for example, Paul Courbin, "Dans la grèce archaïque: Valeur comparée du Fer et de l'Argent lors de l'introduction du monnayage," *Annales Economies Sociétés Civilisations* 14 (1959) 209-233, where earlier bibliography is cited. This proposition has little to recommend it, however, for the spits are badly oxidized and their exact weight and length cannot be determined. It is less than likely, moreover, that they were in fact dedicated by Pheidon. If he dedicated spits anywhere, it would have to have been in the Old Temple of Hera. This building burned in the fifth cnetury, and the spits could hardly have survived the conflagration. One might, of course, argue that these spits were a fifth-century copy of Pheidon's original dedication. But this cannot be proven, and we know that spits were part of temple furniture at Argos and elsewhere. Caskey, *Hesperia* 21 (1952) 183, notes others found at the Heraeum, interestingly enough in a closed deposit dating from the second quarter of the seventh to the second quarter of the sixth century B.C.

28. The fifth-century temple of Hera employed the standard Doric foot of 0.326 meters, but there is no reason to suppose, as does Vollgraff, *BCH* 82 (1958) 520-521, that this standard was introduced by Pheidon. William B. Dinsmoor, "The Basis of Greek Temple Design: Asia Minor, Greece, Italy," *Extrait des rapports des XIe congrès international des sciences historiques* (Stockholm, 1960) 355-368, has shown that it was widely employed throughout the Greek world.

29. Ephorus, *FGrH* 70 F 115; Strabo 8.3.33 (358); see also Ridgeway, *The Origin of Metallic Currency and Weight Standards*, 213-215.

30. The pertinent passages are Ephorus, *FGrH* 70 F 115 and 176; Strabo 8.3.33 (358) and 8.6.16 (376); Orion, *Etymologicum Magnum*, *s. v.* "οβελός"; *Marmor Parium* 1.30; and Pollux, *Onomasticon* 9.83, who also mentions a number of other claimants for the honor of minting the first coins.

31. Ure, *The Origin of Tyranny*, 164-167, firmly believed that Argos controlled Aegina, and he attempted to show that Herodotus 5.88 offers proof of such control. But Dunbabin, *BSA* 37 (1936-37) 83-91, argues convincingly that this is not true.

32. Pausanias 2.29.5; Ephorus, *FGrH* 70 F 176.

33. Even during the Peloponnesian War, Argive troops were transported aboard Athenian ships; see Thucydides 7.20.1-3 and 8.86.8-9. At 8.27.5, however, Thucydides seems to imply that the Argives had some ships of their own.

34. See, for example, Will, *Korinthiaka*, 352-353, and Kagan, *TAPA* 91 (1960) 129.

35. Strabo 8.6.14 (374), and see *AJA* 70 (1966) 113-121.

36. On this war see Herodotus 5.82-88; it is impossible to date the war from his account. It is worth noting, however, that the Argives who aided the Aeginetans fought on land not on the sea.

37. This argument has been used many times; see, for example, E. Babelon, *Traité des monnaies grecquest et romaines* 1 (Paris, 1901) 642-643, 827, and Ridgeway, *The Origin of Metallic Currency and Weight Standards*, 215.

38. Both B. V. Head, *Historia Numorum* (Oxford, 1887) 366-368, and Percy Gardner, *Catalogue of Greek Coins in the British Museum* 6 (London, 1887) liii-liv, date the earliest Argive coins to about 500 B.C., a date followed by Babelon, *Traité des monnaies grecques et romaines* 1:827-835. Coins from the recent excavations at Argos have not been published nor have they been given more than passing mention in the preliminary reports that have thus far appeared.

39. One might, of course, argue that before the Argives began to mint their own coins they were content to use coins minted at Aegina. Although Aeginetan coins were widely respected and used in the sixth century, it is worth noting that, so far as I am aware, no Aeginetan coin has ever been found at Argos.

40. This assumption is so widespread it hardly needs citation, but see, for example, Charles Seltman, *Greek Coins*[2] (London, 1955) 37, and Mabel Lang, *The Athenian Agora* 10: *Weights, Measures, and Tokens*, 9.

41. P. Gardner, *History of Coinage*, 112-113, suggests, for example, that Pheidon did introduce a weight standard into Greece which was later used by the Aeginetans when they began to mint coins and that it was this that confused later writers such as Ephorus and led them to credit Pheidon with the invention of the first Greek Coins.

42. This was long ago suggested by Beloch, *GG*[2] 1: Pt. 2, 348-349, and see also J. Johnson, "Solon's Reform of Weights and Measures," *JHS* 54 (1934) 180-184, and most recently C. M. Kraay, *Essays in Greek Coinage Presented to Stanley Robinson* 4.

43. This is clear from the inscription cited in n. 25 above.

44. This conclusion is by no means new nor is it universally accepted. Heinrich Chantraine, "Literaturüberblicke der griechischen Numismatik," *Jahrbuch für Numismatik und Geldgeschichte* 8 (1957) 70-76, provides a useful annotated bibliography of the many modern works dealing with Pheidon and the introduction of coinage. The two extremes are well represented by Brown, *NC* 10 (1950) 177-204, who argues against a Pheidonian introduction, and Kagan, *TAPA* 91 (1960) 121-136, who attempts to refute Brown's arguments. Kagan is most likely correct in his belief that the Heracleides of Pontus mentioned by Orion in the *Etymologicum* (*s.v.* "οβελός") is the Heracleides who lived in the fourth century B.C. and, therefore, that Ephorus was not the only fourth-century scholar who connected Pheidon with the introduction of coinage. But there is no assurance that fourth-century writers knew a great deal about the event, and it is worth

noting that Orion on occasion used the work of another Heracleides of Pontus who probably lived in the first century A.D. It is not always easy to determine which Heracleides Orion is citing. For some interesting observations on the works of these two men with the same name see Fritz Wehrli, *Die Schule des Aristotle 7. Herakleides Pontikos* (Basle, 1953) 110-111, 117-119. Wehrli also believes that Orion got his information about Pheidon from the fourth-century Heracleides.

45. Herodotus 8.137-138; Thucydides 2.99.3. It is worth noting, too, that Euripides also shared the belief that the Macedonian monarchy was founded from Argos, but for Euripides, Archelaus, not Perdiccas, was the founder of the dynasty; see fragments of the *Archelaus* in A. Nauck, *Euripides Tragoediae 3* (Leipzig, 1892). On the story related by Herodotus see Hermann Kleinknecht, "Herodot und die makedonische Urgeschichte," *Hermes* 94 (1966) 134-146.

46. Theopompus, *FGrH* 115 F 393; Diodorus 7.17.1; both fragments are preserved only by Syncellus 499.

47. The fragments of Satyrus have been assembled by Carolus Müller, *Fragmenta Historicorum Graecorum* (Paris, 1841-70) 3:159-166; see especially fr. 21.

48. See Beloch, *GG*² 1: Pt. 2, 191-196; Busolt, *GG* 1:616-620; and especially Jacoby's commentary on *FGrH* 115 F 393. The fullest and most recent discussion is that of A. Dascalakis, *The Hellenism of the Ancient Macedonians*, 97-146, and also his " Ἀργεάδι-Τημενίδαι: Καταγωνὴ καὶ Ἱστορικὴ ἀπαρχὴ τοῦ βασιλικοῦ οἴκου τῆς Μακεδονίας," Ἐπιστημονικὴ Ἐπετηρὶς τῆς Φιλοσοφηκῆς Σχολῆς τοῦ Πανεπιστήμιου Ἀθηνῶν (1957-58) 35-110, who believes that the legend contains at least a kernel of truth. N. G. L. Hammond, *A History of Macedonia 1: Historical Geography and Prehistory* (Oxford, 1972) 432-433, seems to go even further.

49. Syncellus, 373 and 498, calls Pheidon the brother of Caranus, but at 499 he quotes Theopompus as referring to Pheidon as the father of Caranus.

50. Most modern scholars, including those cited in n. 48 above with the exception of Jacoby, believe that Theopompus (*FGrH* 115 F 393) dated Pheidon seventh in descent from Temenus, but this is not what the text of Syncellus, who preserves the fragment, says. Theopompus is quoted as saying that Caranus was seventh in descent from Temenus and that he was the son of Pheidon, who must, therefore, have been sixth in descent from Temenus.

51. Ephorus, *FGrH* 70 F 115.

52. On the Marmor Parium see Jacoby, *Das Marmor Parium* and *FGrH* 239 F 30, with commentary. Busolt, *GG* 1:616-617, argued that the author of the work got his genealogical information about Pheidon from Theopompus, but Jacoby rightly rejects this view.

53. Herodotus 6.127; Plutarch, *Moralia* 89e; Pausanias 2.19.2.

54. Pausanias 6.22.2 dated Pheidon's march on Olympia to 748 B.C., but he mentions at least three kings, Eratus, Damocratidas, and Meltas, who ruled Argos after that date; see 2.36.4; 4.35.2; and 2.19.2.

55. Diodorus 7.14.1; the fragment is preserved only by the Byzantine chronographer Malalas. The quotation comes from A. Andrewes, "Ephoros Book I and the Kings of Argos," *CQ* 45 (1951) 44, n. 3.

56. Diodorus's chronology and the problems it raises has been discussed by Jacoby in his commentary on Ephorus, *FGrH* 70 T 10 and F 223, and Apollodorus, *FGrH* 244 F 62. The pertinent passage of Diodorus is 16.76.5, which may

contain a scribal or computational error that would require a date of 1089 for the beginning of the Temenid line. The Diodorus figure 549 undoubtedly was derived genealogically; in all probability, it represents 16 1/2 generations of 33 1/3 years. The half generation is easily understandable since Meltas was deposed before his reign came to a natural end.

57. The bibliography on the chronological problems in Herodotus's history is lengthy. A good general discussion of the strengths and weaknesses of his chronology is given by How and Wells, *A Commentary on Herodotus* 1:437-442. More recent studies have reached conclusions that diverge widely. Hermann Strassburger, "Herodots Zeitrechnung," *Historia* 5 (1956) 129-161, and Molly Miller, "Herodotus as Chronographer," *Klio* 46 (1966) 109-128, argue that he had a definite and precise chronology, but F. W. Mitchel, "Herodotus' Use of Genealogical Chronology," *Phoenix* 10 (1956) 48-69, and Willem Den Boer, "Herodot und die Systeme der Chronologie," *Mnem.* 20 (1967) 30-60, argue, and rightly I believe, that he dated vaguely and by genealogical reckoning only. On the lack of chronological precision in this period see Chester G. Starr, *The Awakening of the Greek Historical Spirit*, (New York, 1968) 57-77, 137-140.

58. See, for example, F. Hiedbüchel, "Die Chronologie der Peisistratiden in der Atthis," *Philologus* 101 (1957) 70-89, who holds, among other things, that Herodotus was the "einzige" source of the Atthides for the chronology of the Peisistratids.

59. Herodotus 6.127.

60. The wooing of Agariste is discussed by Herodotus at 6.127; on Cleisthenes's anti-Argive policy see Herodotus 5.67-68. Malcolm F. McGregor, "Cleisthenes of Sicyon and the Panhellenic Festivals," *TAPA* 72 (1941) 266-287, discusses many of the problems surrounding Herodotus's account of the marriage and provides a useful bibliography on the subject. I cannot, however, accept his assumption (p. 274) that "a son of Pheidon seeking a sixth century bride is incredible." James W. Alexander, "The Marriage of Megacles," *CJ* 55 (1955) 129-134, has argued that there is nothing surprising in an Argive suitor turning up among the hopefuls.

61. Most modern scholars simply refuse to take Herodotus's date seriously; see, for example, the statement of McGregor quoted in the previous note. Only a few scholars have greeted the date favorably; see Conrad Trieber, *Pheidon von Argos*; Thomas Lenschau, "König Pheidon von Argos," *Philologus* 91 (1936-37) 385-395; and W. Vollgraff, *BCH* 82 (1958) 536-537.

62. The evidence for a Pheidonian empire will be discussed in the next chapter. On the distortion and misinterpretation of early Peloponnesian history by later writers see above Chapter V with the accompanying notes. E. N. Tigerstedt, *The Legend of Sparta in Classical Antiquity* (Stockholm, 1965), provides a carefully detailed study of the misinterpretation of Spartan history by later Greek writers, and see also Chester G. Starr, "The Credibility of Early Spartan History," *Historia* 14 (1965) 257-272.

63. The most recent discussion is D. M. Leahy's, "The Dating of the Orthagorid Dynasty," *Historia* 17 (1968) 1-23, where references to earlier works will be found.

64. F. W. Mitchel, "Megacles," *TAPA* 88 (1957) 127-130, in an interesting

article has argued that Herodotus provides evidence that requires us to believe that Cleisthenes was still ruling at Sicyon toward the middle of the sixth century.

65. The evidence has been discussed by McGregor, *TAPA* 72 (1941) 266-287, who opts for the year 572, as does Luigi Moretti, "Olympionikai, i vincitori negli antichi agoni olimpici," *Memorie della classe de scienze morali, storiche e filologiche: Atti dell' accademia nazionale dei Lincei* 8 (1957) 70. If the argument of Mitchel cited in the previous note is accepted, however, it would be necessary to believe that the announcement was made at a later Olympiad.

66. Cleisthenes's archonship is known only from epigraphical evidence; see Donald Bradeen, "The Fifth Century Archon List," *Hesperia* 32 (1963) 187-208. His archonship in 525/524 is in conflict with Herodotus 1.64, where it is reported that the Alcmeonids were in exile during the period of the Peisistratid tyranny, but see Peter J. Bicknell, "The Exile of the Alcmeonidai during the Peisistratid Tyranny," *Historia* 19 (1970) 129-131, who argues that the Alcmeonids were exiled only after the murder of Hipparchus and that Herodotus was misled by later Alcmeonid propaganda.

Chapter VII

1. Wilhelm Vollgraff, *BCH* 28 (1909) 192-195, has suggested that Pheidon created the Argive phratries, and in "De titulo Argivo antiquissimo anno MCMXXVIII recuperato," *Mnem.* 59 (1932) 369-393, he has argued that Pheidon instituted the office of demiourgos and first held it himself, but see the objections of Hammond, *CQ* 54 (1960) 33-36. W. Vollgraff, "De Erasino Argivo," *Mnem.* 60 (1932-33) 231-238, also suggests, on the evidence of nothing more than a fifth-century inscribed vase (*SEG* 11.329), that Pheidon constructed a fountain house in the city. Karl Schefold, "Kleisthenes," *Museum Helveticum* 3 (1946) 88-89, has suggested that Pheidon was responsible for the erection of the Old Temple at the Heraeum. Pheidon has recently been connected with the fine style of Late Geometric pottery at Argos by Courbin, *CGA*, 565, and Coldstream, *GGP*, 362, where it is suggested that this pottery may be a "Pheidonian Palace Style." On Pheidon and the introduction of hoplite warfare see Andrewes, *The Greek Tyrants*, 39-42, followed by A. R. Burn, *The Lyric Age of Greece* (London, 1960) 177-179, and Huxley, *ES*, 30. Ure, *The Origin of Tyranny*, 154-183, and Kophiniotou, *IA*, 224-225, greatly overemphasize the commercial interests of Pheidon; see also Z. Rubinsohn, "Pheidon of Argos: Military Reformer or Capitalist?," *Istituto Lombardo Rendiconti* 105 (1971) 636-642.

2. Herodotus 6.127; Ephorus, *FGrH* 70 F 115; Strabo 8.3.33 (358); Aristotle, *Politics* 1310b.

3. On the origin and nature of tyranny see Andrewes, *The Greek Tyrants*, 7-30; M. P. Nilsson, *The Age of the Early Greek Tyrants* (Belfast, 1936); Helmut Berve, "Wesenszüge der griechischen Tyrannis," *Historische Zeitschrift* 177 (1954) 1-30, and *Die Tyrannis bei den Griechen* 1:3-13, 164-167; and most recently Claude Mossé, *La tyrannie dans la grèce antique* (Paris, 1969) 3-9, and Robert Drews, "The First Tyrants in Greece," *Historia* 21 (1972) 129-144.

4. As has been suggested, for example, by Ure, *The Origin of Tyranny*, 154-183.

5. It is probably no more than coincidence, but Argos seems to have been one

of the first Greek states to publish its laws. The earliest inscribed law that I am aware of at Argos (*SEG* 11.314) dates from the first half of the sixth century.

6. On Pheidon of Corinth see Aristotle, *Politics* 1265b; Will, *Korinthiaka*, 317-318; and Lenschaus, *s.v.* "Pheidon" (2), *RE* (Stuttgart, 1938) 1939. Ancient writers obviously had difficulty keeping Pheidon of Argos and Pheidon of Corinth separate in their own minds; a good case in point is the author of the scholia to Pindar's *Ol.* 13. In his comments on *Ol.* 13.20 the scholiast says that weights and measurers were invented by "Pheidon, a man of Corinth." In his comments on *Ol.* 13.27, however, the scholiast says that the Pheidon who first struck Corinthian measures was an Argive.

7. The passage quoted comes from Ephorus, *FGrH* 70 F 115 as preserved in Strabo 8.3.33 (358); I have used the Loeb translation of H. L. Jones (London, 1927). On the Pheidonian mint on Aegina see Ephorus, *FGrH* 70 F 176; Strabo 8.6.16 (376).

8. See above pp. 75-76 ff. with the accompanying notes.

9. On this battle see Herodotus 1.82. It is referred to by a number of later writers; full references will be found in Luigi Moretti, "Sparta alla metà del VI. secolo II: La guèrra contro Argo per la Tireatide," *RFC* 26 (1948) 204-222.

10. On the development of the Peloponnesian League see Moretti, *Ricerche sulle leghe greche*, 5-81, and Wickert, *Der peloponnesische Bund von seiner Entstehung bis zum Ende des archidamischen Krieges*, 7-33.

11. For what it may be worth, this is implied by Ephorus's assertion that Pheidon recovered the Lot of Temenus. The cities traditionally included within this Lot were not controlled by Sparta at any time before their inclusion in the Peloponnesian League in the very late sixth and for the most part early fifth centuries.

12. The pertinent passages of Herodotus are: Olympic games, 6.127; Cynouria, 8.73; west coast of the Argolid and Cythera, 1.82; Epidaurus and Aegina, 5.82-88, 6.92; Sicyon, 6.92.

13. Plutarch, *Moralia* 772d-773b; scholiast to Apollonius 4.1212. Both passages and the confusion and contradictions in them have been discussed by Will, *Korinthiaka*, 180-187.

14. Nicolaus of Damascus, *FGrH* 90 F 35. It is entirely possible, of course, that later writers confused Pheidon of Argos with Pheidon of Corinth.

15. Periander's relations with other Peloponnesian states have been examined by Will, *Korinthiaka*, 540-547.

16. Little sixth-century pottery was uncovered during the original excavations at the Argive Heraeum; see *AH* 2:165-173, and Dunbabin, *BSA* 37 (1936-37) 83-84. Later excavation at the site produced a more substantial amount of sixth-century Corinthian material; see *Hesperia* 21 (1952) 187-193. Recent excavation has also revealed sixth-century Corinthian material from the city of Argos; see *BCH* 91 (1967) 825 (T 233) and 833 834 (T 211); see also *BCH* 92 (1968) 1027.

17. Herodotus 5.94 mentions that Peisistratus married an Argive woman. Aristotle, *Ath. Pol.* 17.4, supplies her name and the fact that she was previously married to a Cypselid. The use of the Pheidonian medimnos at Ambracia was discussed in the previous chapter. The traditional date for the foundation of

Ambracia is generally supported by the archaeological evidence from the site; see Boardman, *The Greeks Overseas*, 233.

18. Scholiast to Pindar, *Ol.* 13.27; but on the ancient confusion of the two Pheidons see above n. 6.

19. Strabo 8.6.14 (374) does not include Troezen among the states in the Calaurian Amphictiony, but Ulrich von Wilamowitz-Moellendorff, "Die Amphiktionie von Kalaurea," *Gött. Nachr.* (1896) 158-170 (*Kleine Schriften* 5:100-113) has argued that since the temple of Poseidon which served as the sacred center for the league was located in territory controlled by Troezen, this city must have been a member of the league.

20. On Procles see Herodotus 3.50-52.

21. Procles can be dated only through his connection with Periander, whose dates are far from secure but who was apparently tyrant of Corinth in the late seventh and early sixth centuries. The evidence for dating the Cypselids has been examined many times and various dates have been arrived at. See, for example, Will, *Korinthiaka*, 363-440, who opts for the so-called low chronology, and Jean Ducat, "Note sur la chronologie des Kypsélides," *BCH* 85 (1961) 418-425, and more recently Jean Servais, "Hérodote et la chronologie des Cypsélides," *AC* 38 (1969) 28-81, who prefer the so-called high dating.

22. Herodotus 5.82-87.

23. Ten pins from a tomb dating to the second quarter of the fifth century have been published by Semne Papaspuridi-Karouzou, " Ἀνασκαφὴ τάφων τοῦ Ἄργους," *AD* 15 (1933-35) 16-53. Jacobsthal, *Greek Pins*, 90, notes that they are no longer than earlier pins; he concludes, therefore, that Herodotus is incorrect on this point.

24. On Attic pottery imported at Aegina see Kraiker, *Aigina: Die Vasen des 10. bis 7. Jahrhunderts v. Chr.*, 25-26. For attempts to date the event from the material found at the Argive Heraeum see J. C. Hoppin, "The Argive exclusion of Attic Pottery," *CR* 12 (1898) 86-87; *AH* 2:174-176; Ure, *The Origin of Tyranny*, 314-320. Dunbabin, *BSA* 37 (1936-37) 83-91, is surely correct in arguing that the war cannot be dated on the basis of the archaeological evidence. However, Dunbabin's attempt to date it on the basis of the literary evidence is no more successful.

25. Both Ure and Dunbabin in the works cited in the previous note believe the war must have occurred in the time of Pheidon, whom they date to the early seventh century; see also Wade-Gery, *CAH* 3:540, and Bradeen, *TAPA* 78 (1947) 232.

26. It may be worth noting here that according to Thucydides 5.53.1 Epidaurus owed some sort of payment to Argos, but the reason for this payment is far from certain.

27. Herodotus 1.82, and see, for example, Ure, *The Origin of Tyranny*, 176.

28. I have discussed the evidence for this in *AHR* 75 (1970) 980-983, where a full bibliography is given.

29. This is the date suggested by Wade-Gery, *CAH* 3:556.

30. Herodotus 6.92.

31. On the reforms of Cleisthenes see Herodotus 5.67-69; on his military ability see Aristotle, *Politics* 1315b.

32. In addition to the report of Pheidon's usurpation of the Olympic games we might also note the erection of the monumental statue of Cleobis and Biton at Delphi about this time. These statues have been much discussed and variously dated, generally between ca. 615 and 580 B.C.; see Ludger Alscher, *Griechische Plastik* 1 (Berlin, 1954) 85-86; Jenkins, *Dedalica*, 74-75; Gisela M. A. Richter, *Kouroi. Archaic Greek Youths: A Study of the Development of the Kouros Type in Greek Sculpture* (New York, 1960) 81-82; Kaulen, *Daidalika*, 98-101. Perhaps the lowest date was advanced by Caskey, *Hesperia* 21 (1952) 173, who would place the statues in the second decade of the sixth century. The presence of an Argive suitor at Sicyon competing for the hand of Agariste (Herodotus 6.127) may also be a reflection of this interest in a wider world.

33. The ancient evidence for this war has been carefully examined by Marta Sordi, "La prima guerra sacra," *RFC* 21 (1953) 320-346, and see also W. G. Forrest, "The First Sacred War," *BCH* 80 (1956) 33-52, who has shown that it certainly was not a holy war. Callisthenes, *FGrH* 124 F 1, reports as one of the causes of the war that the people of Cirrha carried off the daughters of certain Argives who were returning home from the shrine. This would imply that the Argives might have participated in the war on the side of Sicyon, but there is no other evidence for Argive participation in this war, and Jacoby in his commentary on this fragment rightly rejects Callisthenes's account as an imitation of the Trojan War.

34. The notion that Cleisthenes was actually the founder of the Pythian games rests on no ancient evidence, though it has been widely accepted since the publication of J. B. Bury, *The Nemean Odes of Pindar* (London, 1890) 248-263. Bury (p. 249) cites as his evidence for this assertion Dunker, *History of Greece* 2:369, 370, which I have not seen.

35. The Sicyonian treasury at Delphi would appear to have been constructed in the fifth century; see Jeffery, *LSAG*, 142, for bibliography. P. de la Coste Messelière, *Au Musée de Delphes* (Paris, 1936) 77-95, sought to prove, however, that some older blocks and metopes lying near this fifth-century building actually belonged to an earlier construction on the site, which he believed was built by Cleisthenes. He argued, moreover, that the metopes bore pictographic representation that was unfavorable to Argos and that, therefore, Cleisthenes used the monument to put forth anti-Argive propaganda as part of his anti-Argive domestic policy. This is a fanciful but surely oversubtle interpretation; even a cursory viewing of these metope fragments shows nothing that need necessarily be interpreted as an affront to Argos.

36. Herodotus relates these events at 5.67-68. Cleisthenes's actions are almost universally considered anti-Dorian, but Eduard Will, *Doriens et Ioniens: Essai sur la valeur du critère ethnique appliqué à l'étude de l'histoire et de la civilisation grecques* (Paris, 1956) 39-55, has argued that his program was surely anti-Argive and antiaristocratic, but not as such anti-Dorian.

37. See, for example, Charles Skalet, *Ancient Sicyon*, 57, who simply assumes that "Cleisthenes proceeded to dissolve the union existing between the two cities, and to make his city fully independent of Argos."

38. The principal passages are Plutarch, *Moralia* 401d, 553a-b, and Pausanias 10.18.5.

39. The most strained interpretation of the evidence is Bury's *Pindar's Nemean Odes*, 248-263, but see also H. T. Wade-Gery, *CAH* 3:555-556, and McGregor, *TAPA* 72 (1941) 266-287.

40. It must be emphasized that there is no secure chronology for this period, and the dating of the First Sacred War to the decade of the 590's is far from certain. McGregor, *TAPA* 72 (1941) 266-287, believes that Cleisthenes's war with Argos and his anti-Argive policy took place only toward the end of his reign.

41. Pausanias 10.7.4 dates the founding of the Pythian games in the forty-eighth Olympiad, that is, between 588 and 584. The scholiast to Pindar, *Pyth*. 3, dates their founding to the forty-ninth Olympiad, that is, between 584 and 580 B.C. Eusebius gives the same date for the founding of the Isthmian games and dates the first Panathenaic to 566/565, a date generally confirmed by the Panathenaic amphorae.

42. We are better informed about the origin of the Panathenaic games than any of the others, but even for these the evidence is extremely confusing and generally unreliable; see J. A. Davison, "Notes on the Panathenaea," *JHS* 78 (1958) 23 and 82 (1962) 141.

43. The notion that these games were founded by the tyrants was first advanced by Bury, *Pindar's Nemean Odes*, 249-263. McGregor, *TAPA* 72 (1941) 266-287, acknowledges that the Pythian and Olympic games owe some debt to the tyrants but argues that the Nemean and Isthmian games were founded in opposition to the tyrants.

44. Herodotus 5.67 relates that Cleisthenes transferred the sacrifices and festivals from Adrastus to Melanippus. The scholiast to Pindar, *Pyth*. 9, however, asserts that Cleisthenes established Pythian games at Sicyon, and this evidence is accepted by McGregor, *TAPA* 72 (1941) 282-283, and Irene C. Ringwood, *Agonistic Features of Local Greek Festivals Chiefly from Inscriptional Evidence*, 64-65.

45. Pausanias 6.22.2. Although Pausanias says that Pheidon and the Pisatans controlled the games only for one Olympiad, it has often been assumed, largely on the basis of Strabo 8.3.30 (355) and Eusebius, that this began an uninterrupted interlude of Pisatan control of the games; see, for example, H. T. Wade-Gery, *CAH* 3:544-548, and the previous chapter.

46. Ephorus *FGrH* 70 F 115.

47. The evidence for the founding of these games is scattered, and most of it has been referred to in the notes above. Our most trustworthy reports come from Pindar, *Nem*. 4.17 and 10.42, which leave no doubt about the fact that the games were under the direction of the men of Cleonae at least in the early fifth century. The evidence has been assembled by Krister Hanell, " Nemea (Spiele,)" *RE* (Stuttgart, 1935) 2322-2327.

48. Strabo 8.6.19 (377) says that Cleonae aided Argos in the destruction of Mycenae in the 460's and we know from *IG* 1² 931-932 that some men of Cleonae fought with the Athenians and Argives at the Battle of Tanagra.

49. Adrastus's close connection with Argos in Greek mythology is evident from his role as leader of the Argives in the campaign against Thebes. Pindar, *Nem*. 9.9 and 10.28, regards him as the founder of the Nemean games.

50. The earliest reference to these games is found in an inscription (*SEG*

11.305) that was published by Lloyd W. Daly, "An Inscribed Capital from the Argive Heraeum," *Hesperia* 8 (1939) 165-169, and dated by Jeffery, *LSAG*, 169, ca. 525-500 B.C. Herodotus 1.31 indicates, however, that these games were already being celebrated in the period when the statues of Cleobis and Biton were set up at Delphi in the early decades of the sixth century.

51. On the games see Pindar, *Nem.* 10.20.; *Ol.* 7.152 and 9.132. See also, Irene P. Arnold, *AJA* 41 (1937) 436-440, and Axel Boëthius, "Der argivischer Kalendar," *Upsala Universitets Arskrift* (1922) 36-63, and Nilsson, *Griechische Feste von religiöser Bedeutung*, 42-45. In the early period a shield was given as a prize, but from the early fifth century onward we have a number of bronze hydriai which were awarded to the victors. On these vases see Dietrich von Bothmer, "Bronze Hydriai," *Metropolitan Museum of Art Bulletin* 13 (1954-55) 193-200, and Erika Diehl, *Die Hydriai: Formgeschichte und Verwendung im Kult des Altertums* (Mainz, 1964) 23-25. The earliest of these hydriai dates from about 490 B.C. and was found at Sinope; see Ekrem Akurgal and Ludwig Budde, "Vorläufiger Bericht über die Ausgrabungen in Sinope," *Türk Tarih Kurumu Yayinlarindan* 5 (1956) 12-15.

52. On the construction at the site in this period see Hans Lauter, "Zur frühklassischen Neuplanung des Heraions von Argos," *AM* 88 (1973) 175-187.

53. The oracle is preserved in the *Palatine Anthology* 14.73, but there were several versions of the text in antiquity, and it appears to be early. Parke and Wormell, *The Delphic Oracle* 2:1-2, attempt to trace it back to Ion of Chios, but this may be an overstatement. Ion is not referred to in any of the citations that have come down to us, and Jacoby does not include the text of the oracle among the fragments of Ion.

54. The oracle is the one referred to in the previous note. It is commonly dated to the early part of the seventh century, as for example, by Parke and Wormell, *The Delphic Oracle* 1:82-83, and Gschnitzer, *Abhängige Orte*, 77, but only on the assumption that Pheidon ruled in that period.

55. In this connection it may be worth noting that Pausanias 6.22.3 mentions that at the forty-eighth Olympiad in 588 B.C. the Eleans suspected that the Pisatans were intriguing against them and invaded Pisatan territory. The Eleans, however, proceeded to conduct the games that year.

Chapter VIII

1. The inscriptions are *IG* 4.614 (*SEG* 11.336); *SEG* 11.314; *IG* 4.506 (*SEG* 11.302); on their dates see Jeffery, *LSAG*, 156-158, where additional bibliography is cited.

2. This is the interpretation favored by Jeffery, *LSAG*, 157-158, and Hammond, *CQ* 54 (1960) 33-36. However, Vollgraff, *Mnem.* 59 (1932) 369-393, has argued that the verb ἐϝανάσσαντο can not be taken literally here. He noted that the names of the nine demiourgoi were prominent in early Argive mythology and concluded that they were not names of actual men but rather a line of demiourgoi who had held the office of demiourgos before Pheidon, who, Vollgraff believed, initiated the office. He preferred to take the verb in a poetic rather than a literal sense. Vollgraff's arguments have been accepted by Kentarô Murakawa,

"Demiurgos," *Historia* 6 (1957) 386-415, especially 411, but are doubted by Jeffery and effectively refuted by Hammond.

3. This inscription (*SEG* 11.314) was initially published by Vollgraff, *Mnem.* 57 (1929) 206-234, who dated it too early. Carl D. Buck, *The Greek Dialects*[2] (Chicago, 1955) no. 83, offers an English translation

4. This point is made by Wörlle, *UVA*, 65.

5. This inscription *IG* 4.506 (*SEG* 11.302) was initially published by J. D. Rogers, "Fragment of an Archaic Argive Inscription," *AJA* 5 (1901) 159-174, who believed the bronze was broken on both ends. He suggested two rather elaborate restorations, neither of which seems well founded. Indeed, the text seems beyond restoration, but see Jeffery, *LSAG*, 405.

6. The evidence for demiourgoi at Argos, as well as their duties and functions, has been discussed by Wörrle, *UVA*, 61-70, and see also K. Murakawa, *Historia* 6 (1957) 391-392, 411-412.

7. The options are well-stated by Hammond, *CQ* 54 (1960) 35-36.

8. Herodotus 1.82 is the chief source for the battle, but it is referred to by many later writers. Luigi Moretti, "Sparta ala metà del VI. secolo. II: La guerra contro Argo per la Tireatide," *RFC* 26 (1948) 204-222, contains full references to the ancient literature.

9. It may be worth noting here that Chrysermus, *FGrH* 287 F 2, reports that a certain Thersander was in charge of Argive forces in the battle. This information is repeated by Plutarch, *Moralia* 306a-b, but Thersander is otherwise unknown. Pausanias 2.20.7 reports seeing a statue of Perilaus slaying Othryadas, the last Spartan survivor of this battle. At 2.23.7 Pausanias mentions that a certain Perilaus was once tyrant of Argos, but it cannot be determined if this was the same Perilaus mentioned at 2.20.7. Mitsos, *s.v.* "Περίλαυς," *AP* believes they were two different men.

10. Jeffery, *LSAG*, 157, n. 1, has in fact suggested that Meltas was deposed about 560 B.C., but she is not convinced that he is the grandson of Pheidon. She believes, rather, that there were two Argive rulers named Pheidon: one, the famous tyrant, she believes ruled about 670, and the other, who was the grandfather of Meltas, ruled about 610.

11. This is the interpretation of Wörrle, *UVA* 65, though Hammond, *CQ* 54 (1960) 36, believes the nine demiourgoi served as a "board."

12. Huxley, *BCH* 82 (1958) 599-601, has argued that the demiourgoi represented a democratic and anti-Heraclid reaction, but as Wörrle, *UVA*, 64, n. 12, points out, this conclusion is difficult to accept.

13. This point is stressed by Huxley, *ibid.*, and also by Vollgraff, *Mnem.* 59 (1932) 369.

14. Plato. *Laws*, 690d-e, 691a; *Eighth Epistle*, 354b. The authenticity of this epistle has been much disputed, but see most recently G. J. D. Aalders H. Wzn, "The Authenticity of the Eighth Platonic Epistle Reconsidered," *Mnem.* 32 (1969) 233-257.

15. Plutarch, *Lycurgus*, 7.

16. Plutarch, *Moralia*, 340c, where the oracle is preserved. Parke and Wormell *The Delphic Oracle* 1:114-115, argue that the oracle was a later invention.

17. Pausanias 2.19.2, and see Andrewes, *CQ* 45 (1951) 39-40, who argues that Pausanias derived this information from Ephorus. Andrewes may be correct, but it is worth noting here that Ephorus seems not to have been extensively used by Pausanias.

18. Diodorus, fr. 7.13.2; the translation is C. H. Oldfather's in the Loeb Classical Library edition (London, 1939).

19. This point seems not to be generally understood; cf. Huxley, *ES*, 131, n. 394, who believes that Argos and Arcadia must have been allied at the time of the war.

20. If we assume that Ephorus was Diodorus's source, it is worth noting that Andrewes, *CQ* 45 (1951) 39-45, has argued that Ephorus believed Peloponnesian history revolved around a constant struggle between Argos and Sparta. I have elsewhere (*AHR* 74 [1970] 985-988) accepted Andrewes's argument while drawing somewhat different conclusions from it. Since Ephorus was convinced that there was a constant struggle between the two states, it should not be entirely surprising that Diodorus reports that a war with Sparta led to the deposition of the Argive king.

21. It is possible that the fragment of Diodorus, 7.13.2, quoted above, could be interpreted as an Argive attempt to stem the tide of the Spartan advance, but as I have argued, the account presents so many problems that it is difficult to interpret.

22. See above n. 8 and also Angelo Brelich, *Guèrre, agoni e culti nella grecia arcaica*, 24-36.

23. Strabo 8.6.14 (374).

24. This point is made by Wörrle, *UVA*, 70, who also notes that demiourgoi did continue to exist at other communities in the Argolid, including Mycenae.

25. One of these tyrants, Perilaus, is known only from Pausanias; see above n. 9. The other, Archinus, is known only from Polyaenus 3.8, who calls him tyrant, and from a scholiast on Pindar, *Ol.* 7.152, where he is called king. Both men have been dated to the sixth century and also to the third century B.C.; on this see the appropriate entries in Mitsos, *AP*, and Berve, *Die Tyrannis bei den Griechen* 1:35 and 2:537. On the fifth-century king at Argos see Herodotus 7.149 and *SEG* 11.316, where he is clearly an eponymous official.

26. After the Battle of Champions Argos and Sparta did not go to war again until 494; see Herodotus 6.76-83. I have examined later Argive foreign policy in "Argive Foreign Policy in the Fifth Century B.C.," *CP* 69 (1974) 81-99, where I have attempted to show that Argive-Spartan enmity was not the motivating force behind fifth-century Argive foreign policy and that it was only in 421 that the Argives began to show concern about the recovery of Cynouria.

27. On Timonassa and her marriage to Peisistratus see Aristotle, *Ath. Pol.* 17.3-4, 19.4. Herodotus 5.94 notes that Peisistratus had a bastard son by an Argive woman, but he does not mention her name.

28. On the Calaurian Amphictiony see Strabo 8.6.14 (374); on the wars between Athens and Aegina and Argive participation in them see Herodotus 5.82-87 and 6.92.

29. This is nowhere stated explicitly in the ancient literature but has frequently been suggested by modern scholars. Plutarch, *Cato* 24, states that Timonassa

was Peisistratus's second wife and that he married her when he already had grown sons; but Plutarch may well be confused. He lists the sons of the marriage to Timonassa as Iophon and Thessalus but makes no mention of Hegesistratus. Aristotle, however, knew Thessalus only as another name for Hegesistratus. For a discussion of the evidence for the marriages and sons of Peisistratus see Beloch, GG^2 1: Pt. 2, 297-298; Schachermeyr, *s.v.* "Peisistratiden," *RE* 151-153, and "Peisistratos (3)," *RE*, 167-172; and Friedrich Cornelius, *Die Tyrannis in Athen* (Munich, 1929) 26, 41, 78-80.

30. On the troops being mercenaries see Herodotus 1.61; on their being commanded by Hegesistratus see Aristotle, *Ath. Pol.* 17.4; and on the establishment of Hegesistratus at Sigeum see Herodotus 5.94.

31. Tomlinson, *Argos*, 91-92, follows Aristotle slavishly and considers his remarks "definite evidence" that Argos sought closer ties with Athens in this period. He believes, moreover, that the Argive mercenaries at Pallene were not "mercenaries in the conventional sense," but men sent, apparently, with the blessing of the state.

32. Herodotus 1.62-65 implies that the Battle of Pallene occurred before the fall of Sardis; it is entirely possible that it occurred before, not after, the Battle of Champions; though most scholars prefer to date Pallene later. The whole matter is tied up with the chronology of Peisistratus's periods of exile and rule. The most recent discussions of the problem are those of J. G. F. Hind, "The 'Tyrannis' and the Exiles of Peisistratus," *CQ* 24 (1974) 1-18, and J. S. Ruebel, "The Tyrannies of Peisistratus," *GRBS* 14 (1973) 125-136, who would date the Battle of Pallene to 534.

33. Herodotus 1.82 reports that losses were heavy on both sides. It is worth noting here, however, that at 6.92 Herodotus reports that the Argives were able to send 1,000 volunteers to aid the Aeginetans in their war against Athens just a few years after the supposedly costly Battle of Sepeia. For further dicussion of the problems raised by Herodotus's account of this battle, see the works cited in n. 37 below.

34. It has frequently been suggested that the Argives began to erect fortification walls around their city in the latter half of the sixth century; see, for example, Vollgraff, *BCH* 31 (1907) 151-152, and *MKAW* 72 (1932) 72; *BCH* 81 (1956) 366; Robert L Scranton, *Greek Walls* (Cambridge, Mass., 1941) 27, 160. But Franz G. Maier, *Griechische Mauerbauinschriften* (Heidelberg, 1959) 1:145-146, notes that there is really no proof that the walls on the Larissa date from the sixth century. Excavation has recently been resumed in the area, but thus far no reliable evidence for dating the walls has come to light; see *BCH* 89 (1965) 896-897 and *BCH* 90 (1966) 932-933.

35. The war is not mentioned in any literary source and is known from an inscription (*SEG* 11.305) found near the Argive Heraeum and published by Lloyd W. Daly, "An Inscribed Doric Capital from the Argive Heraeum," *Hesperia* 8 (1939) 165-169. On the date of the inscription see Jeffery, *LSAG*, 159.

36. Herodotus 6.92.

37. Herodotus 6.76-83 is our chief source for the Battle of Sepeia, but see also Socrates, *FGrH* 310 F 6; Plutarch, *Moralia*, 223a-c, 245c-f; Pausanias 2.20.8-10, 3.4.1, 3.10.1. Herodotus says the slaves took control of the city and ruled

until a new generation of Argives grew up. Aristotle, *Politics*, 1303a, says that the Argives were forced to admit some of the perioikoi to citizenship, but the ancient evidence for perioikoi at Argos is less than conclusive. It has been examined by Gaetano di Sanctis, "Argo e i gimneti," *Saggi di storia antica e di archeologica offerti a Guilio Beloch* (Rome, 1910) 235-239, and F. Gschnitzer, *Abhängige Orte*, 68-82, who concludes that the sources leave us "im wesentlichen im Stich." On the battle and its consequences for Argos see Franz Kiechle, "Argos und Tiryns nach der Schlacht bei Sepeia," *Philologus* 104 (1960) 181-200; R. F. Willetts, "The Servile Interregnum at Argos," *Hermes* 87 (1959) 495-506; W. G. Forrest, "Themistokles and Argos," *CQ* 54 (1960) 221-241, and most recently M. Zambelli "Per la storia di Argo nella prima metà del V secolo a. C.," *RFC* 99 (1971) 148-158.

38. Herodotus 7.148.

BIBLIOGRAPHY

Bibliography

Alexander, James W. The Marriage of Megacles, *CJ* 55 (1955) 129-134.

Alexandri, Olga. Une broche dédalique laconienne, *BCH* 87 (1964) 525-530.

Ålin, Per. *Das Ende der mykenischen Fundstätten auf dem griechischen Festland: Studies in Mediterranean Archaeology* 1 (Lund, 1962).

Allen, Thomas W. Argos in Homer, *CQ* 3 (1909) 81-98.

Amandry, Pierre. Observations sur les monuments de l'Héraion d'Argos, *Hesperia* 21 (1952) 222-274.

Andrewes, Antony. The Corinthian Actaeon and Pheidon of Argos, *CQ* 43 (1949) 70-78.

———. Ephoros Book I and the Kings of Argos, *CQ* 45 (1951) 39-45.

———. Phratries in Homer, *Hermes* 89 (1961) 129-140.

Arbanitopoulos, A. S. ᾿Ερευναι ἐν ᾿Αργολίδι, *Praktika* (1916) 75-99.

———. ᾿Ανασκαφαί καί ᾿Ερευναι ἐν ᾿Αργολίδι καί Θεσσαλία, *Praktika* (1920) 17-28.

Arnold, Irene P. The Shield of Argos, *AJA* 41 (1937) 436-440.

Balcer, Jack M. The Mycenaean Dam at Tiryns, *AJA* 78 (1974) 141-149.

Barrett, W. S. Bacchylides, Asine, and Apollo Pythaieus, *Hermes* 82 (1954) 421-444.

Berquist, B. *The Archaic Greek Temenos* (Lund, 1967).

Blegen, Carl W. *Prosymna: The Helladic Settlement Preceding the Argive Heraeum* 2 volumes (Cambridge, England, 1937).

———. Post-Mycenaean Deposits in Chamber Tombs, *Arch. Eph.* (1937) 377-390.

———. Prosymna: Remains of Post-Mycenaean Date, *AJA* 43 (1939) 410-444.

———. The Mycenaean Age, the Trojan War, the Dorian Invasion and Other Problems, *Lectures in Memory of Louise Taft Semple* (Princeton, 1967) 1-41.

Boardman, John. *Island Gems: A Study of Greek Seals in the Geometric and Early Archaic Period* (London, 1963).

201

————. Artemis Orthia and Chronology, *BSA* 58 (1963) 1-7.

Boëthius, Axel. Der argivische Kalender, *Uppsala Universitets Årsskrift* (1922) 1-72.

————. Zur Topographie des dorischen Argos, *Strena Philologica Upsaliensis Festskrift Per Persson* (Uppsala, 1922) 248-288.

Bommelaer, Jean-François. Nouveau documents de céramique protoargienne, *BCH* 86 (1972) 229-251.

———— and Grandjean, Y. Recherches dans le quartier sud d'Argos, *BCH* 96 (1972) 155-228.

Bradeen, Donald. The Lelantine War and Pheidon of Argos, *TAPA* 78 (1947) 223-241.

Brelich, Angelo. *Guerre, agoni e culti nella grecia arcaica* (Bonn, 1961).

Brinkmann, A. Die olympische Chronik, *RhM* 70 (1915) 622-637.

Brouwers, Albert. Lycurge et la date de la fondation des jeux olympiques, *Mélanges Georges Smets* (Brussels, 1952) 117-124.

Brown, W. L. Pheidon's Alleged Aeginetan Coinage, *NC* 10 (1950) 177-204.

Bury, John B. *The Nemean Odes of Pindar* (London, 1890).

Busolt, Georg. *Die Lakedaimonier und ihre Bundesgenossen* (Leipzig, 1878).

Callmer, Christian. *Studien zur Geschichte Arkadiens* (Lund, 1943).

Caskey, John L. Investigations at the Heraion of Argos, 1949, *Hesperia* 21 (1952) 165-221.

————. The Ancient Settlement at Lerna in the Argolid, *Geras Antoniou Keramopoullou* (Athens, 1953) 24-28.

————. The Early Helladic Period in the Argolid, *Hesperia* 29 (1960) 285-303.

————. Lerna in the Early Bronze Age, *AJA* 72 (1968) 313-316.

Chantraine, Heinrich. Literaturüberblicke der griechischen Numismatik, *Jahrbuch für Numismatik und Geldgeschichte* 8 (1957) 70-76.

Charitonidis, Seraphim. 'Ανασκαφὴ ἐν ''Αργεη, *Praktika* (1952) 413-426.

————.'Ανασκαφαὶ ἐν Ναυπλία, *Praktika* (1953) 191-204.

————. 'Ανασκαφαὶ Ναυπλίας, *Praktika* (1954) 232-241.

Charles, Robert P. Etude anthropologique des nécropoles d'Argos. Contribution à l'étude des population de la grèce antique, *BCH* 82 (1958) 268-313.

————. *Études Péloponnésiennes* 3: *Étude anthropologique des nécropoles d'Argos. Contribution à l'étude des population de la grèce antique* (Paris, 1963).

Coldstream, J. N. *Greek Geometric Pottery* (London, 1968).

Compernolle, René van. Syracuse, colonie d'Argos?, *Kokalos* 12 (1966) 75-101.

Cook, J. M. The Agamemnoneion, *BSA* 43 (1953) 30-68.

————. The Cult of Agamemnon at Mycenae, *Geras Antoniou Keramopoullou* (Athens, 1953) 112-118,

Courbin, Paul. Un fragment de cratère protoargien, *BCH* 79 (1955) 1-49.

————. Une rue d'Argos, *BCH* 80 (1956) 183-213.

————. Discoveries at Ancient Argos, *Archaeology* 9 (1956) 166-174.

————. Une tombe géométrique d'Argos, *BCH* 81 (1957) 322-386.

————. Dans la grèce arachaïque: Valeur comparée du Fer et de l'Argent lors de l'introduction du monnayage, *Annales Economies Sociétés Civilisations* 14 (1959) 209-233.

―――. Stratigraphie et stratigraphie: Méthodes et perspectives, *Études Archéologiques* 1 (1963) 59-102.

―――. *La céramique géométrique de l'Argolide* (Paris, 1966).

―――. *Études Péloponnésiennes* 7: *Tombes géométriques d'Argos*, 1 (1952-1958), (Paris, 1974).

Croissant, F. Note de topographie argienne (à propos d'une inscription de l'Aphrodision), *BCH* 96 (1972) 137-154.

Daly, Lloyd W. An Inscribed Doric Capital from the Argive Heraeum, *Hesperia* 8 (1939) 165-169.

Dascalakis, A. Ἀργεάδι-Τημενίδι: Καταγωγὴ καὶ Ἱστορικὴ ἀπαρχὴ τοῦ βασιλικοῦ οἴκου τῆς Μακεδονίας, Ἐπιστημονικὴ Ἐπςτηρὶς τῆς Θιλοσοφικῆς Σχολῆς τοῦ Πανεπιστημίον Ἀθηνῶν (1957-58) 35-110.

―――. *The Hellenism of the Ancient Macedonians* (Thessalonike, 1965).

Dawkins, R. M. *The Sanctuary of Artemis Orthia at Sparta* (London, 1929).

Den Boer, Willem. *Laconian Studies* (Amsterdam, 1954).

Desborough, V. R. d'A. *Protogeometric Pottery* (Oxford, 1952).

―――. Four Tombs, *BSA* 49 (1954) 258-266.

―――. Three Geometric Tombs, *BSA* 50 (1955) 239-247.

―――. *The Last Mycenaeans and Their Successors, an Archaeological Survey, c. 1200-c. 1000 B.C.* (Oxford, 1964).

―――. The Greek Mainland, c. 1150-1000 B.C., *Proceedings of the Prehistoric Society* 31 (1965) 213-228.

―――. *The Greek Dark Ages* (London, 1972).

―――. Late Burials from Mycenae, *BSA* 68 (1973) 87-101.

Deshayes, Jean. Les vases mycéniens de la Deiras (Argos), *BCH* 77 (1953) 58-89.

―――. *Études Péloponnésiennes* 4: *Argos: Les fouilles de la Deiras* (Paris, 1966).

―――. Les vases Vollgraff de la Deiras, *BCH* 93 (1969) 574-616.

Drerup, Heinrich. *Griechische Baukunst in geometrischer Zeit* (Göttingen, 1969).

Dunbabin, Thomas J. Ἐχθρη παλαίη, *BSA* 37 (1936-37) 83-91.

―――. *Perachora: The Sanctuaries of Hera Akraia and Limenia* 2: *Pottery, Ivories, Scarabs and Other Objects from the Deposit of Hera Limenia* (Oxford, 1962).

Erzen, Afif. Das Besiedlungsproblem Pamphyliens in Altertum, *AA* (1973) 388-401.

Fischer, Henricus. *Historiae Argivae Fragmenta* (Breslau, 1850).

Forrest, W. G. The First Sacred War, *BCH* 80 (1956) 33-52.

―――. *A History of Sparta 950-192 B.C.* (London, 1968).

Frickenhaus, August and Müller, Walter. Aus der Argolis: Bericht über eine Reise von Herbst 1909, *AM* 36 (1911) 21-38.

Friedländer, Paul. Zur Frühgeschichte des Argivischen Heraions, *AM* (1909) 69-79.

Frödin, Otto and Persson, Axel. *Asine: Results of the Swedish Excavations, 1922-30* (Stockholm, 1938).

Fürst, Carl M. Zur Anthropologie der prähistorischen Griechen in Argolis, *Acta Universitatis Lundensis* 26 (1930) 1-130.

Giovannini, A. *Étude historique sur les origines du catalogue des vaisseaux* (Bern, 1969).

Gschnitzer, Fritz, *Abhängige Orte im griechischen Altertum* (Munich, 1958).

Guarducci, Margherita. L'istituzione della fratria nella grecia antica e nelle colonie greche d'Italia, *Atti della Reale Accademia Nazionale dei Lincei: Memorie della classe di scienze, morali, storiche, e filologiche* 6 (1937) 5-101, 8 (1938-39) 65-135.

Hägg, Inga and Hägg, Robin. *Excavations in the Barbouna Area at Asine* (Uppsala, 1973).

Hägg, Robin. Research at Dendra, 1961, *Opusc. Ath.* 4 (1962) 79-102.

———. Geometrische Gräber von Asine, *Opusc. Ath.* 6 (1965) 117-138.

———. Protogeometrische und geometrische Keramik in Nauplion, *Opusc. Ath.* 10 (1971) 41-52.

———. *Die Gräber der Argolis in submykenischer, protogeometrischer und geometrischer Zeit* (Uppsala, 1974).

Hammond, Nicholas G. L. The Heraeum at Perachora and Corinthian Encroachment, *BSA* 49 (1954) 93-102.

———. An Early Inscription at Argos, *CQ* 54 (1960) 33-36.

Hanell, Krister. *Megarische Studien* (Lund, 1934).

Harl-Schaller, F. Die archaischen "Metopen" aus Mykene, *JdAOI* 50 (1972-73) 94-116.

Hejnic, Josef. *Pausanias the Perieget and the Arachaic History of Arcadia* (Prague, 1961).

Hind, J. G. F. The 'Tyrannis' and Exiles of Peisistratus, *CQ* 24 (1964) 1-18.

Holloway, R. Ross. An Archaic Hoard from Crete and the Early Aeginetan Coinage, *The American Numismatic Society. Museum Notes* 17 (1971) 1-21.

Huxley, George L. Argos et les derniers Téménides, *BCH* 82 (1958) 588-601.

———. *Early Sparta* (Cambridge, 1962).

Jacobsthal, Paul. *Greek Pins and Their Connexions with Europe and Asia* (Oxford, 1956).

Jacoby, Felix, ΧΡΝΣΤΟΤΣ ΠΟΙΕΙΝ (Aristotle fr. 592R), *CQ* 38 (1944) 15-16.

———. *Die Fragmente der griechischen Historiker* (Berlin and Leiden, 1922-1958).

Jameson, Michael H. and Papachristodoulou, Ioannis. Die archaischen Inschriften von Tiryns, *Akten des VI. Internationalen Kongress für Griechische und Lateinische Epigraphik München 1972* (Munich, 1973) 421-425.

Jantzen, Ulf, *Griechische Greifenkessel* (Berlin, 1955).

———. Greifenprotomen von Samos: Ein Nachtrag, *AM* 73 (1958) 26-48.

Jeffery, Lilian H. *The Local Scripts of Archaic Greece. A Study of the Origin of the Greek Alphabet and Its Development from the Eighth to the Fifth Centuries B.C.* (Oxford, 1961).

Jenkins, R. J. H. Archaic Argive Terracotta Figurines to 525 B.C., *BSA* 32 (1931-32) 23-40.

———. *Dedalica: A Study of Dorian Plastic Art in the Seventh Century B.C.* (Cambridge, 1936).

Kagan, Donald. Pheidon's Aeginetan Coinage, *TAPA* 91 (1960) 121-134.

Kaulen, Georg. *Daidalika. Werkstätten griechischer Kleinplastik des 7. Jahrhunderts v. Chr.* (Munich, 1967).

Kelly, Thomas. The Calaurian Amphictiony, *AJA* 70 (1966) 113-121.

———. The Argive Destruction of Asine, *Historia* 16 (1967) 422-431.

———. The Traditional Enmity between Sparta and Argos: The Birth and Development of a Myth, *AHR* 75 (1970) 971-1003.

———. Did the Argives Defeat the Spartans at Hysiae in 669 B.C.?, *AJP* 91 (1970) 31-42.

———. Argive Foreign Policy in the Fifth Century B.C., *CP* 69 (1974) 81-99.

Kiechle, Franz. *Messenische Studien: Untersuchungen zur Geschichte der messenischen Kriege und der Auswanderung der Messenier* (Kallmünz Opf, 1959).

———. *Lakonien und Sparta. Untersuchungen zur ethnischen Struktur und zur politischen Entwicklung Lakoniens und Spartas bis zum Ende der arachaischen Zeit* (Munich and Berlin, 1963).

Kophiniotou, Ioannis K. Ἱστρία τοῦ ᾽Ἀργους μετ᾽ εἰκόνων ἀπὸ τῶν ἀρχαιοτάτων χρόνων μέχρις ἡμῶν (Athens, 1892).

Kraiker, Wilhelm. *Aigina: Die Vasen des 10. bis 7. Jahrhunderts v. Chr.* (Berlin, 1951).

———. and Kübler, Karl. *Kerameikos, Ergebnisse der Ausgrabungen* 1: *Die Nekropolen des 12. bis 10. Jahrhunderts* (Berlin, 1939).

Kübler, Karl. *Kerameikos, Ergebnisse der Ausgrabungen* 5: *Die Nekropole des 10. bis 8. Jahrhunderts* (Berlin, 1954).

———. *Kerameikos, Ergebnisse der Ausgrabungen* 6: *Die Nekropole des späten 8. bis frühen 6. Jahrhunderts* (Berlin, 1959).

Kunze, Emil. *Olympische Forschungen* 2: *Archaische Schildbänder. Ein Beitrage zur frühgriechischen Bildgeschichte und Sagenüberlieferung* (Berlin, 1950),

Lauter, Hans. Zur frühklassischen Neuplanung des Heraions von Argos, *AM* 88 (1973) 175-187.

Lehmann, Herbert. Zur Kulturgeographie der Ebene von Argos, *Zeitschrift der Gesellschaft für Erdkunde zu Berlin* (1931) 38-59.

———. *Argolis: Landeskunde der Ebene von Argos und ihrer Randgebiete* (Athens, 1937).

———. Argeia. Das Anlitz einer griechischen Landschaft, *Die Antike* 14 (1938) 143-158.

Lenschau, Thomas. König Pheidon von Argos, *Philologus* 91 (1936-37) 385-395.

———. Die Siegerliste von Olympia, *Philologus* 91 (1936-37) 396-411.

Lilie, Guilelmus. *Quae ratio intercessit inter singulas Argolidis civitates* (Breslau, 1862).

McGregor, Malcolm F. Cleisthenes of Sicyon and the Panhellenic Festivals, *TAPA* 72 (1941) 266-287.

Mitchel, Fordyce W. Herodotus' Use of Genealogical Chronology, *Phoenix* 10 (1956) 48-69.

———. Megacles, *TAPA* 88 (1957) 127-130.

Mitsos, Markellos Th. ᾽Ἀργολικὴ Προσωπογραφία (Athens, 1952).

Moretti, Luigi. Sparta alla metà a del VI. secolo: La guerra contro Tegea, *RFC* 24 (1946) 87-103.

———. Sparta alla metà del VI. secolo II: La guerra contro Argo per la Tireatide, *RFC* 26 (1948) 204-222.

———. Olympionikai, i vincitori negli antichi agoni Olympici, *Memorie della* classe di scienze morali, storiche e filologiche: Atti della accademia nazionale dei Lincei 8 (1957) 53-198.

———. Ricerche sulle leghe greche (Rome, 1962).

Müller, Kurt. Gebäudemodelle spätgeometrischer Zeit, AM 48 (1923) 52-68.

Nilsson, Martin P. Griechische Feste von religiöser Bedeutung (Leipzig, 1906).

———. Cults, Myths, Oracles, and Politics in Ancient Greece (Lund, 1951).

———. Geschichte der griechischen Religion 1 (Munich, 1955).

Oikonomos, G. Ὁ ἐκ τοῦ Ἀργείου Ἡραίου πήλινος οἰκίσκος κατὰ νέαν συμπλήρωσιν, Arch. Eph. (1931) 1-53.

Page, Denys L. History and the Homeric Iliad (Berkeley and Los Angeles, 1959).

Papadimitriou, Ioannis. Ἀνασκαφαὶ ἐν Μυκήναις, Praktika (1952) 427-472.

Papaspyridi-Karouzou, Semne. Ἀνασκαφὴ τάφων τοῦ Ἄργους. AD 15 (1933-35) 16-53.

Parke, H. W. and Wormell, D. E. W. The Delphic Oracle 2 vols. (Oxford, 1956).

Payne, Humfry G. G. Perachora: The Sanctuaries of Hera Akraia and Limenia 1: Architecture, Bronzes, Terracottas (Oxford, 1940).

Philippson, Alfred and Kirsten, Ernst. Die griechischen Landschaften 4 vols. (Frankfurt am Main, 1959).

Protonotariou-Deïlaki, E. Ἀνασκφὴ λαξευτυῦ Μυκηναϊκοῦ τάφου ἐν Ἡραίῳ Ἄργους, Arch. Eph. (1960) 123-135.

———. Μυκηναϊκὸς τάφος ἐξ Ἄργους. Charisterion eis Anastasion K. Orlandon 2 (Athens, 1966) 239-247.

———. Δύο μυκηναϊκοὶ τάφοι εἰς Λάρισαν Ἄρνους, AAA 3 (1970) 301-303.

Roes, Anne. Une pierre gravée Syro-Hittite trouvée à Argos, BCH 61 (1937) 1-4.

———. Fragments de poterie géométrique trouvés sur les citadelles d'Argos, BCH 77 (1953) 90-104.

———. Les souris d'Argos aux yeux bandés, BCH 93 (1969) 333-336.

———. Les ex voto de bronze de l'époque géométrique, RA (1970) 195-208.

Roux, Georges. Le sanctuaire argien d'Apollo Pythéen, REG 70 (1957) 474-487.

Rubinsohn, Z. Pheidon of Argos: Military Reformer or Capitalist?, Istituto Lombardo Rendiconti 105 (1971) 636-642.

Säflund, Gösta. Excavations at Berbati, 1936-37 (Stockholm, 1965).

Sakellariou, Michel B. La migration grecque en Ionie (Athens, 1958).

Salmon, John. The Heraeum at Perachora and the Early History of Corinth and Megara, BSA 67 (1972) 159-204.

Sanctis, Gaetano di. Argo e i gimneti, Saggi di storia antica e di archeologica offerti a Guilio Beloch (Rome, 1910) 235-239.

Sarian, Haiganuch. Terres cuites géométriques d'Argos, BCH 93 (1969) 651-678.

Schneiderwirth, J. H. Politische Geschichte des dorischen Argos (Heiligenstadt, 1865).

Servais, Jean. Hérodote et la chronologie des Cypsélides, AC 38 (1969) 28-81.

Smith, Emil. Argos hos Homer, Symbolae Osloenses 1 (1923) 71-86.

Snodgrass, A. M. Early Greek Armour and Weapons (Edinburgh, 1964).

———. Barbarian Europe and Early Iron Age Greece, Proceedings of the Prehistoric Society 31 (1965) 229-240.

———. The Hoplite Reform and History, JHS 85 (1965) 110-122.

———. Arms and Armour of the Greeks (London, 1967).

————. *The Dark Age of Greece: An Archaeological Survey of the Eleventh to the Eighth Centuries B.C.* (Edinburgh, 1971).

Stamatakis, P. Περὶ τοῦ παρὰ τὸ ᾽Ηραῖον καθαρισθέντος τάφου, *AM* 3 (1878) 271-286.

Starr, Chester G. The Early Greek City State, *La parola del passato* 12 (1957) 97-108.

————. The Decline of the Early Greek Kings, *Historia* 10 (1961) 129-138.

————. *The Origins of Greek Civilization 1100-650 B.C.* (New York, 1961).

————. The Credibility of Early Spartan History, *Historia* 14 (1965) 257-272.

————. *The Awakening of the Greek Historical Spirit* (New York, 1968).

Styrenius, Carl-Gustaf. *Submycenaean Studies* (Lund, 1967).

Syriopoulos, K. ῾Η Προ-ἱστορία τῆς Πελοποννήσου (Athens, 1964).

Technau, Werner. Griechische Keramik im samischen Heraion, *AM* 55 (1929) 6-64.

Tigerstedt, Eugene N. *The Legend of Sparta in Classical Antiquity* (Stockholm, 1965).

Tomlinson, R. A. *Argos and the Argolid from the End of the Bronze Age to the Roman Occupation* (London, 1972).

Toynbee, Arnold J. *Some Problems of Greek History* (Oxford, 1969).

Trieber, Conrad. *Pheidon von Argos* (Hannover, 1886).

Unger, G. F. Die zeitverhältnisse Pheidons, *Philologus* 28 (1869) 399-424 and 29 (1870) 245-273.

Verdelis, Nicholas M. Neue geometrische Gräber in Tiryns, *AM* 78 (1963) 1-62.

Vollgraff, Wilhelm. Fouilles d'Argos, *BCH* 28 (1904) 364-399.

————. Inscriptions d'Argos, *BCH* 28 (1904) 420-429.

————. Fouilles d'Argos (Les établissements préhistoriques de l'Aspis), *BCH* 30 (1906) 5-45 and 31 (1907) 139-184.

————. Inscriptions d'Argos, *BCH* 33 (1909) 171-200, 445-466.

————. Rhodos oder Argos?, *Neue Jahrbücher* 1 (1910) 305-317.

————. Novae inscriptiones Argivae, *Mnem.* 44 (1916) 46-71, 219-238.

————. Arx Argorum, *Mnem.* 56 (1928) 315-328.

————. Opgravingen te Argos, *MKAW* 66 (1928) 87-107.

————. Inscriptio in arce Argorum reperta, *Mnem.* 57 (1929) 206-234.

————. Nieuwe opgravingen te Argos, *MKAW* 72 (1932) 71-124.

————. De titulo Argivo antiquissimo anno MCMXXVIII recuperato, *Mnem.* 59 (1932) 369-393.

————. De Erasino Argivo, *Mnem.* 60 (1932-33) 231-238.

————. Le decret d'Argos relatif a un pacte entre Knossos et Tylissos, *Verhandeling der Koninklijke Nederlandsche Akademie van Wetenschappen, Afdeeling Letterkunde* 51 (1948) 1-105.

————. *Études Péloponnésiennes 1: Le Sanctuaire d'Apollon Pythéen a Argos* (Paris, 1956).

————. Fouilles et sondages sur le flanc oriental de la Larissa a Argos, *BCH* 82 (1958) 516-570.

————. Observations sur les nom de trois phratries argiennes, *BCH* 83 (1959) 254-257.

Waldstein, Charles, *The Argive Heraeum* 2 Vols. (Boston and New York, 1902-1905).

————. The Argive Heraeum and Bacchylides XI. 43-84, *Classical Review* 14 (1900) 473-464.

Wickert, Konrad, *Der peloponnesische Bund von seiner Entstehung bis zum Ende des archidamischen Krieges* (Königsberg, 1961).

Will, Edouard. *Korinthiaka: Recherches sur l'histoire et la civilisation de Corinthe des origines aux guerres médiques* (Paris, 1955).

Wörrle, Michael. *Untersuchungen zur Verfassungsgeschichte von Argos im 5. Jahrhundert vor Christus* (Munich, 1964).

Zambelli, M. Per la storia di Argo nella prima metà de V secolo a. C., *RFC* 99 (1971) 148-158.

INDEX

Index

Aegina: Argive material imported at, 32, 57, 83; included in the Lot of Temenus, 42, 102, 118; alleged Pheidonian mint at, 102-105, 115; relations with Argos in the time of Pheidon, 102-103, 118-120; involed in war with Argos against Athens and Epidarus, 119-120; mentioned, 39, 44, 67, 82, 117, 140

Agariste, 108-109, 110, 111

Alphabet, 44-45, 49

Anolympiads, 97-98

Apollo, 53, 65, 67-68

Argive Heraeum: date of construction of, 54-55; archaeological material from, 59, 79-83, 90, 119-120; significance of the location of, 60-64, 66-67; perhaps the center of an amphictionic league, 68-69; foreign objects found at, 82-83; games at, 127-128; mentioned, 8, 33, 41, 57, 71, 85, 112, 132

Aristocracy; in the late eighth century, 70-71; in the seventh century, 89-

93; in the time of Pheidon, 113-114; in the sixth century, 134

Aristotle: as a source for Pheidon, 96-97, 101-102, 106, 113; on Pheidon of Corinth, 114; on Peisistratus' relations with Argos, 138-140; mentioned, 110

Asine: archaeological material from, 6, 21, 23, 27, 36, 53, 61; destruction of by the Argives, 45-46, 60, 64-66, 68, 88; mentioned, 9, 11, 13, 14, 20, 29, 62

Aspis, 5-6, 10, 36, 53, 85

Attica, Athens: Submycenaean material from, 21, 22, 23, 24, 25, 26; relationship between Athenian and Argive pottery in the Dark Age, 27-31, 35-36; relationship between Athenian and Argive pottery in the Late Geometric period, 56; Argive pottery found at Athens, 57, 82; Pheidonian measure used at Athens, 101; involved in a war with Epidaurus against Argos and Aegina, 103, 119-120; relations with Argos